TOM WEDGWOOD

TOM WEDGWOOD

TOM WEDGWOOD
THE FIRST PHOTOGRAPHER

AN ACCOUNT OF HIS LIFE, HIS DIS-
COVERY AND HIS FRIENDSHIP WITH
SAMUEL TAYLOR COLERIDGE
INCLUDING THE LETTERS OF
COLERIDGE TO THE WEDGWOODS

AND AN EXAMINATION OF ACCOUNTS
OF ALLEGED EARLIER PHOTOGRAPHIC
DISCOVERIES

By R. B. LITCHFIELD

" A mind perhaps the finest I ever met with."—T. CAMPBELL

LONDON
DUCKWORTH AND CO.
3 HENRIETTA STREET, COVENT GARDEN
1903

" RES OMNES EARUMQUE PROGRESSUS INITIIS SUIS DEBENTUR "

LORD BACON (First words of his letter sending a
copy of the " De Augmentis" to Trinity College,
Cambridge, the place of his early education).

INSCRIBFD TO

GODFREY WEDGWOOD

GREAT-NEPHEW OF THE FIRST PHOTOGRAPHER, AND

GREAT-GRANDSON OF THE FAMOUS POTTER, IN

ADMIRATION OF A LIFE AND CHARACTER

WORTHY OF THE NAME HE BEARS

PREFACE

THIS Memoir appears, it must be confessed, rather late. It was in the year 1806 that the little world of Tom Wedgwood's friends, relations, and acquaintances —a little world, but it included some of the most notable Englishmen of the time—were expecting the appearance of a book which was to give an account of his life and character, with an essay expounding his philosophical theories. This essay was to be written by Sir James Mackintosh, and the Memoir by Coleridge. But neither of these eminent persons did what he promised. It is not certain that either even began to do it. Of Mackintosh, Coleridge once wrote : "He is one of those men with whom the meaning to do a thing means nothing." Of Coleridge himself this was absolutely true, and it was not quite untrue of Mackintosh ; for he was noted for his infinite capacity for procrastination, as if his rule of life was never to do a thing to-day which could possibly be put off till to-morrow. The plan of a joint Memoir by two such collaborators, two men, as it happened, not. the least in sympathy one with the other, was thus virtually hopeless from the first. Mackintosh, moreover, had gone to be a Judge in India, and Coleridge was nearing that saddest time in his life when his best friends could only describe his condition (produced by opium) as one of " paralysis of the will." So it has been Tom Wedgwood's fate to be but faintly remembered—

> carpere lividas ·
> obliviones . . .
> caret quia vate sacro.

But it seemed to me that, in spite of the lapse of time, partly indeed by reason of it, it might now be worth while for the humblest of biographers to essay a modest record of the man, in part reparation of the failure of those two sadly untrustworthy *vates sacri*. The· task seemed to come naturally in my way, as, through the accident of private connection, I had happened to have read a great number of old family letters of the Wedgwoods, preserved by the descendants of the photographer's brother Josiah, including a mass of correspondence formerly in the possession of Mrs. Charles Darwin, the last survivor of his many nieces and nephews, who died at the age of eighty-eight in 1896.

This year 1902, the centenary of the date which justifies our calling him the "first photographer," seemed a fitting time for putting some account of him before the world, and for examining the question, which, so far as I know, has not been critically discussed before, whether that title properly applies to him. It was the more necessary to do this, as the story of what he really did had become confused with a foolish legend, a complete misrepresentation of the facts, which had unluckily been put forward in what was the only book (prior to the recent appearance of a notice in the

" Dictionary of National Biography ") giving information about him.*

Only two persons, as far as I can ascertain, have been described as doing, or possibly doing, anything photographic before the time of Wedgwood, the German Heinrich Schulze, and the French physicist Charles ; but an examination of the accounts of what they did clearly disposes, I think, of both claims. Knowing next to nothing of the technique of photographic processes, I should have no right to say this if the question turned on technical points, but that, as the reader of pp. 218–240 will see, is not the case.

When one thinks of the astonishing developments of the art in these latter years, the now familiar "living pictures," the achievements of the camera in stellar astronomy, and its importance as an aid to various kinds of literary, scientific, and artistic research, with the collateral wonders that have sprung out of photography, the strange mysteries of Röntgen, Becquerel, and Cathode "Rays," with their suggestions of fresh revelations of yet unknown natural forces, the poor little results got by Wedgwood may well seem insignificant. But there remains the fact that the step he took was the first step, the *premier pas*,† and his the original

* "A Group of Englishmen," by Eliza Meteyard, 1872. In this book Miss Meteyard, who had written a life of Josiah the famous potter, gives a pleasant gossipy account of his sons and other relatives. It has been rightly called "an agreeable *mélange*," but it is full of inaccuracy, the authoress habitually mixing up guesswork with fact.

† "Ah! Monsieur le Cardinal, dans de pareilles affaires, il n'y a que le premier pas qui coute." The *affaire* under discussion when Mme. Du Deffand said this was the famous walk of Saint Denis after his decapitation on Montmartre. The Cardinal had been wondering how the saint could possibly have walked *all the way to Paris.*

picture which has never been engraved, nor, I think, publicly exhibited.

I am under like obligation to Mr. Godfrey Wedgwood (of Idlerocks, Staffordshire), who placed at my disposal the whole of the MSS. left by the photographer, and has also very kindly allowed me to reproduce in miniature the very interesting picture by Stubbs, which includes the whole of Tom Wedgwood's family as it was in the year 1780.

For valuable assistance on specific points my thanks are due to Lord Kelvin and to Professor Liveing of Cambridge, who obligingly answered inquiries as to Tom Wedgwood's physical science work ; as also to Mrs. Henry Sandford, who kindly allowed me to see some letters of the Wedgwoods, not printed in her-Life of Tom Poole. I may mention that I should have printed a remarkable estimate of the character of Tom Wedgwood written soon after his death by Tom Poole, had not this been already given at length in that biography, a book, it is needless to say, which should be read by any one interested in Coleridge and his circle.

R. B. LITCHFIELD.

31 Kensington Square, London,
       November 1902.

CONTENTS

CONTENTS

APPENDICES

SHORTENED REFERENCES TO SOME BOOKS CITED

"D. C." "Samuel Taylor Coleridge, a Narrative of the Events of his Life." By James Dykes Campbell (Macmillan's, 1894).

"Coleridge's Poetical Works." The One Volume Edition (Macmillan's, 1893), edited by J. Dykes Campbell, with a Biographical Introduction, being that which was reproduced in 1894 as a separate work.

"T. P." "Thomas Poole and his Friends." By Mrs. Henry Sandford. Two vols. 1888.

"Coleridge Letters." The Collection edited by Mr. E. H. Coleridge, 1895. Two vols. 8vo, paged continuously.

ILLUSTRATIONS

* For these four views the author is indebted to the kindness of the Editors of
Photography.   They are from photographs taken in 1902 for the Centenary number
(May 6, 1902) of that publication.

SKETCH OF WEDGWOOD—ALLEN—DARWIN RELATIONSHIPS.

Josiah Wedgwood = Sarah Wedgwood
of Etruria   (a distant cousin),
(1730–1795), m.1764.   d. 1815.

Susannah (1765–1817)
m. (1796) Dr. Robert
Darwin, of Shrewsbury,
son of Dr. Erasmus,
the poet.

John (1766–1844)
(of Cote House,
Bristol), m. Jane
Allen,* who d.
1836.

Many
children.

Caroline
Darwin
(1800–88),
m. (1837)
her cousin
Josiah.

Erasmus Alvey
Darwin
(1804–1881),
d. unm.

Charles Darwin
(1809–1882), (author
of "The Origin of
Species"), m. (1839)
his cousin, Emma
Wedgwood.

Richard,
(1767–68).

Josiah (1769–1843)
(of Maer Hall,
Staffs), m. Eliza-
beth Allen,* who
d. 1846.

Three
other
children.

Josiah (1795–1880),
of Leith Hill Place,
m. Caroline Darwin,
his cousin.

Thomas
(1771–1805),
photographer,
d. unm.

Catharine
(1774–1823),
d. unm.

Sarah
(1776–1856),
d. unm.

Mary Anne,
b. 1778,
d. in
childhood.

Emma (1808–1896),
m. (1839) her
cousin, Charles
Darwin.

Six other
children.

* Elizabeth and Jane Allen were daughters of John Bartlett Allen, of Cresselly, Pembrokeshire. Catherine, another sister (1765–1830),
was the second wife (m. 1798) of Sir James Mackintosh (1765–1832).

CHAPTER I

EARLY YEARS

1771—1790

---

* The house still exists ; for many years past it has belonged to the Duchy of Lancaster, which owns the minerals under it and the surrounding lands, and is now used for purposes connected with the mines.

Thomas is often called the third son, one of his elder brothers having died in infancy.

A

While this work was still in the press, Mr. Litchfield died at Cannes on January 11, 1903. Owing to his absence from England and other causes there had been delay in its appearance. He had greatly hoped that it would appear in 1902, the Centenary of Tom Wedgwood's photographic work

CHAPTER I

EARLY YEARS

1771—1788

THOMAS WEDGWOOD, fourth son of Josiah Wedgwood, the famous potter, was born on May 14, 1771, at Etruria Hall, near Stoke-upon-Trent. The hall was a new house which his father had built as a residence for the family, hard by the Pottery, the potting business having been removed from Burslem to this site a year or two previously.* When only six years old the boy was sent to a school kept by Mr. Holland, a Unitarian minister at Bolton, where his brothers already were, and remained there two years. The method of his education was a matter which gave his father many doubts. Josiah Wedgwood's letters to his partner and friend, Bentley, contain frequent speculations on the questions as to what his boys should learn, and how to secure their having a healthy bodily life while the schooling went on.

"Erasmus Darwin," he says in one letter (October 1779), "has approved my idea of curtailing the educa-

---

* The house still exists ; for many years past it has belonged to the Duchy of Lancaster, which owns the minerals under it and the surrounding lands, and is now used for purposes connected with the mines.

Thomas is often called the third son, one of his elder brothers having died in infancy.

A

tion of my boys in order to establish their health, and give the more strength to their constitution." Dr. Darwin advises him to keep them at home, and this he does. They are to have four Latin lessons a week, "only to keep up what they know, till I have decided as to this part of their learning." "I am distressed to find out a sort of compromise between the body and the mind that shall do the least injury to either."

In another letter he describes the *régime* at length. They "read English before breakfast, newspaper or travels, writing one hour with Mr. Swift; writing French exercises; then ride or drive their hoop or jump over a cord, or use any exercise they please for an hour." Later in the day there are two French lessons, and "some accounts in the evening, in which the girl takes part."

The earliest letter of Tom which has been preserved is one written when he was nearly twelve years old, giving an account of a scene during the bread riots, which broke out in the Potteries in 1783. His father is in London.

Tom Wedgwood to his father, Josiah

ETRURIA,
Wednesday, March 11, 1783.

DEAR PAPA,—

As I thought you would like to hear how the mob went on I will tell you.

On Sunday all was quiet. There was a meeting at Newcastle (at which my brother John was present) to consider what was the best way to quell the Mob and to keep up the market. John subscribed £10; a good many others also subscribed.

On Monday the mob came to Bilington's where there was

a meeting of the Master Potters, Dr. Falkener, Mr. Ing, Mr. Sneyd of Bellmont, and harrangued to the Mob on the bad way they had begun in to lessen the price of corn, as did my brother John and also Major Sneyd. (who came with the Militia) was exceedingly active in speaking to them. He said, "Why do you rise," and he answer'd him "on the same account that your father went out of the country." This distressed him so much that he cried. All their speaking was to no effect.

They then raised a subscription. John subscribed £20. This they said would not have been raised without we had risen. This speech pussled them much. They then read the riot act and said if they did not disperse in a hour's time they would fire on them. An hour gone and they did not disperse. Dr. Falkener had got the word "Fire" in his mouth when two men dropt down by accident which stopt him and he considered about it more. The Woemen were much worse than the men ; as for example, Parson Sneyd had got about 30 men to follow him he hurraing and the an all [sic] but a woman cried Nay, nay that wunna do, that wunna do, and so they turned back again; it was agreed that the corn taken in the boat* should be sold at a fair price.

Bolton, Barlow are taken up and gone to Stafford the rest of the days have been quiet. John and Mr. Lomas are gone to Stone. They all send their love to you and comts. to Mr. and Mrs. Byerley.

I am,

Your dutifull son,

THOMAS WEDGWOOD.

Turn over.

P.S.—I would have written this letter well but I have got the head ach, but did not like to miss the opportunity of a box.   T. W.

---

* A barge which was stopped and plundered at Etruria, as it was making its way to Manchester, the mob imagining that, as the corn

Another letter to his father, of about a year later, gives a pleasant glimpse of his home life, and shows him as certainly very much grown up for a boy of thirteen. It shows, too, that he was on charmingly easy terms with his father.

Tom Wedgwood to his father

ETRURIA,
April 20, 1784.

DEAR PAPA,—

By the time this letter reaches you I hope you will have had a pleasant journey and got safe and sound to London. Matthew Mills is very busy at the Garden Pools repairing the dams at the lower Pool, which the cows have damaged very much that go to drink there, and unless some remedy is thought of to secure the dam, it will be considerably damaged. Now making a drinking place just below the lower Pool with the water that runs from the Pool and fencing a post and railing round the dam, will be good security. If you will give me the post of Superintendant of your pools, I will see that they are done properly and soon. My hotbed is compleated all but glazing. The Bricklayers have pulled down part of the lower wall and are building it up again and will finish at the end of the week.

I have had several large fish at my line lately (fishing with a Gudgeon) and leaving it in all night. Some large fish at the top Pool struck at my Bait as I lifted it up. Another, my rod drawn in the water and the bait eat of. Still another, half my bait eat of and the other half drawn up the line.

I'd be very glad if you would give me that post for indeed

---

was going out of the district, the owners were trying to raise prices against the Staffordshire people. John Wedgwood, Tom's eldest brother, is at this time a lad of seventeen. The reply of the mob to Major Sneyd is enigmatical. Possibly Mr. Wedgwood would understand why it made him cry. The two men taken to Stafford were convicted, and Barlow executed.

I would take very good care and always keep them in good order. Mathew only waits only for Command to go on and finish his job.

My Aunt is much better and will drink Beer and brandy and I don't know what. I wish you would get me a pair of Buckles and send them immediately, for I have got none but a broken pair. I shall furnish all your pools with plenty of baits as I have now near a dozen hands under employment. I have got leave to fish of Mr. Stockley and the miller will get leave of the tenant of Mr. Allen and J. Beech of Mr. Jarvis, so then for Wilkes and liberty.

Give my love to my sister and will answer her letter very soon. Mary Anne is very well indeed and was much pleased with her journey.

Almost everybody have colds but I have escap'd yet. Mr. Chisolm is very well and sends his best respects to you and family.

Give my best love to my Mother, sister and John and should be happy in hearing from them. Pray remember me to Mr. and Mrs. Byerley and believe me to be,

Your dutifull son,
THOS. WEDGWOOD.

Would have written it better but had not time.

(Address on cover : Mr. Wedgwood, London.—No postmark ; it no doubt went in the box.)

The person who had most to do with the education of Tom * Wedgwood, after his father, was Alexander Chisolm, Josiah Wedgwood's faithful secretary and chemical assistant. Chisolm came to Etruria, a man of middle age, in 1780, when Tom was nine years old.

---

* I shall refer to him thus throughout the book, as he was always so-called, both in and outside of the family circle.

He was a good chemist, a man of education, and at least something of a classical scholar. The boys became much attached to him. The various other influences which would help to mould the mind and character of a boy growing up in the Etruria household may be easily imagined from what we know of Josiah Wedgwood and his life.*   Among the friends of the great Potter were some of the foremost Englishmen of the time.   He was intimate with James Watt from 1768 onwards.   Priestley, who settled in Birmingham in 1780, owed much to his friendship. Wedgwood sent him annually twenty-five guineas in aid of his expenditure on scientific experiments.   With Erasmus Darwin and his family there was constant intercourse.   Derby, where Darwin lived from about 1781, was not far off, and the children of the two houses were intimate as well as the parents.   James Keir of West Bromwich, ex-captain of foot and glass manufacturer, whom James Watt called "a mighty chemist and very agreeable man," was one of the group. Richard Lovell Edgeworth was another.   It was a circle in which "advanced" ideas prevailed, ideas which

---

* Unfortunately there is no satisfactory biography of Josiah, the Potter.   Miss Meteyard's two bulky volumes give a large amount of information about him, but, as sufficiently appears from her entirely mythical account of Tom Wedgwood's photography (see p. 241) no statement of hers can be trusted which is not confirmed by other evidence, while her persistent strain of magniloquent eulogy is a constant irritation to the reader.   The little book by Mr. Smiles (1894) is a lively sketch of the man and his career, but it has many technical errors, and was evidently put together in great haste.   The memoir in the "Dictionary of National Biography," by Professor Church, F.R.S., is (I am told by a high authority on the subject) excellently well done.

THE WEDGWOOD FAMILY AT ETRURIA HALL, ABOUT 1780

were in great part a reverberation from the pre-revolutionary movement in France. All this could not fail to give a strong bent to Tom Wedgwood's mind. His training was scientific rather than literary, but we find him working hard at the Latin classics with Chisolm, and also with a tutor by name Lomas, who however, according to his brother Josiah's account, was a quite uninspiring teacher. A French prisoner was found to teach the boys French.

In the autumn of 1786 (*æt.* fifteen), Tom joined his brother Josiah at Edinburgh University. The lads lived with Dr. Blacklock, the blind poet, who must have been an interesting man in many ways. He was one to whom the world owes something, for it was he who, at a critical moment in the life of Robert Burns, when the young poet, despairing of a career in Scotland, had resolved to leave his native country for ever and was on the point of embarking for the West Indies, induced him to give up the scheme and come to Edinburgh.*

The letters of the two young men from Edinburgh show them, as one would expect, plentifully interested in the place and its student life. They are busy with their lectures and their various societies, and take a good deal of exercise—golf, apparently, is the chief

---

* " My chest was on its way to Greenock" (writes Burns to Dr. Moore, August 2, 1787) "when a letter from Dr. Blacklock to a friend of mine overthrew all my schemes, by opening new prospects to poetic ambition. His opinion that I would meet with encouragement in Edinburgh for a second edition fixed me so much that away I posted for that city without a single acquaintance or a single letter of introduction." ("Currie's Life," Ed. 1800. See also Sir Leslie Stephen's account in "Dict. Nat. Biog.")

form of it, which Jos expects will keep off Tom's headaches. Jos tells his father " the students here are not very genteel ; the Divinity students are the dirtiest set I ever saw ; a company of old potters look like gentlemen compared to them."

Tom corresponds with Chisolm, chiefly on chemical topics ; his letters bristle with rows of the queer old symbols for gases, acids, and metals which were still then in use among chemists. Chisolm gives him wise advice about his studies ; his letters are big folio sheets, closely written in a clear and careful hand. Some read like chapters out of a chemical journal, discussions on what Priestley or Lavoisier is doing, and the conflicting theories of the day. He addresses the boy (who is only fifteen) with the ceremonious formality of the time.

Alexander Chisolm to Tom Wedgwood

ETRURIA,
Dec 23, 1786.

DEAR SIR,—

I wrote to you a few lines two or three days ago along with some books, which I understand are not yet gone, and therefore I cannot let slip the opportunity of thanking you for the very sensible letter I received from you last night, and expressing my unfeigned pleasure in the avidity I observe in you for useful knowledge, and your assiduity in acquiring it. Your plan of study has my perfect approbation. . . . The classics I could wish to be a principal object this winter ; you can now read them with understanding ; you will soon read them with pleasure.

[Here follows much about the question of using translations, the Latin of Livy and of Buchanan, &c. ; then advice as to how to read to the blind Dr. Blacklock, not sinking the voice in the final syllables. At present let him not try to study Moral Philosophy or "Belles Lettres," but let Classics and Chemistry take his whole time.]

Your elaboratory shall be taken care of [and this leads to a long chemical excursus.]

I will only add that I am sincerely glad the salubrious exercise of golf is agreeable to you, and I recommend it to you as strongly for Saturdays as I would Chemistry or Classics any other day.

> Interpone tuis interdum gaudia curis,
> Ut quemvis animo possis perferre laborem.

Remember me to Jos, and believe me to be,
Dear Sir, Your faithful & Obedient servant,
ALEX^r. CHISOLM.

Tom Wedgwood to his Father

Dec. 31, 1786.

DEAR SIR,—

* * * * *

I have just got into a new society here, called the Philological Society, in which I must exert all my oratory powers, which, as I never yet tried them in public, you know, *may* be very great ; but I dinna ken. There are some very clever members of it . I shall have to write a paper in a little time, but am as yet quite undetermined of the subject of it, and should be very thankful if you would help me a little in this.

* * * * *

There has been a very disagreeable thing here [story of a student having tried to pass a forged bill at a shop]. He was sent to the Tolbooth (the prison). He stands no chance for his life. This unlucky affair will confirm the townspeople a bad opinion of the Irish gentry (He was one). There has already been one hanged, and several have taken French leave.

* * * * *

I am come to the end of my paper, and so I shall finish with desiring you to

Believe me,
Yours affectionately,
THOS. WEDGWOOD.

Auld Reekie, Dec^r., Saturday before New Year's Day, 1786.

Josiah Wedgwood to Alex^r Chisolm

January 11, 1787.

DEAR SIR,—

Tom began this letter and I shall finish it. . . . The Philological Society consists of 13 or 14 young men, among which are two or three very clever. I intend to write on the *sublime* . . . I like Dr. Blacklock more every day. . . . We had three visits from Mr. Burns, a natural poet; his brother is a farmer and he was the ploughman, but had a very uncommon poetic turn. He is now publishing a second edition of his poems, to which I shall subscribe. Many of them are in the Scottish dialect.

My love to all at Etruria,
I am your much obliged friend,
JOSIAH WEDGWOOD.

Tom Wedgwood spent two winter sessions, apparently, at Edinburgh, 1786–7 and 1787–8. In the spring of 1788 there was a scheme for his going to Rome; but this dropped, and he remained at Etruria, taking part in the work of the pottery. We find him writing to his father, in March 1790, about such matters as the dismissal of apprentices at Etruria for over much swearing, and the colouring and furnishing of the London show-room in Greek Street. But his letters show him to be keenly eager, all this time, to go on with his studies in Natural Philosophy. This was the main motive of a scheme which he now proposed to his father.

While at Edinburgh he had made the acquaintance of John Leslie, a young man about five years older than himself who had come there as a student of Theology, but had given up the intention of becoming a minister and was working at natural science. Tom and he had not been particularly intimate at Edinburgh, but they had since corresponded at intervals. Leslie, who had no private means—his father was a carpenter—had been to America as a travelling tutor, and was now without any definite plans, supporting himself in a precarious way by teaching and lecturing. Tom's proposition to his father was that Leslie should be asked to come to stay at Etruria to assist him and his brother Josiah in their laboratory work and scientific studies generally. His father agreed to this, and Leslie received the offer with rapturous delight.

John Leslie to Tom Wedgwood

LONDON,
April 13, 1790.

MY DEAREST SIR,—

To-day I received your very kind and flattering letter of the 9th instant. Your uncommon manner of writing throws me into a maze of wonder, and transports me with heartfelt joy. What a charming picture of a polished, elegant, and feeling mind ! I am at a loss to answer your kindness. That warmth of affection, and that goodness of heart, give a lovely cast to human nature. A crowd of ideas at once rush upon me. That diffidence and extreme delicacy is highly pleasing ; but to me is unnecessary. Talk freely—from you nothing can displease. . . . The idea of residing with a young man whose heart is of the same mould, and whose mind is so benevolent, so generous, and so enlarged, is beyond measure delightful. Every other view vanishes in an instant. Money, my dear friend, is to me no object. The situation which you describe is the most fortunate, the most happy I could picture in my imagination. . . .

I am afraid, my dearest friend, you over-rate my real merit. . . . The smallness of my acquisitions will I hope be compensated by steady attention and warm affections. [Then follows an eulogy of the genius of Josiah Wedgwood, the father.] I have long been accustomed to admire the ingenuity and boldness which created a manufacture, that contributes more to the real glory and wealth of our country than our fleets and armies. . . .

But I exhaust your patience and precious time with long epistles. I wait with trembling anxiety—my happiness hangs upon your decision.

I am, my dear Sir,
Yours ever sincerely,
Jo. LESLIE.

Excuse this scrawl.

This letter is a characteristic specimen of Leslie's epistolary style. Except when he happens to be writing of thermometers or gases, we seem to be reading Mr. Collins in " Pride and Prejudice." The " scrawl " for which he excuses himself is a piece of quite perfect penmanship, without sign of erasure or alteration.

It was a part of Tom Wedgwood's plan that he and Leslie should live together, not in the family house at Etruria, but in a separate house hard by. His father did not see the advantage of this, but Tom is urgent in arguing the point. Here is one of several letters in which he expounds his views. They disclose intensely "earnest" views of life and duty.

ETRURIA HALL AND POTTERY WORKS
From view taken about 1775

He is full of exalted ideas of self-culture, and of devotion to the service of mankind.

Tom Wedgwood to his Father

May 8, 1790.

     *   *   *   *   *

I rather suppose that you have formed a wrong idea of my intention. . . . Be assured there is no danger of my entering into the selfish, insignificant character of a hermit. I know too well the purposes of my creation. I have conceived too exalted a notion of the real dignity of man, existing in *Action from principle*, and despise too heartily those mistaken beings who amuse themselves unprofitably in the mazes of metaphysical refinements and abstruse philosophy. My aim is to strengthen the power of reason by the habit of reflection, and by cultivating the virtues of the heart in a *temporal* [*sic*] retirement from the *world at large ;* to purify the motives of conduct —for what is Action unless the sources be pure? With that openness which should subsist between a father and a son, I joyfully acquaint you that I have already made considerable progress in this most important work—a thousand sensations convince me that in this confidence I am not misled by the illusions of vanity. . . .

I am well aware that the next three or four years of my life are the most important. Manhood is the seal of man. Our passions and affections are all to be moderated and corrected in the season of youth. In this critical moment I shall strive hard to fashion myself so, that I may best perform the grand dutys [his spelling is not impeccable] of this life. I reflect every day on the nature of the relation between the creator and creature, and hope by these instructive speculations to arrive at the knowledge of the purposes of creation, and hence of what these dutys consist in. The question is extremely intricate and comprehensive, and can never receive a full decisive answer from human reason. . . . An inactive and virtuous life are incompatible,

and I mean to exert myself for the good of my fellow creatures. . . .

[In another letter]. Our main dutys are Beneficence and the
Social. I can say for myself that whatever my situation and
circumstances may be, I shall never sleep in the service of my
fellow creatures.

Promiscuous company has no allurements. . . . I have a
strong desire of enjoying the blessing—the right, perhaps, of
choosing my own company and of avoiding that I dislike, by
easier methods than I have now recourse to.

One may smile at many things in this letter, but
we must remember that the writer is just nineteen
years old, and that the time is ten months after the
fall of the Bastille. In his aspirations after a life of
" beneficence and virtue " one feels the ring of the new
ideas which the great upheaval of 1789 was stirring in
the young and ardent souls of the time. How Josiah
Wedgwood replied to his son's eager pleadings we do
not know. We may be sure that the wise father did
not laugh at his young enthusiasm, though he may
have been amused at the didactic solemnity with which
the lad expounds his ideal of life. Nor do we know
whether he and Leslie were allowed to set up house
apart from the family at Etruria Hall. We might
guess that Tom's friend and tutor was treated with
Josiah Wedgwood's usual liberality, and received cordially as one of the family. Leslie lets us know, in his
magnificent language, that this was the case.

John Leslie to Tom Wedgwood

LONDON,
April 29, 1790.

* * * * *

How shall I make a proper return ? I hope the magnitude of the offer will be an additional spur to my exertions. There is a circumstance, my dear friend, which gives me peculiar pleasure. From the generosity of your nature I am convinced that I shall be upon an easy footing. I am a *moderate* lover of liberty, but I am every day more riveted in a settled aversion to the fawning arts of the sycophant, and to be submitted to the caprices and tyranny of an *Aristocrate* [*sic*] would to me be the more dreadful of punishments. At the same time my dear Sir, I hope this disposition does not arise from any overweaned conceit of myself, but springs from the consciousness of the unalienable rights and native dignity of man. . . .

I am filled with a mixture of wonder and gratitude. . . . United with a gentleman who possesses all the warmth of disposition and the acuteness of discernment of our friend T. M. Randolph, but who possesses, besides, a virtue the most essential to the dignity and success of life, steadiness of conduct and resolution of character, whose passions are subordinate to his reason, and who has imbibed more of the spirit of the Stoic than the Epicurean philosophy—and not yet *nineteen !* I upbraid myself that I am five years older. This is the age of bliss, the head not hardened by jarring interests is susceptible of every delicate impression, and the soul springs unbounded. . . . What character is so benevolent and so generous as that of a young man who has just left college. You feel the justness of the remark.

* * * * *

I am, my dear Sir,
Yours affect^{ly}.,
Jo. LESLIE.

Leslie remained at Etruria about two years, from June 1790. His stay there was doubtless a great help to Tom Wedgwood in his scientific work. One may doubt whether his influence was good in other ways. He pours out his admiration for his pupil in language which is too exuberant to sound sincere, and whether sincere or not, it was hardly wholesome reading for a lad of nineteen.

"Our dispositions, you say, are congenial. I esteem this the highest compliment I could receive."

"I derived great advantage from it [Edinburgh University], but what I am confident is the greatest of all, I commenced at Edinburgh an acquaintance with yourself."

"To reside with a young man whose heart is of the same mould, and whose mind is so benevolent, so generous and so enlarged, is altogether delightful."

"Your time is too precious to *spend* much of it with me— but to enjoy your company in your intervals of leisure is the most flattering prospect."

These are specimens of Leslie's outpourings; but his career as a man of science showed him to be a man of more real capacity than one would have inferred from the absurd pomposity of his letters.

CHAPTER II

THE three years which followed Tom Wedgwood's stay at Edinburgh University, 1789–91, were spent mainly at Etruria, and they may be said to have been the only working years of his short life, for this was the only time during which health allowed him to set himself to any definite occupation. Early in 1790 he became a partner in his father's business, and began taking part in the management of the pottery. During these years he was also working at physical science. The laboratory and the pottery processes at Etruria gave him special facilities for experiments bearing on the relations between heat and light, and he gave much time to a course of experiments of this kind. The results of his work were embodied in two papers which were read before the Royal Society. The first of these, read on December 22, 1791 (*Transactions* for 1792, pp. 28–47), is entitled " Experiments and Observations on the production of Light from different bodies by heat and attrition," by Mr. Thomas Wedgwood, communicated by Sir Joseph Banks, Bart., F.R.S. The second paper is described as a continuation of the first. This special field of investigation was apparently a new one. He corresponded with Priestley on the subject, and we

B

find the great chemist telling him : " I do not know that any experiments have been made on the curious and important subjects that you mention," and again, " they (your experiments) will throw some new light on a very important subject, about which we as yet know very little."*

In his first paper, after a brief summary of the results of previous observations, beginning with the discovery of the stone which went by the name of " Bolognese Phosphorus," he describes how a great variety of substances, some fifty or more, can be rendered luminous by the method of reducing the substance to powder and sprinkling it on a warm plate of iron, and then gives an account of the processes whereby he has been able to obtain phosphoric effect by attrition.

In his second paper he gives the particulars of various experiments showing the results of making different substances red hot. In the first of these (to take an instance) he fixes two equal cylinders of silver, half an inch long and a quarter of an inch in diameter, with polished surfaces, in a tube of earthenware. 'One cylinder is painted over, one not so. Both are put into a red hot crucible surrounded by burning coals, and he observes that the blackened silver shines much before that with the non-blackened surface.

A particular interest attaches to one of these experiments (the seventh), as it was the first announcement, apparently, of a law at that time unknown. He " gilded a piece of earthenware in lines running across "

* Quoted by Miss Meteyard ("Group of Englishmen," p. 53) from letters described as Finch MSS.

and gradually made it red hot; and he "could not, after many trials, perceive that either the gold or the earthenware began to shine first." Whereon he adds: "As it appears from this experiment that gold and earthenware begin to shine at the same temperature, and as no two bodies can well be more different, in all their sensible properties, may it not be inferred, that almost all bodies begin to shine at the same temperature?" The inference, it will be seen, is put in an interrogative form; but though this experiment would not in itself establish the suggested law, it is the fact that all bodies "begin to shine at the same temperature," or, as it sometimes is expressed, have the same point of incandescence.

I have been unable to ascertain to whom the first discovery of this law has usually been attributed, but I have not at present found any reference to it, other than that in Tom Wedgwood's paper, earlier than the year 1847. (See Appendix, p. 241.)

While working at the long series of experiments described in the two papers, Wedgwood was corresponding on the subject with Priestley, and with another chemist of note, James Keir, of West Bromwich.*

---

* James Keir was a man of mark, and had a singular career. He had been a medical student at Edinburgh, where he was a great friend of Erasmus Darwin, and afterwards, for about nine years, an officer in the army. His proclivities to science ultimately led him to settle at West Bromwich and devote himself to chemistry and geology. Then he became a glass manufacturer, and was concerned in other manufacturing works, being at one time associated with Boulton and Watt. He, like so many of Tom Wedgwood's friends, was a sympathiser with the French Revolution, and became conspicuous in that character by taking the chair at the meeting at Birmingham on July 14, 1791 (second anniversary of the fall of the

Spent ½ year in endeavouring to suspend a thermometer in vacuo — olive oil seemed to promise better than mercury — I thought that the thermometer might be raised to a great height by exposing it with a blackened bulb to the rays of the sun, suspended by a very fine wire or hair —. as I concluded that a true vacuum wou'd not conduct the heat away from the bulb, all it wou'd lose wou'd be by the wire or hair. I proposed to converge the rays of the moon on it also to try if their heat cou'd be thus appreciated. I proposed likewise to have balls upon a delicate axis to turn round by the impulse of light. But not succeeding in my tries at a vacuum, & finding my health impaired, I resolved to give up experimenting.

April 1792

Thos Wedgwood.

FACSIMILE OF T. WEDGWOOD'S WRITING

direction of photography is wholly uncertain. At present there seems to be no evidence definitely showing that he did; but this point will be touched on in the chapter dealing with his photographic work.

Other problems connected with light and heat occupied him for a long time in these years. But by the year 1792 the ill health from which he had suffered more or less from childhood had become so constant as to make him unfit for any serious or continous work, and from that time onwards he seems to have done nothing in physical science save in a fragmentary and occasional way.

A memorandum in his writing, preserved among his letters, records this arrest of what promised to be a fruitful course of scientific work. It is on a half-sheet of letter paper, and bears marks of wafers, by which it seems to have been closed up as if for special preservation, with the endorsement " Account of proposed experiments *in vacuo*." It runs as follows :

" I spent half a year in endeavouring to suspend a thermometer in vacuo. Olive oil seemed to promise better than mercury. I thought that the thermometer might be raised to a great height by exposing it with a blackened bulb to the rays of the sun, suspended by a very fine wire or hair, as I concluded that a true vacuum would not conduct the heat away from the bulb, all it would lose would be by the wire or hair. I proposed to converge the rays of the moon on it also to try if their heat could be thus appreciated. I proposed likewise to have sails upon a delicate axis to turn round by the impulse of light. But not succeeding in my trials at a vacuum, and finding my health impaired, I resolved to give up experimenting.

" April, 1792.*   Thos. Wedgwood."

---

* This date is so placed (the word " experimenting " being at the

His object, I should imagine, in writing this, was to keep some record of ideas which he might pursue at a future time if his health should mend, or which might be useful as suggestions to future experimenters. The first sentence testifies to his perseverance as well as his enthusiasm. To spend six months in struggling with a single mechanical problem shows something of the "infinite capacity for taking pains," in which we have been told that genius mainly consists. But the interest of the record is in the date, which shows that at least as early as April 1792 his health had become too bad to allow of his going on with any continuous work. He was then some weeks short of twenty-one years old. There is a pathos in the thought of so eager a student being forced, when still only at the outset of his work, to abandon the hope of doing anything effective.

His idea of getting sails upon a delicate axis to turn round by the action of light may perhaps remind a modern reader of the curious radiometer of Sir William Crookes, in which something like this appears to be going on. But of course Wedgwood could have had no real prevision of what happens in the radiometer. Reasoning on Newton's emission theory of light, he thought that if the opposing pressure of the air could be got rid of, the shock of the little particles of light knocking on the sails would make them turn round. In the radiometer, as I understand, the turning of the little vanes has to do with light only in the sense that

---

end of a line) that it may signify either the date on which the paper was written, or the date when he "resolved to give up experiment-ing."

the heat accompanying it makes inequalities of temperature in the gas surrounding the instrument, whence come differences of pressure causing the motion. Tom Wedgwood, naturally, had no glimmering of these mysteries of molecular action, which were to be expounded nearly a century later by Clerk Maxwell and other physicists.*

The detection and measurement of the heat sent to the earth by the moon was another problem which had to wait long for a solution. Lord Rosse attempted it some forty years ago, but it has only recently, I believe, been settled by means of Mr. Boys's "micro-radiometer," a wonderful instrument, which measures very minute changes of temperature by means of a test founded on the electrical action of one metal on another.

Tom Wedgwood's "resolve to give up experimenting" on account of impaired health brings us to what was the dominant fact of his life. He never had any health. In his early years he was weakly; we hear of headaches troubling him as a boy, and in his student days at Edinburgh. As years went on it became clear that he had a grave constitutional disease, which, as we shall see, made the last ten years of his life utterly miserable. What the ailment was the best medical skill of the time failed to discover. The doctors seem to have generally agreed that it had to do with the digestive system. Some called it a paralysis or semi-paralysis of the colon. One considered it to be

---

* Clerk Maxwell in *Phil. Tr.* of 1879 on Stresses in rarefied gases, &c. "Enc. Brit." Art. "Pneumatics," p. 249.

the sequel of an attack of dysentery which he had when a student at Edinburgh. Others would only call it "hypochondria." Whatever the physical cause was, a main feature of the disease was a continual recurrence of fits of depression, sometimes lasting for weeks together. His mental misery at these times, especially towards the close of his life, made his condition hardly distinguishable from one of insanity. The impression, however, left by the letters is that the disease was not primarily mental. There is not the slightest trace in them of anything approaching a delusion, and in letters written in moments of the deepest despondency we find him discussing practical matters in the manner of a man who is in complete possession of his faculties. There were intervals when he was well capable of bodily and mental labour, but as time went on the periods of depression became longer and more frequent, making his life well-nigh unbearable. Thus it came about that, broadly speaking, his whole adult life, from about 1792 on to the end in 1805, was devoted to a single object, the fighting this terrible and mysterious enemy. He went the round of the most notable physicians of the day, Clive, Baillie, Erasmus Darwin, Beddoes, and many more. He tried all manner of cures, strange and fantastic *régimes*, new modes of life. "Change of scene" was continually recommended as a remedy; hence he was perpetually travelling, in England and abroad, and continually visiting relatives and friends. It was not till nearly the end of his life that he had a house of his own, and that was only nominally a home. Its acquisition hardly arrested his wandering course of life.

To revert to the year 1792—it was then that he was for the first time out of England, making a flying visit to Paris in order to be present at the great "Federation" fête held on July 14, on the Champ-de-Mars, to celebrate the third anniversary of the fall of the Bastille. Like most of his friends and belongings he was ardently in sympathy with the revolutionary movement in its early stages. The following letter gives some of the impressions made by this first sight of a foreign country. At this moment, it will be remembered, the fall of the French monarchy was imminent. Another month was to see the attack on the Tuileries and the massacre of the Swiss Guard (August 10, 1792). Six months later Louis had been guillotined and France and England were at war.

Tom Wedgwood to his Father

PARIS,
July 7, 1792.

DEAR SIR,—

We have had a most delightful journey from London to this place. We spent near three days at Brighton, waiting for a good packet, and the wind being favourable got to Dieppe in nine hours. We were about 25 passengers, all groaning under sickness. . . . Mr. Biddulph made a third in a cabriolet with us from Dieppe to Paris. . . . The last 50 or 60 miles to Paris is all vineyard and a charming country. We stopped near a day at Rouen with Mr. Wild; nine-tenths of the people are Aristocrats; nearly three dozen churches are turning into shops and dwellings by a decree of the N. Assembly, and yet seventeen Parish Churches are left. I lodge here in the same house with young Watt—he is a furious democrat—detests the King and Fayette. The latter seems to be pretty generally suspected of treachery—Condorcet is equally so. It is entirely impossible for me to give you any good account of French politics ; they are mutable as the wind.   Watt says that a new revolution must inevitably take place, and that it will in all probability be fatal to the King, Fayette, and some hundred others.   The 14th of this month will probably be eventful. He means to join the French Army in case of any civil rupture. I have this morning been to some of the principal buildings of Paris with him as a guide.   The Thuilleries are shut up by the King's order, though they are *national* property.   I am this moment risen from a dinner at Bouvilliers (which John knows) where everything is given in a style far superior to what they do in London, and very much cheaper. . . . The streets of Paris stink more than the dirtiest hole in London, and you cannot walk even in this dry time, without repeated splashes.   I have been most completely lost many times already, and find the little French I know of the greatest use.   Poor John Turner * has never yet given utterance to a single word. I shall endeavour to get some intelligence about the safety with which one may be a spectator at the Federation.   I do not intend to run any risk in the matter, though every one agrees that the sight will be grand beyond conception.   I shall write again before I leave Paris. . . . The English here are all Aristocrats, and I do not intend to dine again at the Table d'Hote, as politics are discussed with such freedom that it is difficult to avoid disagreeable disputes. . . .

Believe me, Yours affectionately,

THO. WEDGWOOD.†

Best love to all.

P.S.—You cannot write to me in Paris.

---

* Who he was does not appear , perhaps an employé from Etruria, going over to France on a business errand.

† This and the letter next mentioned are the only letters of his among the family papers between the years 1791 and 1795.

The P.S. probably means that he is hurrying home after the fête. His making the journey for such a short stay is a sign of his revolutionary ardour. One can well imagine him making, like Wordsworth at the same time, a pilgrimage to the site of the Bastille, and piously bringing away a bit of stone from the fallen fortress.

> Bliss was it in that dawn to be alive,
> But to be young was very heaven !

It was only for about two years that Tom Wedgwood was a partner in the Etruria works. Whether he really worked at the business it is impossible to say— probably he did very little, considering his poor health and his laboratory work. A letter of April 1792 gives a glimpse of him as attending to sundry matters relating to the pottery, and sending a string of memoranda thereon to his father and brother in London. " Our common jasper is not yet at all as it should be ; it is too soft and all the things made of it drop in firing. . . . This is a great disappointment." Then come questions as to purchases of adjacent land, and as to what can be done with a tipsy coachman or postilion. Twice in a fortnight " Dan has got very drunk at Mr. Fletchers, and had like to have fallen off his horses. He alarmed my sisters by his bad driving and was very saucy to George this morning."

But by April in the next year, 1793, we have discussions as to the terms on which he and John Wedgwood are to retire from the partnership, and in June they ceased to be members of the firm. Tom had now some thoughts, apparently, of settling in America. To the young enthusiasts of that revolutionary time the lately born republic seemed, as we know, a blessed land of promise, a land where men might live in "freedom and virtue," untrammelled by the corruptions and superstitions of the old world. Leslie, who had spent a year or two in the States, argues with Tom against this project.

"I am afraid you will hardly find a situation in America where you could settle comfortably. The society is neither sufficiently enlightened for you, nor sufficiently refined. That country, seen at a distance, will present its fairest aspect ; and, though the slavish disposition of the people of Britain is mortifying to a generous man, we may reasonably hope that the impulse lately given to men's minds will soon triumph over every obstacle, and finally produce a general renovation of things."

Wedgwood, in turning his thoughts to America, probably had in his mind the notable example of Priestley, who, shrinking from the idea of returning to Birmingham after the destruction of his home in the riots of 1791, was on the point of migrating to Pennsylvania. But Leslie's advice was sensible, whatever we may think of his reasons. Priestley's own experience a year or two later was a good commentary on the hint that America was not altogether an ideal abode for the "friends of liberty." The unorthodox theologian and savant did not find it at all a peaceful retreat.*

At some time in the year 1793 Tom Wedgwood

* See Appendix, p. 253.

made the acquaintance of William Godwin,* then a prominent figure among the "friends of liberty." His "Enquiry concerning Political Justice" had appeared early in that year, and it had made him known as the philosophical representative of English Radicalism. Wedgwood, a youth of twenty-two, still in the stage of vehement revolt against things as they were, readily fell into the attitude of a reverent disciple, and we may be sure that to the impecunious and much-borrowing philosopher, the devoted allegiance of a young man belonging to a circle in which there was no lack of money, and himself on the way to being rich, would be more than welcome. The earliest of the extant letters addressed to Godwin (November 9, 1795) is on the subject of a proffered gift. It would seem that Wedgwood had proposed to send him a copying machine, and that Godwin had declined the gift, explaining at the same time his "sentiments on the giving and taking of presents."† This evoked from Wedgwood a lengthy reply, in which he treats the matter from the high ethical standpoint.

---

* William Godwin, born at Wisbech in 1756, began life as a Presbyterian minister, but at about thirty became a "complete unbeliever"; published "Political Justice" in 1793, and "Caleb Williams" in 1794; married Mary Wollstonecraft (father by her of Shelley's second wife); and afterwards Mrs. Clements or Clairemont, mother of the "Claire" who was mother of Byron's "Allegra"; got the sinecure post of yeoman-usher of the Exchequer in 1833, and died in 1836.

† One would like to know what these "sentiments" were Godwin's delicacy in the matter of gifts was of a singular kind. In after years he did not mind begging of Shelley, but stipulated that his son-in-law's drafts should be made out without his own name appearing on them.

Tom Wedgwood to Godwin

November 9, 1795.

[After an elaborate preamble] " Prostituted as we all are to the customs and opinions of Society, the attempt to build all our actions on motives of vestal purity is obviously impracticable. I durst not give, nor could another accept, an invitation to my table. . . . But what would result from the total suspension of good offices ? A disposition of mind unalloyed by selfishness ? No, our selfishness would increase with our wants and our principles would become every day weaker and weaker from not being brought into action. . . . I will now explain to you the precise motives of the action which gave birth to this speculation." [This he does at great length, beginning with the " pleasure that curious mechanical inventions afford." Copying machines had just lately been invented by James Watt. Then he proceeds :]

" I was glad when it occurred to me that by thus becoming useful to your pursuits and by cautiously avoiding at the same time any interruption of them from unseasonable visits, it was not improbable you might connect some agreeable associations with my person, and conceive some interest in my fellowship. . . . The above is a perfectly ingenuous and accurate review of the ideas that determined and grew out of an action of my life that I can never wish to retract. There may be a speck of selfishness on the face of it, but it is sound and untainted at heart. . . . May I solicit from you an explication as unreserved of the feelings that accompanied your passive situation ? If more agreeable to you, defer it till our next meeting. I confess that on some accounts I prefer writing to conversation. But this preference is owing entirely to my want of a frank and clear expression of my thoughts which exercise alone can supply.

" THOMAS WEDGWOOD."

Wedgwood's early letters are written, as this specimen shows, in an elaborately formal dialect, which we may set down in part to the fashion of the time. Later they became less stiff. In this instance, doubtless, the reverential attitude of the disciple to the master is accountable for the solemnity with which he discusses Godwin's pragmatical refusal of a small present. Like many older and wiser people, he was completely taken in by the audacious vigour with which Godwin expounded an utterly preposterous theory of human life. Mr. Kegan Paul tells us that the two men did not really get on very well together; they were "antipathetic when they met, and suited each other only at a distance." Wedgwood, while helping his friend with liberal loans, "preferred that they should not meet, and that their discussions should be conducted on paper." *

It is rather entertaining, when one remembers the philosopher's many borrowings, euphemistically so called, to find that he was annoyed at his disciple being so indelicate as to prepay the postage of his letters. Mrs. Shelley tells us that at one time Tom Wedgwood and her father "contemplated making a common household together." Such a common household would not have lasted many days without an explosion.

Wedgwood's papers include one or two bits of what appear to be compositions sent to Godwin for correction and comment. The criticisms in Godwin's hand are not of a kind to suggest that the master's help was of much value to the pupil. They are minute verbal corrections, in the manner rather of the schoolmaster

---

* Kegan Paul's "Life of Godwin," i. 311.

than of the philosopher. Wedgwood, for instance, writes: "This feeling, from the cradle to the death bed, never once deserts us." Godwin comments: "'Once,' pleonastic." Wedgwood describes a man as being in a "live" mood. Godwin says, "for 'live' read 'vigilant,' the other is scarcely English." Wedgwood's English is lax (*e.g.*, the odd use of the word "prostituted" in the above letter), but Godwin's corrections are of the kind which would take the life out of any style.

CHAPTER III

BEDDOES AND THE PNEUMATIC INSTITUTE

1793—1794

Soon after the rearrangement of the Wedgwood partnership in 1793, when Tom Wedgwood and his eldest brother John retired from the firm, the latter took up his abode at Cote House, a country place not far from Bristol, and there Tom was a frequent visitor. That, apparently, led to his becoming acquainted with Dr. Beddoes, the noted physician, who had lately come to settle in Bristol. The two men became intimate. Their views of things were in general accord, as would be sufficiently shown by the fact that it was Beddoes' sympathy with the French Revolution which had in some way been the cause of his having to give up the post of reader in chemistry at Oxford.* Both men · shared the passion for reforming and improving the world, which moved so many of the younger men of the time. Beddoes was a singularly interesting man. His letters give the impression of a mind overflowing with new ideas, a nature full of energy and initiative,

---

* Beddoes was born in 1760 at Shifnal in Shropshire, and died in London, where he had a large practice in his later years, in 1808. He was father of Thomas Lovell Beddoes, the half-mad poet, author of "Death's Jest Book." See the notices of both in the "Dict. Nat. Biog."

sanguine, optimistic, rebelling against antiquated routine, keen on striking out new paths. One of the things he preached was the importance of "preventive" medicine. He must have been one of the earliest workers in that field, and one of his schemes was a plan for setting a staff of young doctors to go about Bristol lecturing on the prevention of disease. " By this plan," he tells Wedgwood, " I think £550 a year would confer the full benefit of preventive and to a great extent of curative medicine upon all Bristol and the counties within attending distance." " This preventive medicine," he says, in another letter, "is much the most important of the two divisions." At another time we find him advocating a new system of "rational toys," and at another a new method of teaching geometry. But his chief enterprise was the " Pneumatic Institute," a scheme which aimed at giving a full trial to the method of treating consumption, cancer, and other diseases by the use of "factitious airs "—i.e., by the inhalation of certain gases, or of chemically modified atmospheric air. The institute was to be a small hospital for the reception of patients thus to be treated. Various eminent men, such as Dr. Erasmus Darwin, Keir the chemist, Professor Black, James Watt the great engineer, and some leading physicians, supported the scheme. Watt invented apparatus for making and administering the gases. The Wedgwoods, father and sons, gave substantial contributions. Tom Wedgwood was also active in helping Beddoes to collect the needful funds; and when there seemed to be a difficulty in  getting together what was wanted, he gave an additional thousand pounds in order that the plan might

be at once started.* His feeling about it is shown by
a few words he puts on a letter of Beddoes (dated
August 12, 1794), which he sends on to his brother
Josiah. "I think I shall contribute" (this was at the
first inception of the scheme), " as the attempt must be
successful in part if it only goes to show that 'airs'
are *not* efficacious in medicine.")

The Institute was duly opened in 1798, the patients
being taken into a house in Dowry Square, on the
Clifton side of Bristol, but it did not, alas! answer the
sanguine hopes of Beddoes. Consumption, cancers,
and internal ulcers refused to yield to the new treatment. The experiment had only the negative success
guessed at in Tom Wedgwood's wise and suggestive
words. It showed that "airs are not efficacious in
medicine." After two or three years the Institute was
given up, and in 1801 Beddoes left Bristol for London.
During these years Tom Wedgwood was one of
Beddoes' patients, stopping at Clifton at intervals to be
under his care. The "airs," however, did him no
good, nor had he better success with other strange
sorts of treatment which he tried, apparently, under
Beddoes' advice. One was the "warm-room plan."
His brother Josiah (December 1799) describes him as
living in a completely closed room, with a stove,
double windows, and double doors, in a temperature
kept up to 70 degrees, without once going out of the
room for seventy-two hours. He tells us also of con-
sumptive patients living in cow-houses, "three cows in

---

* In the notice of Josiah Wedgwood (the father) in the " Dict.
Nat. Biog.," it is implied that he gave this large contribution, but it
seems to have been Tom Wedgwood's.

each of the cow-houses," warmed by stoves.   Whether
Tom Wedgwood lived with the cows does not appear.
"For mere temperature," says Beddoes in his beautiful
optimistic way," "living with cows is the most
delicious thing imaginable; perhaps the fumes would
give a salutary stimulus to the surface of the lungs,
which might communicate itself to the whole system.
I find this much better than living with a butcher."
(Beddoes to T. W. November 12, 1799.)   The last
words seem to show that Beddoes had other patients
living with butchers, presumably on the theory that the
meaty atmosphere would do them good.   In another
letter (Beddoes to Tom Wedgwood, August 3, 1792)
he says: "I have had strict inquiry made concerning
the state of health among the Bristol butchers.   The
information is curious and satisfactory, and the result
will be of great use to my essay on consumption."   We
come across this strange cow-cure in the "Life and
Letters of Maria Edgeworth," whose sister Anna
Beddoes married.   "One of his hobbies," it is there
asserted, "was to introduce cows into invalids' bed-
rooms, that they might inhale the breath of the
animals, a prescription which naturally gave umbrage
to the Clifton lodging-house keepers."   De Quincey,
many years afterwards, described Tom Wedgwood as
having at one time kept a butcher's shop.   This myth
may perhaps have arisen from some twisted account of
the theory held, and apparently practised, by his
doctor.*

---

* The story is in De Quincey's gossiping account of Coleridge in
the "Autobiographic Sketches," first published in *Tait's Magazine*,
and afterwards republished (1854) among the "Selections Grave and

It was 'through Beddoes' " Pneumatic Institution" that the world first heard of the afterwards famous chemist, Humphrey Davy, of whom we shall have more to say as collaborating with Tom Wedgwood in his photographic work. The Wedgwoods had met him at Penzance, his native place, where he was an apothecary's apprentice, when staying there in the winter of 1797-8 for the sake of the warm climate. Beddoes, hearing that the youth knew something of chemistry, engaged him as assistant in the laboratory at Dowry Square. There, doubtless, he and Tom Wedgwood became more closely acquainted. One of the excitements of the time was Davy's discovery of the so-called " laughing gas." He had found a way of making nitrous oxide safely respirable, and was trying its effects on troops of friends who came to the laboratory to see and feel the new wonder. Southey called it " the wonder-working gas of delight." Here is Tom Wedgwood's written report of his sensations :

I called on Mr. Davy at the Medical Institution on July 23. . . . I had six quarts of the oxide given me in a bag undiluted, and as soon as I had breathed three or four respirations, I felt myself affected, and my respiration hurried, which effect increased rapidly until I became as it were entranced, when I

Gay." "As a desperate attempt to rouse and irritate the decaying sensibility of his system, I have been assured, by a surviving friend, that Mr. Wedgwood at one time opened a butcher's shop, conceiving that the affronts and disputes to which such a situation would expose him might act beneficially upon his increasing torpor." "Which, however" (he adds in a note to the reprint of 1854), " his brother Josiah denied as a pure fable."

De Quincey's account of Tom Wedgwood, in the passage of which this is a part, has all his accustomed charm of manner, but is too full of inaccuracies and confusions to be worth quoting.

threw the bag from me and kept breathing on furiously with an open mouth, and holding my nose with my left hand, having no power to take it away, though aware of the ridiculousness of my situation. . . . Before I breathed the air I felt a good deal fatigued from a very long ride I had had the day before; but after breathing, I lost all sense of fatigue.*

After the Institute was given up and Beddoes went to London, Tom Wedgwood appears to have seen little of him. In letters of the year 1803 we find him collecting funds for some project the nature of which is not mentioned, to which Tom gives £100 and his brother Josiah £50.

---

* Printed in the collected works of Davy with reports of other like experiences.

JOSIAH WEDGWOOD
Of Gunville, Dorset, and Maer Hall, Staffordshire

CHAPTER IV

THE FAMILY CIRCLE
1795—1796

IN the last few pages I have departed from chronological sequence in order to give an account of Tom Wedgwood's relations with Beddoes. I will now take up the thread of his life from the time when the death of old Josiah Wedgwood of Etruria led to a dispersion of the family circle.

That death happened in January 1795. The fortune the great potter left to be divided among his children was large, and thus at the age of twenty-three Tom became a fairly rich man. His broken health forbade him to think of taking up any regular pursuit, and his frequent fits of dejection and restlessness drove him to seek relief in a wandering life. Of marriage he cannot have thought, it was too plainly impossible; and neither his extant letters nor family tradition tell us of his caring for any woman outside the circle of his relations. But he had a warmly affectionate nature; he clung closely to his family, and could not endure to be for long away from his brothers and sisters and their children. Among them he may be said to have lived, though in an intermittent way. And here it may be convenient to say what were his family surroundings in this year 1795 and thereafter.

Josiah Wedgwood of Etruria left behind him a widow and six children : three sons, John, Josiah, and Thomas, and three daughters, Susannah, Catharine, and Sarah. John, the eldest son, who had given up his partnership in the pottery in 1793, had become a London banker, and was living in Devonshire Place, Marylebone. A year or two later he took up his abode at Cote House, a country place about two miles out of Bristol. Josiah, the next brother, remained for a time at Etruria, carrying on the works in conjunction with his cousin, Thomas Byerley, who for many years was the working head of the business. He not long afterwards sought an abode in the south of England, fixing himself first at Stoke d'Abernon, near Cobham, in Surrey, and ultimately (1799–1800) at Gunville House, near Blandford, in Dorsetshire. Josiah had married, in 1792, Elizabeth Allen, the eldest of many daughters of John Bartlett Allen of Cresselly, a Pembrokeshire squire, and John, about a year later, had married Jane Allen, another of the sisters. Both brothers had children. Susannah Wedgwood, Tom's eldest sister, married, a few months after her father's death, Dr. Robert Darwin of Shrewsbury, son of Dr. Erasmus the poet. One of her many children was Charles Darwin, author of the " Origin. of Species " (born 1809). The two younger sisters, Catharine and Sarah Wedgwood (always spoken of as Kitty and Sally), aged twenty and eighteen, lived with their mother for a few years in Staffordshire, and afterwards moved with her into Dorsetshire to be near Josiah's family. The person who counted for most in Tom Wedgwood's life was his brother Josiah. An intense affection united these two men. It was to Josiah that Tom turned in all his troubles. Intellectually, the two were not much alike. Josiah was a man of solid character, wide-minded and high-minded; an upright, calmly judging person, a man whom every one trusted, and on whom every one near him leant. He had intellectual tastes, but these were quite secondary to the practical interests of life, and warm affections, but no man could have been more inexpressive. His letters are the *ne plus ultra* of dryness. As he was his poor sick brother's mainstay, so he was a rock of support at all times of doubt and difficulty to the whole of his family, including his wife's relations. The strong family belief in his excellent judgment was well shown at a critical moment in the life of his nephew, Charles Darwin. The turning-point in Darwin's career was his going as naturalist on the voyage of the *Beagle*. When the offer was made to him—he was then twenty-one—his father strongly objected to his accepting it, and he was on the point of sending a refusal; but his " Uncle Jos " backed him up in his desire to go, and wrote to Dr. Darwin, discussing *seriatim* the latter's objections. His reasonings convinced the father, and the son became a naturalist, instead of, as he had intended, a clergyman. Darwin, in the brief autobiography which he wrote (in 1876) for his wife and children, describes his uncle thus :

I greatly revered him ; he was silent and reserved so as to be rather an awful man ; but he sometimes talked openly with

me.   He was the very type of an upright man, with the clearest
judgment.   I do not believe that any power on earth could
have made him swerve an inch from what he considered the
right course.   I used to apply to him in my mind the well-
known ode of Horace, now forgotten by me, in which the
words, " nec vultus tyranni," &c., come in.*

Josiah had had the happiness to marry a delightful
woman.   His " Bessy" was the best beloved of the
whole family circle, and her letters give the reflection
of an ideally beautiful character.   The family tradition
tells the same story with one voice, and we can well
believe it when we look at the " radiantly cheerful
countenance " that beams upon us out of one of the
loveliest of Romney's portraits.†

Cote House, the abode of John Wedgwood, was
Tom's most frequent resort after that of his brother
Josiah.   There, too, he had always an affectionate welcome from another charming sister-in-law.   Louisa
Jane Wedgwood (always called " Jenny " in the family)
was the beauty of the Wedgwood-Allen circle, and the
family letters give ample proof that she must have been
a singularly attractive woman.   The Robert Darwins
of Shrewsbury seem to have seen but little of Tom.

---

* "Life of C. Darwin," by F. Darwin, I. 44.   (The ode is that
beginning "Justum et tenacem propositi virum.")   The interesting
letter of Josiah's about the *Beagle* business is given on p. 198 of the
same volume.

† Now belonging to her grand-daughter, Miss Wedgwood, of
Leith Hill Place.   "She has her mother's radiantly cheerful countenance," are the words used by Maria Edgeworth, a life-long friend
of the family, in describing Mrs. Charles Darwin, Mrs. Josiah's
youngest daughter, then in her thirty-third year.   (Letter of December 26, 1840, to Fanny Butler.)

MRS. JOSIAH WEDGWOOD, BORN ELIZABETH ALLEN
From Portrait by Romney

Of his two unmarried sisters, both of whom were cultivated and intelligent women, Sally was the one with
whom he had most in common intellectually. During
his wanderings in search of health it is to her that he
most often sends affectionate messages.*

Through his two sisters-in-law he became intimate
with the family at Cresselly. Fanny Allen,† the
youngest, gayest, and most keen witted of the group
of sisters, became, during the last few years of his life,
one of his best friends.

Catherine Allen, another of the Cresselly sisters,
married Mr. Mackintosh (afterwards Sir James) in
1798. They naturally became friends of Tom Wedgwood, and the two men were brought the closer
together by their common interest in metaphysical
speculation.

Such was the family *entourage* of Tom Wedgwood
when he ceased to live at Etruria after his father's
death. What plan of life, if any, he formed at that
time, there is nothing to show. Metaphysical study
and speculation was evidently, as always, one of his
chief interests.‡ Physical investigations he had put

---

* Sarah Wedgwood lived to the age of eighty and died in 1856.
She spent her last years at Down, in Kent, living near her nephew
and niece, Charles and Emma Darwin.

† Fanny Allen lived to be ninety-three, dying in 1875, and was
the last link between Tom Wedgwood's generation and that of his
great-nephews and nieces. They remember her as a most entertaining old lady, with a sharp tongue and caustic wit ; a fiercely
bigoted whig of the old school, full of Holland House traditions,
including the worship of Napoleon. Mackintosh and Sydney Smith
were among her particular friends. When the news of Waterloo
came, she wrote of it as "a splendid victory, but in a terribly bad
cause." (As to Jessie Allen, Mme. Sismondi, see p. 123.)

‡ See chap. xiv.

aside, at least for a time. Such active work as his
letters disclose always took the form of helping forward some scheme aiming at the improvement of the
world. [Anything of the kind we now call a social or
philanthropic "movement," any plan for teaching
mankind to mend its ways, if it ran on what he
thought sound philosophical or liberal lines, found in
him a zealous supporter. To such plans he would
give work as well as money. To spread, for instance,
a knowledge of inoculation as a preventive of small-
pox was one of the things with which he busied himself. He corresponded with people in various parts of
England who were engaged in the same effort, and
used his local influence in the cause. We find him
getting a thousand copies printed of an "address to
parents" on the subject, for distribution among the
people of the Potteries.] This was in 1795, after
which time I find no more letters on the subject.
Jenner was just then completing the investigations
which led to vaccination taking the place of inoculation.

[Another correspondent is a worthy Quaker book-
seller, Mr. Samuel Phillips, whom he has commissioned
to send him a supply of books fit for popular reading.
Mr. Phillips applauds "thy praiseworthy attempts to
improve the minds of the labouring poor in your
neighbourhood," and sends a supply of books.] He
has severe views as to what reading is beneficial, and
sternly bars all fiction. "I was much pleased with the
hesitating *perhaps* to ' two or three novels.' *Experto
crede Roberto.* Let them read *none.* Few of them are
true pictures of life. The best of them fill the mind

with dreams of imaginary happiness not to be enjoyed in this life."

In 1796, Tom Wedgwood took the first of many tours out of England in search of health, spending some five months in Germany and Switzerland, with Leslie for his companion.   As a rule his letters during such absences are not cheerful reading, being but too full of his health troubles ; but this journey was comparatively prosperous.   He does much of it on foot, at one time walking 200 miles, as he reckons, in fourteen days ; and he apparently walks without difficulty over mountain passes in the Swiss Oberland. The two friends follow the now familiar route, Lucerne, Rigi, Brunig, Meyringen, Grindelwald, Lauterbrunnen, Thun ; and his long, cheerful letters, telling his brother Jos of each day's experiences, show that at this time he had a spell of fair health.

It is merely through the accidental preservation of a few letters from his friends that a record has survived of some of his charitable and public-spirited deeds during the years immediately following his father's death ; * but enough appears to show that he was acting out the scheme of life and duty which was the burden of those enthusiastic outpourings to his father in his early youth.

"I mean," he had said at nineteen, "to exert myself for the good of my fellow creatures."   He had become

---

* His only letters of this time are those from abroad.   He was an enjoying traveller, and every word must have been interesting to the readers of a century ago in Staffordshire.   But travel-letters have too often proved the bane of biographers, and these would be no exception to the rule.

a rich man, and this was what he was trying to do, though a cruel fate had cut him off from the possibility of trying to do it by direct personal work. He believed, evidently, that advance in knowledge was the surest means of bettering the condition of the world. This belief, doubtless, quite as much as personal friendship, was the governing motive which led him to promise John Leslie an annuity of £150 a year, to be increased to £250 in the case of his marrying, with the view of putting him in a position to go on working at physical science, unhampered by anxiety as to his daily bread. Leslie at this time (1797) was thirty-one years old. He had been pursuing his physical researches, but had not got any post suitable to his powers, or any other prospect of making a regular income. He was at a loose end, and had vague intentions of seeking his fortune on the continent or in India. The query on which Wedgwood hung the offer of the annuity was : "would it materially increase the sum total of your philosophical product?" Leslie's response to this (August 18, 1797) is in his customary strain of magniloquence :

"Your letter I have perused with surprise and with admiration. Sentiments so remote from vulgar apprehension, so pure, so refined, so far exalted above the cold maxims that govern the world ! I well know your elevation of mind, fired by every generous resolve, yet attempered by the calm dictates of philosophy. But how wide the difference between the aspirations of beneficence and that vigour of character which successfully spurns the low, the incessant whisperings of opinions and interest, and in spite of sacrifice carries its plans into deliberate effect !"

In another letter, after taking time to consider the ✓ query, he answers it (at great length) in the affirmative.⌐

Of the letter offering the annuity there is no copy among the Wedgwood papers. But we may take the motives of the generous act to have been the same as we shall see expressed, a little later, in the offer of an annuity to Coleridge. What degree of personal attachment existed between Tom Wedgwood and Leslie it is not easy to say. It was apparently a warm feeling, on Wedgwood's side at any rate, in the early days of their acquaintance at Edinburgh, but the impression given by the later letters is that it afterwards subsided into no more than an intellectual friendship. In Wedgwood's letters during their five months touring in 1796, he hardly ever mentions his companion, and the elaborate pomposity of Leslie's style effectually masks any feeling there may have been on his side.

Wedgwood's generosity, in this instance, may be said to have borne good fruit in the way which he desired. Leslie's contributions to the advance of physical science were substantial, and they rested on long-continued experimental researches which he certainly could not have pursued without some assurance of a maintenance. His "Experimental Inquiry into the Nature and Properties of Heat," has been described as "an important contribution to the scientific study of the subject," and his discoveries as to the radiation of heat made his name widely known. His "differential thermometer" is, I understand, still a familiar instrument in physical laboratories. He is mentioned by Clerk Maxwell as

having " given the first correct explanation of the rise
of liquid in a tube " (capillary attraction). Ice-making ⁄
machines were his invention.*

---

* He received the annuity up to the year 1812. He became
Professor of Mathematics at Edinburgh in 1805, and Professor of
Natural Philosophy there in 1819. He was knighted in 1832 and
died in the same year.

CHAPTER V

POOLE AND COLERIDGE—THE COLERIDGE ANNUITY

1797—1798

THE year 1797 brought with it a notable extension of Tom Wedgwood's friendships. He was staying in the summer with his brother John at Cote House (near Bristol), and it was probably there that he made the acquaintance of that interesting and singular man Thomas Poole, or "Tom Poole" as every one called him, tanner, farmer, and land agent, of Nether Stowey. The acquaintance soon became a very close friendship, and out of it sprang an equally close friendship with Coleridge the poet.

The admirable biography of Poole by Mrs. Henry Sandford,* gives a vivid picture of his life, besides much information, some of it new, as to Coleridge and . as to Tom Wedgwood. Poole was a man of rough exterior, and for the most part self-educated, but what we now know of his mind and character fully explains

---

* "Thomas Poole and his Friends," 2 vols. Macmillan, 1886. See also the notice of Poole in "Dict. Nat. Biog." by Sir L. Stephen. Mrs. Sandford is, I believe, the grand-daughter of one of Poole's first cousins. He was born in 1765, lived practically his whole life at Nether Stowey, and died in 1837. The group of friends among whom Tom Wedgwood now found himself were all young together. Their birth dates all fall within the range of a few years : Coleridge 1772, Wedgwood 1771, Wordsworth 1770, Dorothy Wordsworth 1771, Poole 1765, Lamb 1775.

how it was that he became the attached friend of some
of the most remarkable Englishmen of his time.
Here is De Quincey's description of the man as he
found him in 1807, ten years later than the time of
his first acquaintance with Tom Wedgwood :

> I found him a stout, plain-looking farmer, leading a bachelor
> life, in a rustic, old-fashioned house, the house, however, upon
> further acquaintance, proving to be amply furnished with
> modern luxuries, and especially with a good library, superbly
> mounted in all departments bearing upon political philosophy ;
> and the farmer turning out a polished and liberal Englishman,
> who had travelled extensively, and who had so entirely dedicated
> himself to the service of his humble fellow countrymen—the
> hewers of wood and drawers of water in this part of Somerset-
> shire —that for many miles round he was the general arbiter of
> their disputes, the guide and counsellor of their difficulties ;
> besides being appointed executor and guardian to his children
> by every third man who died in or about the town of Nether
> Stowey.*

Coleridge had at this time (Midsummer 1797) been
living for six months in a cottage at Stowey with his
wife and their infant child.   He and Poole were almost
next door neighbours, for a walk of a few yards along
a back lane led from the garden of the cottage to the
garden of Poole's house.   Wordsworth and his sister
Dorothy were just then taking up their abode at
Alfoxden House in the Quantocks, where they lived
for a year, about three miles away ; and it was then

---

* From an article contributed to *Tait's Magazine* in 1834, vol. ii.
p. 139 of Professor Masson's Ed. of De Quincey, 1889. The epithet
"polished" as applied to Poole, is absurdly out of place. But De
Quincey's inaccuracies of detail are innumerable, especially when he
is writing from recollections of thirty or forty years back.

that they and Coleridge first became intimate. Dorothy's journal gives a delightful picture of the three friends. There were almost daily meetings, continual walkings to and fro between Stowey and Alfoxden, wanderings among the glades and over the downs of the Quantocks—they were, as Coleridge said, " three people and one soul." In much of this intimacy Poole shared. He had been a good friend to Coleridge since 1794, the days of the wild Pantisocracy scheme, had helped him much, and was still helping him. For some years past he had been his chief stand-by in all trouble. Into this remarkable group of friends Tom Wedgwood came through his acquaintance with Poole. Unfortunately we have none of his letters of this date, and it is only through a few words in a note book kept for jotting down memoranda bearing on his metaphysical studies that we know that in September of this year he paid a visit of five days to the Wordsworths at Alfoxden. The note is as follows :

Time, entering the garden at Langford, September 15, 1797. Went down to Wordsworth's with ——n. Spent 5 days there. Remarked to ——n on the 5th day at Alfoxden that the time had gone like lightning. He agreed with me. Entering the garden at L——, it struck me as being very long since I had entered it before, though I knew it was only five days. Might not this be owing to my having never "intermediately" thought of the garden ? Its recollection was faint, and suggested remoteness of time, as faint objects do distance in sight.*

---

* Tom Wedgwood evidently did much of his metaphysical thinking while travelling, and it was his habit to keep by him a notebook wherein he could record at the moment anything that occurred to him. The front page of the one containing the above observation

One would have liked to have heard something of
the impressions left by those five days spent in the
company of Coleridge and Wordsworth, and of that
delightful woman, Dorothy Wordsworth, who was so
much to both of them.   The moment was one of
supreme interest.   For what was stirring those three
minds was to be the beginning of a new departure in
English poetry.   Wordsworth was still unknown to
the world, but most of the " Lyrical Ballads " lay on
his table, ready for the press; and it was only a few
weeks later that the three happy people started on that
memorable walk to Porlock and Lynton, during the
first few miles of which the " Rime of the Ancient
Mariner " began to take shape.   The talks which went
on during those autumn days, when, as Wordsworth
has it in the Prelude :

> Upon smooth Quantock's airy ridge they roved
> Unchecked, or loitered 'mid her sylvan combes,

or in the many walks between Stowey and Alfoxden,
were giving form and force to ideas which were to issue
in a literary revolution, to mould, more or less, the
poetry of the coming century, and to colour the whole
of its intellectual movement.   Wedgwood, probably,
could have had little prevision of what was to come out
of the association of his new group of friends.   The
poetic side of Coleridge's genius would appeal to him

---

bears the words : " If this book is sent by coach or other conveyance
to A. R. BUSH TAVERN, BRISTOL, to lie till called for, one
crown will be given to the person sending it."   I should guess that
his companion " ——n," was the James Tobin with whom both he
and the Wordsworths were intimate.   (See note p. 143)

less than the outpourings of that wonderful mind upon the subjects which most occupied his own thoughts—Ethics and Metaphysics.* In any case the impression he carried away was a deep one, as is sufficiently shown by what occurred three months later.

Coleridge's whole existence was made up of visions, and his then plan of life, if plan it could be called, was one of these. He was living in the cottage found for him by Poole. There he was trying, or professed to be trying, to support himself with his wife and child by a "combination of literature and husbandry." Charles Lloyd, the young man who had been living with him for a time as pupil and friend, paying £80 a year, had left him. The cottage stood in a garden of an acre and a half. On this he thought he could · "raise vegetables and corn enough for myself and wife, and feed a couple of grunting cousins from the refuse." His evenings he was to devote to literature. "By reviews in the magazine and other shilling-scavenger employments, I shall probably gain £40 a year, which economy and self-denial, gold-beaters, shall hammer till it cover my annual expenses." The ever kind Poole, who let him have the cottage rent free, was also apparently to supply the family with milk, and no doubt with other incidentals. Before Tom Wedgwood came on the scene, this arcadian dream, hardly less

---

* I feel it difficult to imagine that Tom Wedgwood cared deeply for poetry. Hazlitt quotes Coleridge as saying that "Mackintosh and Tom Wedgwood (of whom, however, he spoke highly) had expressed a very indifferent opinion of Mr. Wordsworth, on which he remarked to them, 'he strides on so far before you that he dwindles in the distance.'"

absurd than the Pantisocracy of a few years earlier, must have nearly faded away. The "Watchman" enterprise of the previous year (1796) had utterly failed, and Coleridge was in great straits. Poole had then got together a sum of £35 to £40, six or seven friends contributing five guineas each, which was given him as a "testimonial," with the expressed intention that the like help should be continued annually for a time. The gift seems to have been repeated in 1797.

It was in December of this year that Coleridge was invited to preach in a Unitarian Chapel at Shrewsbury, with the prospect of being appointed its minister at a salary of £150 a year. "This coming to the knowledge of Josiah and Thomas Wedgwood, they hastened to send him a present of £100, to relieve his immediate necessities, and to dissuade him from abandoning poetry and philosophy for the ministry. The cheque was immediately returned by Coleridge with a grateful letter, explaining that the £100 would soon be consumed, and prospectless poverty recur."* Immediately after writing this, he went to Shrewsbury, and on the next Sunday, January 14, 1798, preached there the sermon so graphically described many years later by William Hazlitt in an often quoted passage. Meanwhile, on the preceding Saturday (January 13), there had reached Stowey the following letter, addressed to him by Josiah Wedgwood, writing on behalf of himself and his brother.

---

* These are the words of Mr. Dykes Campbell, p. 81, but see note on p. 56 *infra*. There is nothing in the Wedgwood papers referring to this matter. A copy of Coleridge's letter declining the £100 exists in Tom Poole's letter-book (T. P., i. 256), but Mrs. Sandford does not print it.

Josiah Wedgwood to S. T. Coleridge

PENZANCE,
January 10, 1798.

DEAR SIR,—

In the absence of my brother, who has an engagement this morning, I take up the pen to reply to your letter received yesterday. I cannot help regretting very sincerely that, at this critical moment, we are separated by so great a length of the worst road in the kingdom. It is not that we have found much difficulty in deciding how to act in the present juncture of your affairs, but we are apprehensive that, deprived of the benefit of conversation, we may fail somewhat in explaining our views and intentions with that clearness and persuasion which should induce you to accede to our proposal without scruple or hesitation—nay, with that glow of pleasure which the accession of merited good fortune, and the observation of virtuous conduct in others, ought powerfully to excite in the breast of healthful sensibility. Writing is painful to me. I must endeavour to be concise, yet to avoid abruptness. My brother and myself are possessed of a considerable superfluity of fortune ; squandering and hoarding are equally distant from our inclinations. But we are earnestly desirous to convert this superfluity into a fund of beneficence, and we have now been accustomed for some time, to regard ourselves rather as Trustees than Proprietors. We have canvassed your past life, your present situation and prospects, your character and abilities. As far as certainty is compatible with the delicacy of the estimate, we have no hesitation in declaring that your claim upon the fund appears to come under more of the conditions we have prescribed for its disposal, and to be every way more unobjectionable, than we could possibly have expected. This result is so congenial with our heartfelt wishes, that it will be a real mortification to us if any misconception or distrust of our intentions, or any unworthy diffidence of yourself, should interfere to prevent its full operation in your favour.

After what my brother Thomas has written,* I have only to state the proposal we wish to make to you. It is that you shall accept an annuity for life of £150, to be regularly paid by us, no condition whatsoever being annexed to it. Thus your liberty will remain entire, you will be under the influence of no professional bias, and will be in possession of a "*permanent income not inconsistent with your religious and political creeds*," † so necessary to your health and activity.

I do not now enter into the particulars of the mode of securing the annuity, &c.—that will be done when we receive your consent to the proposal we are making ; and we shall only say that we mean the annuity to be independent of everything but the wreck of our fortune, an event which we hope is not very likely to happen, though it must in these times be regarded as more than a bare possibility.

Give me leave now to thank you for the openness with which you have written to me, and the kindness you express for me, to neither of which can I be indifferent, and I shall be happy to derive the advantages from them that a friendly intercourse with you cannot fail to afford me.

I am very sincerely yours,

JOSIAH WEDGWOOD.‡

---

* What Tom had written we do not, and probably never shall, know. Presumably Josiah is alluding to the letter sending Coleridge £100, which Mr. Dykes Campbell describes as written " to dissuade him from abandoning poetry and philosophy for the ministry." The terms of that letter have never, I believe, been published, and probably it does not exist. Coleridge's mention of it in a letter of January 30, 1798, to Thelwall (" Letters of S. T. C.," 234), shows nothing to connect it with the Shrewsbury invitation, save the fact that it and the invitation reached him at the same time. But the Wedgwoods may have known before that time that Coleridge was thinking of becoming a Unitarian minister

† A " quotation," says Mrs. Sandford, "from S. T. C.'s last letter."

‡ Poole entered a copy of Josiah's letter in his own letter-book, from which copy it was printed for the first time by Mrs. Sandford (T. P., i. 259). She describes it as a reply to the letter of Coleridge declining the £100, which letter I take to be the one

This letter was opened by Poole, who at once wrote to Coleridge, sending him a copy of it ; and strenuously urging him to accept the offer.   This found Coleridge at Wem, a village near Shrewsbury, where he was staying for a few days with the Hazlitts.   He accepted the proposal at once.   Hazlitt's account * says :

When I came down to breakfast, I found that he had just received a letter from his friend T. Wedgwood, making him an offer of £150 a year if he chose to waive his present pursuit, and devote himself entirely to the study of poetry and philosophy. Coleridge seemed to make up his mind to close with this proposal in the act of tying on one of his shoes.

The letter conveying the acceptance is apparently not now extant; that it expressed his deep gratitude may be safely inferred from his allusions to the brothers' generosity in other letters and at other times. " You know, of course," he writes to Wordsworth, " that I have accepted the magnificent liberality of Josiah and Thomas Wedgwood."   And to Thelwall (January 30, 1798), he says : " Astonished, agitated, and feeling as I could not help feeling, I accepted the offer in the same worthy spirit, I hope, in which it was made."   (Letters of S. T. C., pp. 234, 235.)

Josiah mentions as " received yesterday."   Poole's letter to Coleridge sending him a copy of Josiah's (also printed by Mrs. Sandford) is curiously argumentative, as if he were afraid Coleridge would decline the offer.

* First published in 1817 by Hazlitt in the *Examiner* and reprinted by him with additions more than once.   The whole story evidently made a deep impression on him, so that his recollections were probably accurate, notwithstanding the lapse of twenty years.

The following letter has more than once been printed as being that conveying the acceptance. This it was not, but a reply to a note from Tom Wedgwood asking him to come at once to Cote House, whither, no doubt, Tom was then going from Penzance. The "Friday night" must have been January 26, 1798.*

S. T. Coleridge to Tom Wedgwood

Friday night,
Twelve o'clock.

MY DEAR SIR,—

I have this moment received your letter, and have scarcely more than a moment to answer it by return of post. If kindly feelings can be repaid by kindly feelings, I am not your debtor. I would wish to express the something that is big at my heart, but I know not how to do it without indelicacy. As much abstracted from personal feelings, as is possible, I honour and esteem you for that which you have done. I must, *of necessity*, stay here till the close of Sunday next. On Monday morning I shall leave it, and on Tuesday will be with you at Cote House.

Very affectionately yours,

S. T. COLERIDGE.

Shrewsbury.

The letter making the offer of the annuity was written, it will be seen, by Josiah Wedgwood, but this, as the first words show, was an accident. I think it is

---

* (See T. P., i. 261, and Dykes Campbell, p. 84.) This point of detail would be of no consequence if Coleridge's hasty note had not been wrongly read as representing his feelings on receiving the offer of the annuity. Cottle's print of the letter is, as usual, inaccurate in several places. The original is at Leith Hill Place.

certain that the act was due to Tom's initiative. Subsequent correspondence shows that Coleridge was much less intimate with Josiah than with his brother, and there can be little doubt that it was the impression which Tom took away from those autumn days at Stowey and Alfoxden that impelled him to come to Coleridge's assistance at the critical moment of the Shrewsbury candidature. It was in the preceding summer that he had promised the. annuity to Leslie. In that Josiah had no share ; but there was the closest possible union between the brothers, and we may easily suppose that he would be anxious to take his part in this new exercise of a wise generosity.

Wordsworth called it an act of " unexampled liberality," and this it probably was. There have been, of course, in all times " patrons " of poets and men of genius. But this act had nothing of patronage in it, nor anything savouring of selfishness. It sprang from the same kind of impulse as prompted that memorable legacy of £900 left by the dying Raisley Calvert to Wordsworth, upon which little sum, with a few slight windfalls, he and his sister managed to live during those seven or eight years at Alfoxden and Dove Cottage which gave to the world the most imperishable of his poems. The history of the world, perhaps, could show no case of a little money better used than that. The act differed from the Wedgwoods' only in being a bequest while theirs was an immediate gift. But whether " unexampled " or not, their liberality was of a rare kind.* The brothers were acting out, in a

---

* The nearest parallel to it which I can remember, is that of the

very uncommon way, that high conception of wealth as
a trust which is so often heard of but so seldom translated into deeds.   How far the annuity worked for the
good of Coleridge, or for the benefit of the world,
except as a fine example of public spirit, is a question
not to be answered with certainty. No one can be
sure that if he had taken for a time the charge of the
Shrewsbury chapel, the pressure and stimulus of regular
work might not have saved him from the weakness
which practically spoilt his life. One can hardly say
that the relief from pressing money cares stimulated
his poetic faculty.   The " Ancient Mariner " was begun

---

annuity secured to Beethoven by three Viennese grandees, in order
to deliver him from the necessity of teaching for a livelihood, and
give him the leisure to which we owe the grandest of his music.
Their wise liberality has given a secure immortality to the names
of the Archduke Rudolph, Prince Lobkowitz, and Prince Kinsky ;
but their act was not clear of a touch of selfishness ; for they did
it partly to keep Beethoven in Vienna, fearing lest he might be
tempted by some royal or noble music-lover to migrate to Berlin or
elsewhere.   Similarly the world has reason to be grateful to the
Esterhazys for maintaining Haydn in ease and plenty for many
years ; but that, of course, was only in a secondary sense an act of
public spirit, to keep an orchestra and a composer as part of a
princely establishment being in that time and country much the
same thing as an English peer's keeping a pack of foxhounds.
  Southey had, from 1797 (*æt.* 23), an annuity settled on him by
his old schoolfellow Charles Wynn, which he insisted on relinquishing
when Wynn married, but private friendship counted for much in
that case.
  The case of Auguste Comte and his English admirers, Grote,
Molesworth, Mill, and Currie, who came to his assistance on his
losing an official income, is another example of public spirit.   But
it ended somewhat uncomfortably, for when the philosopher began
to claim payment of the subsidy as a right, the donors, partly perhaps
because they had cooled in their estimate of his philosophy, did
not see their way to continue it.

in November 1797, before the annuity was thought of, and finished in March 1798; the first part of "Christabel" was produced in that same year 1797. Save the second part of "Christabel," which was completed in 1800, little of his work after 1797 can be said to be of substantial value.* That the "shaping spirit of imagination" which produced such a marvel as the "Ancient Mariner" should have thus gone to sleep, only to wake again at rare moments, is one of the sad wonders of Coleridge's life. The annuity, however, had one immediate result, the effects of which were far-reaching. Coleridge's stay in Germany was from September 1798 to June 1799. It was there that he got his knowledge of the language and began to make a close acquaintance with German poetry and philosophy. German literature was at that time practically unknown in England, though there had been signs here and there, towards the end of the century, that we were beginning to take note of its existence. It was Coleridge who played the leading part in bringing German philosophy within the range of English ideas, and the residence in the country which enabled him to do this was the first result of the annuity.† The

---

* "Kubla Khan was written about April 1798 (D. C., p. 88), "Love" in 1798–99, "France" in February 1798, "Dejection" and the "Chamounix Sunrise-hymn" in 1802. Sara Coleridge, herein agreeing with all the world, calls 1797 her father's "annus mirabilis," his "poetical zenith" ("Biog. Lit." ed. 1847, ii. 421).

† Sir L Stephen, in the "History of English Thought in the Eighteenth Century," calls Coleridge "the interpreter of Germany to England." See also the same writer's Essay on the "Importation of German" ("Studies of a Biographer"), in which he brings together a number of curious particulars as to the first beginnings of the study of German literature and philosophy in England. "Cole-

project had been talked over, apparently, between him
and the Wordsworths at Alfoxden, and it took shape
almost immediately after they gave up that abode at
Midsummer 1798. By September they and Coleridge
were on their way to Hamburg, he leaving his wife and
child at Stowey. The route they took, by Göttingen,
Goslar, and the Hartz Mountains, was exactly that
which Tom Wedgwood had followed with Leslie a year
and a half earlier. This was probably more than a
coincidence. We may suppose the whole scheme to
have been planned at Alfoxden, where Wedgwood
would naturally have talked about his travels of the
preceding year in the country the three friends were
about to visit. In any case it was the annuity which
made the journey possible to Coleridge.* His meeting
with Tom Wedgwood was the turning-point of his
life.

He was then twenty-five, and had yet thirty-seven
years to live. During many of these years he was
under the bondage of the opium-slavery, which so
nearly wrecked his life. But from this he was to recover, as we all know, and to such effect that one of

---

ridge," he says, " must be regarded as the main channel through
which German philosophy began to influence Englishmen."

* It has been stated that the Wedgwoods supplied the funds for
Coleridge's journey, besides giving him the annuity : but I know of
nothing to show that they did this. Professor Knight (" Life of
Wordsworth," vol. 1.) seems to think that they also defrayed part
of the Wordsworths' expenses, but I think any help they gave him
was only by way of loan, and by enabling him to get his drafts
cashed through their German correspondents. A letter of Josiah
(February 5, 1799) mentions drawings of this kind, and in another
letter (July 31, 1800) he alludes to the repayment of an advance
of £100 which he made to Wordsworth for the tour.

the greatest thinkers of the succeeding generation, one
whose words were as oracles to the English youth of
his time, could speak of him as "one of the two
seminal minds of the century." Thus wrote John
Stuart Mill in 1840, coupling him with Bentham—a
curious collocation, but one that shows, at least, the
breadth of view on which the judgment was founded.
If Coleridge's far-reaching influence on many of the
finest minds of the next generations has tended to the
benefit of the world, we may well "count it for right-
eousness" to Tom Wedgwood that he had the insight
to discern, in the unknown young man of twenty-five,
during these five days at Stowey and Alfoxden, a rare
and original genius, and that when the opportunity
came he did what he could to set that genius free for
doing the highest service to the world. How it was
that such a life as Coleridge's, made up of visionary
schemings, with only fitful intervals of fragmentary
effort, and with hardly any accomplished result save
the few pages of poetry which have enshrined him
among the immortals, should have left such an influence behind it, is a standing wonder. His earlier and
his later life seem like the lives of two different men.
Any attempt to estimate the extent of that influence
would be here out of place. I may perhaps recall
one example which to myself has always been a con-
vincing proof of its reality and power, the life and
work of Frederick Denison Maurice. The aims and
beliefs of that "spiritual splendour" (as Gladstone
called him, quoting Dante's description of St. Dominic
in the *Paradiso*), whose mind and character became, in
their turn, a living and inspiring influence still felt in

various spheres of English life, were a direct out-
come of Coleridge's teaching.*

---

* Whatever may be the true view of Coleridge's teaching we
need not, I think, take any serious account of Carlyle's famous
caricature of him in the "Life of Sterling." ("Coleridge sat on
the top of Highgate Hill," &c.) That I prefer to think of as merely
a piece of picturesque satire, thrown in for the sake of literary
effect, and a good example of the rule that in writing history the
picturesque is the deadly enemy of the true. This, perhaps, was
what Jowett chiefly meant when he wrote of Carlyle as "a man
totally regardless of truth." He certainly had in him, with all his
virtues, a strain of churlish jealousy which made him incapable of
heartily admiring genius in a contemporary. A man who was
always talking of the "eternal verities," and yet never told the
world how much he himself believed of any known creed, should
not have scoffed at another man's religion as "Coleridgean moon-
shine." "Coleridge was not," says Carlyle, "without what talkers
call wit"! Did ever a sneer go more hopelessly wide of the mark?
But perhaps what looks like malice may have only been dyspepsia.

CHAPTER VI

WANDERINGS—SETTLEMENT IN DORSETSHIRE
1798—1800

In the winter of 1797–98, Tom Wedgwood, as we have seen, was at Penzance with his brother, making one of his many experiments on change of climate as a means of combating his disease. During the latter part of 1798, Josiah's house at Stoke d'Abernon in Surrey was apparently his temporary home, and here we find Coleridge visiting them shortly before his departure for Germany. Writing hence to Poole (in June), he says :

> The Wedgwoods received me with joy and affection. I have been metaphysicizing so long and so closely with T. W. that I am a *caput mortuum*, mere lees and residuum. . . . This place is a noble, large house in a rich, pleasant country ; but the little toe of Quantock is better than the head and shoulders of Surrey and Middlesex.*

During a great part of these two years (1798–99) the brothers were making journeys and inquiries in various parts of the South of England, trying to find an estate which they could make their permanent home. In this search Poole joined very zealously, and

---

* T. P., i. 271.

E

at one time they were on the point of settling near Taunton, in his immediate neighbourhood. They had nearly purchased an attractive estate there, and were planning to get an abode in the same country for their mother and sisters. This project, however, broke down, another purchaser having anticipated them. Poole had set his heart upon securing them as life-long neighbours, and his disappointment at this failure was intense. Here is his letter announcing it :

T. Poole to T. Wedgwood

TAUNTON,
Wednesday (Feb. 1799).

This morning I got to Combe Florey, and was too much sickened with the intelligence I heard to proceed upon the business I was upon. I heard that Gwyn had actually yesterday sold Pigott the Mansion House and fifty acres of land and Lethbridge Coomdown Estate. To be certain I came here and have seen Gwyn. *It is true.* . . . I hope this disappointment is not severe to you, but it is indeed to me the greatest I ever sustained. . . . I will never set my heart upon anything again.

Yours ever,
THOMAS POOLE.

A letter of Poole to Coleridge brings in this grievous disappointment as to the estate in a curious way. Mrs. Coleridge had just lost her youngest boy, the baby Berkeley.

I have advised her [writes Poole to Josiah Wedgwood] not to inform Coleridge of his death. For he indulges in such tumultuous feelings upon every possible occasion where his wife and children are concerned, and his untired imagination is so active in conjuring up every possible scene of distress which could have occurred to them, that I am persuaded the knowledge of this event would either hurry him home, or at least prevent for a long time his exerting himself to any advantage.

Poole accordingly writes himself to Coleridge to tell him the sad news in a judicious fashion. After detailing the circumstances of the baby's death, he launches into an argument to the effect that as a parent's love of an *infant* is not "a thing of reason," but only "a wise law of nature," "a mere instinct, destined to preserve man in his infant state," such a death ought not to be a serious grief to the parent.

Let your *mind* act [he says] not your *feelings*. . . . Mrs. Coleridge is now perfectly well, and does not make herself miserable by recalling the engaging, though, remember, mere instinctive "attractions" of an infant a few months old. Heaven and Earth ! I have myself experienced disappointments more weighty than the death of ten infants. There are two particular friends of mine who offered, ten days ago, £22,000 for a delightful estate within seven miles of Stowey. But for an untoward circumstance, they would have had it. . . . The loss to the neighbourhood is incalculable. . . .*

This odd outburst is not in keeping with Poole's undeniable kindness of heart, and it betokens a strange lack of imagination. But it also shows the warmth of his attachment to the Wedgwoods. His letters, of which many remain, show that no man can have had a truer friend than Tom Wedgwood had in him. Many were evidently written with no other purpose than to

---

* Letter of March 15, 1799. T. P., i. 290.

put a little hope and brightness into the gloomy life of the poor, sick, broken man. With the same object he was always ready to go to him, to be his companion in travel or to welcome him to Stowey—and a most burdensome guest he must have been—whenever it seemed likely that a change of surroundings would help to mitigate his troubles. It was a quite brotherly devotion.

When Coleridge's stay in Germany was drawing to a close, Josiah had from him the following letter:

S. T. Coleridge to Josiah Wedgwood

GOTTINGEN,

May 21, 1799.

MY DEAR SIR,—

I have lying by my side six huge letters, with your name on each of them, and all excepting one have been written for these three months. About this time Mr. Hamilton, by whom I send this and the little parcel for my wife, was, as it were, setting off for England; and I seized the opportunity of sending them by him, as without any mock-modesty I really thought that the expense of the Postage to me and to you would be more than their worth. Day after day, and week after week, was Hamilton going, and still delayed; and now that it is absolutely settled that he goes to-morrow, it is likewise absolutely settled that I shall go this day three weeks, and I have therefore sent only this and the Picture by him, but the letters I will now take myself, for I should not like them to be lost, as they comprise the only subject on which I have had any opportunity of making myself thoroughly informed, and if I carry them myself, I can carry them without danger of their being seized at Yarmouth, as all *my* letters were, yours to the Von Axens, &c., excepted, which were luckily not sealed. Before   left England, I had read the Book of which you speak.* I must confess that it appeared to me exceedingly illogical. Godwin's and Condorcet's extravagancies were not worth confuting; and yet I thought that the Essay on Population had not confuted them. Professor Wallace, Derham, and a number of German Statistic and Physico-theological writers had taken the same ground, namely, that Population increases in a geometrical but the accessional nutriment only in an arithmetical ratio ; and that vice and misery, the natural consequences of this order of things, were intended by Providence as the Counterpoise. I have here no means of procuring so obscure a book as Rudgard's; but to the best of my recollection, at the time that the Fifth Monarchy enthusiasts created so great a sensation in England, under the Protectorate and the beginning of Charles the Second's reign, Rudgard or Rutgard (I am not positive even of the name) wrote an Essay to the same purpose ; in which he asserted, that if War, Pestilence, Vice, and Poverty were wholly removed, the World could not exist two hundred years, &c. Süssmilch, in his great work concerning the divine order and regularity in the Destiny of the human Race has a chapter entitled a confutation of this idea ; I read it with great eagerness, and found therein that this idea militated against the Glory and Goodness of God, and must therefore be false, but further confutation found I none ! This book of Süssmilch's has a prodigious character throughout Germany ; and never methinks did a Work less deserve it. It is in 3 huge octavos, and wholly on the general Laws that regulate the Population of the human species ; but is throughout most unphilosophical, and the tables, which he has collected with great Industry, proved nothing. My objections to the Essay on Population you will find in my sixth letter at large ; but do not, my dear sir, suppose that because unconvinced by this Essay, I am therefore convinced of the contrary. No, God knows I am sufficiently sceptical, and in truth more than sceptical, concerning the possibility of universal Plenty and

---

* Malthus's "Essay on the Principle of Population" was published (anonymously) in 1798.

Wisdom, but my doubts rest on other grounds. I had some conversation with you before I left England on this subject; and from that time I had proposed to myself to examine as thoroughly as it was possible for me the important question, Is the march of the Human Race progressive, or in cycles? But more of this when we meet.

What have I done in Germany? I have learned the language, both high and low German; I can read both, and speak the former so fluently, that it must be a torture for a German to be in my company—that is, I have words enough and phrases enough, and I arrange them tolerably; but my pronunciation is hideous. 2ndly, I can read the oldest German, the Frankish, and the Swabian. 3rdly, I have attended the lectures on Physiology, Anatomy, and Natural History, with regularity, and have endeavoured to understand these subjects. 4thly, I have read and made collections for a History of the Belles Lettres in Germany before the time of Lessing, and 5thly, very large collections for a Life of Lessing, to which I was led by the miserably bad and unsatisfactory Biographies that have been hitherto given, and by my personal acquaintance with two of Lessing's Friends. Soon after I came into Germany, I made up my mind fully not to publish anything concerning my *Travels*, as people call them; yet I soon perceived that with all possible economy my expenses would be greater than I could justify, unless I did something that would to a moral certainty repay them. I chose the Life of Lessing for the reasons above assigned, and because it would give me an opportunity of conveying, under a better name than my own ever will be, opinions * which I deem of the highest importance. Accordingly my main business at Göttingen has been to read all the numerous Controversies in which L. was engaged; and the works of all those German Poets before the time of Lessing, which I *could not* or could not *afford* to buy. For these last four months, with the exception of last week, in

---

* Here he wrote, apparently, and then struck out, the words "on History and Metaphysics."

which I visited the Hartz, I have worked harder than, I trust
in God Almighty, I shall ever have occasion to work again ;
this endless transcription is such a body-and-soul-wearying
Purgatory. I shall have bought thirty pounds worth of books,
chiefly metaphysics, and with a view to the one work to which
I hope to dedicate in silence the prime of my life ; but I believe
and indeed doubt not, that before Christmas I shall have
repayed myself; but before that time I shall have been under
the necessity of requesting your permission that I may during
the year *anticipate* for 40 or fifty pound. I have hitherto
drawn on you for 35 & 30 & 30 & 30 = 125£. Of this sum
I left about 32 or 33 pounds in your hands, of Mr. Chester's,
when I left England, and Chester has since desired his brother
to transmit 25£, and again in his last letter 30£. Wordsworth
has promised me that he will pay into your hands 4£ for me,
33 & 25 & 30 & 4 = 92£. Hitherto, therefore, I have drawn
as it were about 33 or 34 pound, but this week, to pay both our
Göttingen Bills, and our journey to England, I must draw for
70£. So that altogether I shall have in this year drawn for
103 pound.

I never, to the best of my recollections, felt the fear of Death
but once ; that was yesterday when I delivered the picture to
Hamilton. I felt, and shivered as I felt it, that I should not
like to die by land or water before I see my wife and the little
one that I hope yet remains to me. But it was an idle sort of
feeling, and I should not like to have it again. Poole half
mentioned, in a hasty way, a circumstance that depressed my
spirits for many days, that you and Thomas were on the point
of settling near Stowey, but had abandoned it. " God Almighty ! what a dream of happiness it held out to me ! " writes
Poole. *I* felt disappointment without having had hope !

In about a month I hope to see you. Till then may heaven
bless and preserve us ! Believe me, my dear sir, with every
feeling of love, esteem, and gratitude,

Your affectionate Friend,

S. T. COLERIDGE.

The object of this letter was evidently to satisfy the natural wish of the brothers to hear what Coleridge was doing. They would not understand as well as we do how little, alas! was signified by the large literary projects he tells them of. Neither the Lessing biography, as we know, nor the pre-Lessing history of Belles Lettres, came to anything. One is half inclined to wonder whether the "six huge letters," which had waited so mysteriously three months for a means of conveyance, ever had any objective existence. If they ever reached Josiah's hands it seems strange that they should not be found with other letters of Coleridge carefully kept by him.

In August 1799 the brothers' long hunt for a place of abode was ended by their hearing of what seemed a suitable property in Dorsetshire, a house with an estate of moderate size round it, which Josiah soon agreed to take. This was Gunville House (or Park) at Tarrant Gunville, some five or six miles from Blandford. Josiah's plan was to live here during most of each year, migrating to Staffordshire for about three months every summer, in order to look after the works at Etruria. A year later Tom bought the Eastbury estate, a property separated only by a road from Gunville, and here soon afterwards his mother and sisters joined him. The place was remote from any considerable town, the nearest being Salisbury, about seventeen miles away. One may judge from the present old-world look of the little village how utterly rural must have been its aspect in 1800. The house at Eastbury Park was (and is) a singular one, being but a remnant of a magnificent mansion built by Vanbrugh, about 1718, for Bubb Dodington, at a cost, it is said, of about £150,000. Earl Temple, who inherited the estate, found the vast building a burdensome possession. He offered to pay any gentleman £200 a year to inhabit it, and when this failed to secure a tenant, he took it down, selling it piecemeal, all but one wing. This was done about 1795.

Josiah's life at Gunville became that of a country gentleman. He hunted, shot, did his share of county business, and became deeply interested in improving his breed of sheep.*

This would have been a happy family settlement but for the gloom thrown over it by Tom's sad condition of health. He had long given up all serious work, and his life was devoted to the wearying struggle to get the better of his disease. The " warm-room cure " had had no good result ; but cold, apparently, was his great enemy, and we now find him busy with the problem how to adapt a part of Gunville House to carrying out some *régime* of the same kind. Herein he sought the aid of his and his father's old friend, James Watt, who had already been the deviser of the apparatus for generating Beddoes' medicinal " airs." How eager the great engineer was to help him is shown by

---

* Tom Wedgwood's educational theories (p. 208) absolutely ignored any such thing as inheritance or congenital character. And yet he must have seen his brother taking vast pains to get rams of the right sort. Strange that this object-lesson never, apparently, led him to question the omnipotence of education, a theory which seems to assume that all human infants are born with substantially the same character !

five or six very long letters, in which Watt describes,
with careful drawings by his own hand, various elaborate appliances, special grates, window fittings, and
ventilating contrivances, which he thinks will suit
Wedgwood's purpose.   But Gunville is not yet in a
condition fit for an invalid's occupation, and in the
beginning of 1800 Tom is planning a voyage to the
West Indies, hoping that a year of tropical heat may do
something for him.

The following two letters from Coleridge are of this
time.   The first gives an idea of his life in London,
where he is writing for the *Morning Post*, and of his
various shadowy literary projects.   The other answers
a letter from Josiah about the West India scheme.

S. T. Coleridge to Tom Wedgwood

No. 21 Buckingham Street, Strand.

[*Jan.*] 1800.

[Address : Cornwallis House, Clifton, Bristol.]

My dear Sir,—

I am sitting by a fire in a rug great coat.   Your room is
doubtless to a greater degree air-tight than mine, or your notion
of Tartarus would veer round to the Greenlander's creed.   It
is most barbarously cold, and you, I fear, can shield yourself
from it only by perpetual imprisonment.   If any place in the
southern Climates were in a state of real quiet, and likely to
continue so, should you feel no inclination to migrate ?   Poor
Southey, from over great industry as I suspect, the Industry, too,
of a solitary Composition, has reduced himself to a terrible state
of weakness, and is determined to leave this Country as soon as
he has finished the poem on which he is now employed.   'Tis

a melancholy thing—so young a man, and one whose life has ever been so simple and self-denying ! Oh, for Peace, and the south of France ! I could almost wish for a Bourbon king, if it were only that Sieyes and Buonaparte might finish their career in the old orthodox way of Hanging. Thank God; I have *my health perfectly* and I am working hard ; yet the present state of human affairs presses on me for days together, so as to deprive me of all my chearfulness. It is probable that a man's private and personal connections and interests ought to be uppermost in his daily and hourly Thoughts, and that the dedication of much hope and fear to subjects which are perhaps disproportionate to our faculties and power is a disease. But I have had this disease so long, and my early Education was so undomestic, that I know not how to get rid of it ; or even to wish to get rid of it. Life was so flat a thing without enthusiasm, that if for a moment it leaves me, I have a sort of a stomach-sensation attached to all my Thoughts, like those which succeed to the pleasurable operation of a dose of opium. *Now* I make up my mind to a sort of heroism in believing the progressiveness of all nature, during the present melancholy state of Humanity ; and on this subject I am now writing ; and no work on which I ever employed myself makes me so happy while I am writing.

I shall remain in London till April. (The expences of my last year made it necessary for me to exert my industry ; and many other good ends are answered at the same time. Where I next settle I shall continue, and that must be in a state o retirement and rustication. It is therefore good for me to have a run of society, and that various, and consisting of marked characters. Likewise by being obliged to write without much elaboration I shall greatly improve myself in naturalness and facility of style ; and the particular subjects on which I write for money are nearly connected with my future schemes. My mornings I give to compilations, which I am sure cannot be wholly useless, and for which by the beginning of April I shall have earned nearly an 150£; my evenings to the Theatres, as I am to conduct a sort of Dramaturgy or series of Essays on the

Drama; both its general principles, and likewise in reference to the present state of the English Theatres. This I shall publish in the *Morning Post.* The attendance on the Theatres costs me nothing, and Stuart, the Editor, covers my expences in London. Two mornings and one whole day, I dedicate to the Essay on the possible Progressiveness of man and on the principles of Population. In April I retire to my greater work, The Life of Lessing. My German chests are arrived, but I have them not yet, but expect them from Stowey daily; when they come I shall send a little pacquet down to you.

To pay my wife's travelling expences in London I borrowed 29£ from my friend Purkis, for which I gave him an order on your Brother, York Street, dating it Jan. 5, 1800. Will you be kind enough to excuse my having done this without having previously written; but I have every reason to believe that I shall have no occasion to draw again till the year 1801; and I believe, that as I now, [*sic*] I have not anticipated beyond the year, if I have wholly anticipated that. I shall write to Jos. to-morrow for certain.

I have seen a good deal of Godwin, who has just published a novel. I like him for thinking so well of Davy. He talks of him everywhere as the most extraordinary human Being he had ever met with. I cannot say that, for I know one whom I feel to be the superior, but I never met with so extraordinary a young man. I have likewise dined with Horne Tooke. He is a clear headed old man, as every man needs must be who attends to the real import of words; but there is a sort of charlatannery in his manner that did not please me. He makes such a mystery and difficulty out of plain and palpable things, and never tells you any thing without first exciting and detaining your curiosity. But it were a bad Heart that could not pardon worse faults than these in the author of the Epea Pteroenta.*

Believe me, my dear sir, with much affection,

Yours,

S. T. C.

---

* Horne Tooke, ex-clergyman, radical politician, and philologist,

S. T. Coleridge to Josiah Wedgwood

[Address : CORNWALLIS HOUSE, CLIFTON, BRISTOL.]
Tuesday Morning, 4 *Feb.*, 1800.

21 BUCKINGHAM STREET, STRAND.

MY DEAR SIR,—

Your brother's health outweighs all other considerations ; and beyond a doubt he has made himself acquainted with the degree of heat which he is to experience there. The only objections that I see are so obvious, that it is idle in me to mention them : the total want of men with whose pursuits your brother can have a fellow feeling ; the length and difficulty of the return, in case of a disappointment ; and the necessity of Sea-voyages to almost every change of Scenery. I will not think of the Yellow Fever ; that, I hope, is quite out of all probability. Believe me, my dear friend, I have some difficulty in suppressing all that is within me of affection and grief ! God knows my heart ; wherever your Brother is, I shall follow him in spirit ; follow him with my thoughts and most affectionate wishes.

I read your Letter, and did as you desired me. Montagu* is very cool to me. Whether I have still any of the leaven of the citizen and visionary about me,—too much for his present zeal ; or whether M. is incapable of attending to more than one man at a time ; or whether from his dislike of my pressing him to do something for poor Wordsworth ; or perhaps from all these causes combined—certain it is that he is shy of me. Of

---

(born 1736, died 1812), published his " Eπεα Πτεροεντα, or the Diversions of Purley," an entertaining medley of Etymology, Metaphysics, and Politics, in the years 1786–1805.

* Basil Montagu (b. 1770, d. 1851), friend of Wordsworth, Coleridge, Mackintosh, and Godwin, was at this time beginning his legal career. He became known in later life by the edition of Bacon which Macaulay made the text of his famous Essay. It was some ten years after this that he was the cause of an unfortunate estrangement between Wordsworth and Coleridge by misreporting something Wordsworth had said to him.

course, I am supposed to know but little of him distinctly from himself; this however in Montagu's case implies no loss of any authentic source of Information. From his friends I hear that the pressure of his immediate circumstances increases, and that (as how could it be otherwise, poor fellow !) he lives accumulating Debts and Obligations. He leaves Wordsworth without his Principal and Interest, which of course he would not do, W.'s daily bread and meat depending in great part on him, if he were not painfully embarrassed. Embarrassed I should have said ; for Pinny tells me that he suffers no pain from it. As to his views, he is now going to Cambridge to canvass for a fellowship in Trinity Hall. Mackintosh has kindly written to Dr. Lawrence, who is very intimate with the Master ; and he has other interest. He is also trying hard for and in expectation of a Commissionership of Bankruptcy, and means to pursue the Law with all ardour and steadiness. As to the state of his mind it is that which it was and will be. God love him ! He has a most incurable Forehead. John Pinny called on him and looking on his table saw *by accident* a letter directed to himself. "Why, Montagu ! that letter is for me, and from Wordsworth !" "Yes ! I have had it some time." "Why did you not give it me ?" "Oh ! it wants some explanation first. You must not read it now, for I can't give you the explanation now." And Pinny, who you know is a right easy-natured man, has not been able to get his own Letter from him to this Hour ! Of his success at Cambridge Caldwell is doubtful, or more than doubtful. He says that men at Cambridge don't trust overmuch these sudden changes of Principle. And most certainly, there is a zeal, an over acted fervour, a spirit of proselytism that distinguishes these men from the manners, and divides them from the sympathies, of the very persons to whose party they have gone over. Smoking hot from the oven of conversion they don't assort well with the old Loaves. So much of Montagu ; all that I know, and all, I suspect, that is to be known. A kind, gentlemanly, affectionate-hearted man, possessed of an absolute *Talent* for Industry ; would to God ! he had never heard of Philosophy !

I have been three times to the House of Commons; each
time earlier than the former; and each time hideously crowded.
The two first Days the Debate was put off, yesterday I went
at a quarter before 8, and remained till 3 this morning; and
then sat writing, and correcting other men's writing till 8—a
good twenty four hours of unpleasant activity! I have not felt
myself sleepy yet. Pitt and Fox completely answered my pre-
formed ideas of them. The elegance and high finish of Pitt's
Periods, even in the most sudden replies, is *curious*, but that is
all. He *argues* but so so, and does not *reason* at all. Nothing
is rememberable in what he says. Fox possesses all the full and
overflowing Eloquence of a man of clear head, clean heart, and
impetuous feelings. He is to my mind a great orator; all the
rest that spoke were mere creatures. I could make a better
speech myself than any that I heard, except Pitt's and Fox's.
I reported that part of Pitt's which I have enclosed in crotchets,
not that I report ex-officio; but curiosity having led me there,
I did Stuart a service by taking a few notes. I work from morning to night, but in a few weeks I shall have completed my purpose; and then adieu to London for ever! We newspaper
scribes are true Galley-Slaves. When the high winds of Events
blow loud and frequent then the Sails are hoisted, or the ship
drives on of itself. When all is calm and Sunshine, then to our
oars. Yet it is not unflattering to a man's vanity to reflect that
what he writes at twelve at night will before twelve hours is over
have perhaps 5 or 6000 Readers! To trace a happy phrase,
good image, or new argument, running through the town and
sliding into all the papers! Few Wine-merchants can boast of
creating more sensation. Then to hear a favourite and often-
urged argument repeated almost in your own particular phrases
in the House of Commons; and quietly in the silent self-com-
placence of your own heart chuckle over the plagiarism, as if
you were grand Monopolist of all good Reasons! But seriously,
considering that I have newspapered it merely as means of
subsistence while I was doing other things, I have been very
lucky. The New Constitution, the Proposals for Peace, the Irish

Union, &c. &c.—they are important in themselves, and excellent Vehicles for general Truths. I am not ashamed of what I have written.]

I desired Poole to send you all the papers antecedent to your own. I think you will like the different Analyses of the French Constitution. I have attended Mackintosh regularly. He was so kind as to send me a Ticket, and I have not failed to profit by it. What I think of M. and all I think I will tell you in some future Letter. My affectionate respects to Mrs. W. God love you, my dear Sir !

I remain, with grateful and most affectionate Esteem,

Your faithful Friend,

S. T. COLERIDGE.

It was while Tom Wedgwood was preparing for his voyage to the West Indies, that he must have been, as we may suppose, startled by receiving from Leslie a letter making a proposal for the hand of one of his sisters. It was of quite prodigious length, and of course a most ornate and poetical composition, one so remarkable indeed that I am tempted to insert part of it here, as a curiosity of amatory literature. Leslie having left no descendants, we may hope that no one's feelings will be hurt by our taking this liberty with a century-old love-story. We may remember that his first sight of Kitty and Sarah Wedgwood was when he came to stay with the family at Etruria in 1790. When he left it in 1792, Sarah, the younger, was about sixteen years old. She was now in her twenty-fourth year. He does not mention the lady's name, but it is believed that Sarah was the adored one. The letter begins without any introductory words.

John Leslie to Tom Wedgwood

ISLINGTON,
10 *Feb.*, 1800.

On the eve of bidding a tender adieu, may I venture at last to communicate a matter of the most serious and delicate nature? Long has the thought fired and tortured my brain. Often have I been on the point of disclosing it and as often have I been restrained by timidity or a sense of propriety. Still I hesitate. Shall I, by one rash step, provoke your displeasure? That reflection would be the torment of my life. Yet to whom should I unbosom myself but to my early and tried friend, who has felt such a lively interest in all my concerns, and who on this occasion is called by the most sacred ties to interpose his counsel? By dwelling on a loved object which absorbs the imagination, by cherishing a sort of forlorn hope amidst obstacles seemingly almost insurmountable, a passion full of delicious anxiety has gradually sprung up, has acquired consistency, and has at length mounted to such a pitch as to threaten my repose. I need your indulgence. I will submit to your direction. And as the ardour of my attachment is chastened by sentiments of deference and distant respect, I have some room to expect you will judge me with tenderness. Not to keep you longer in suspense, I have had the temerity to think of soliciting an alliance in your family.

You startle at this declaration. It may appear presumptuous and romantic. I must intreat you to suppress your emotions until you have finished the perusal of this letter. I owe it to my conscience to disclaim the idea of being stimulated by ambitious motives. Calculations of interest would on this occasion ill comport with the warmth of my feelings. I am indeed convinced that riches would in a very slight degree, if at all, augment my happiness. I have hitherto betrayed no disposition to outstep the bounds of mediocrity. The close and artificial garb of ambition is foreign to my heart. By disguising or retracting my sentiments it was more than once in

F

my power to have obtained situations which the bulk of men
considered respectable.   I have sought only the approbation of
my own mind and that of a few discerning friends.   My
attachment to the fair object of all my vows is founded on a
certain sympathy of character, rendered irresistible by the
fascination of personal charms.   Her fortune and condition, so
far from inviting the suit, present the most formidable bar to
the accomplishment of my wishes.

I have seen very few, indeed none of their sex, with whom
I would compare your younger sisters.   What a bewitching
assemblage of all the qualities fitted to inspire love, affection
and esteem !   One of them, and I believe your particular
favourite, to great personal attractions unites the most uncommon powers of mind.   But her sister seems to possess those
soft feminine charms which touch and melt, the soul.   The
impression I first received can never be effaced.   In the bloom of
health and beauty—but what a sweetness was expressed on every
feature !   I was confused, intoxicated.   Fortune soon placed
me beside her, and the memory of that happy period will always
affect me with delight.   My prepossessions were surpassed by
experience.   That species of mild beauty which is most capti-
vating, and those qualities of head and heart which justify the
triumph !   The image was realised which my fancy had framed,
of the most amiable of women.   Gentle, kind, frank and open
—invariably, habitually chearful, without levity, and without
the smallest particle of affectation.   Blessed with the finest
dispositions on earth, she seemed formed to be happy herself
and to diffuse happiness around her.   Such admirable equality
of temper !   Never a frown was seen on her brow.   Endued
with good sense, a correct judgment, and a cultivated understanding, with considerable accomplishments, she yet appeared
unconscious of her merits, and showed on all occasions a
hesitation and a modesty bordering on timidity, which in her
sex is altogether irresistible.   When I remarked, too, the interior
economy of the family, those excellent patterns exhibited, the
ease, simplicity, and decorum which prevailed, that knowledge

and liberality of sentiment which seasoned every conversation—
I envied the happy man who was destined to enjoy those
reflected charms. For my part, I durst not aspire—I sighed
in secret. I strove to repress every symptom that might excite
suspicion. Yet a gleam of hope would at times flit across my
mind and lift it to extacy.

A long separation followed, but she remained undisputed
mistress of my heart. . . . How I longed to see her, without
daring to signify a wish! How often my attempts were traversed!
At length I enjoyed that supreme satisfaction last summer. I
found her fresh as Hebe; and if possible more amiable than
ever. What kindness and condescension! My senses were
overpowered. In the delirium of imagination, I even fancied
that she betrayed some marks of partiality. I formed the
resolution to disclose my passion, but I wanted courage and
opportunity. The most imperious urgency only, the obligation
of previously consulting your sentiments, could compel me to a
confession.

But why fatigue you with this amorous tale? . . . If I am
guilty of an offence, I have endeavoured to make it as light as
possible. Never shall the young lady need to . . . [words torn
away] . . . on my account. The secret has not been entrusted
to mortal; it shall rest in my breast, it shall perish with me. I
shall religiously avoid hurting her feelings or those of the family.
Yet such is my opinion of her perfect goodness that I am
persuaded she is incapable of conceiving hatred or disdain, and
that even a repulse from her would be couched in obliging
terms.

I owe a thousand apologies for abusing your patience. It is
the first time I have written in such a strain—the first time I ever
made profession of love. You see the state of my mind. I am
agitated by conflicting passions. This is the most momentous
crisis of my life. My heart swells with anxiety. I tremble to
hear your advice. A few words will suffice, but let it be from
your own hand. If it shall be in the least consolatory, it will
give buoyancy to hope—it will in part open the prospect of

earthly elysium. A contrary presentiment weighs me down. Alas ! is all the future to be shrouded in despondency ? I fear I have already committed folly. Destroy this letter.

Farewell !

JOHN LESLIE.

On one of the flaps is a P.S. as to some commissions, with the following sentences : . . .

> Your brother's note has at this moment fallen into my hands. It rends my heart. I had still some lingering hopes. I have a thousand things to say, and your [sic] torn prematurely from me.

How the "amorous tale" ended appears from Leslie's next letter, which also gives us a glimpse of the lady's attitude towards her lover during his visit-to Stoke in the preceding year.

John Leslie to Tom Wedgwood

(Address : COMMERSON'S HOTEL, FALMOUTH.)

No date,

Postmark . Feb. 21, 1800.

Each new incident raises my admiration of your character, and makes me feel more intensely the pang of separation. In your last letter you appear in a light peculiarly endearing. The circumstances under which it was written, the indulgent and friendly tone of admonition all affect me extremely. There is a solemnity in the scene. It is a precious relict—the last perhaps I shall receive for many months. Yet it has dashed all the gay visions of hope. I submit, whatever the effort may cost. Here the matter shall rest. My spirits are now more composed and I shall listen to the dictates of reason. Be assured that my conduct shall during your absence give no ground of uneasiness or suspicion. I will testify my devotion by observing a religious silence. That rapturous attachment can never be extinguished, but I may hope that it will finally soften down into permanent esteem.

What a disclosure the letter contains! I am indeed astonished. Nothing could have betrayed me but my embarrassed manner and fixed absent looks, circumstances which I imagined would naturally be confounded with my ordinary habits. Is it possible that I may have hurt inadvertently the feelings of the tenderest, gentlest nymph on earth? If I have, I am heartily concerned for it. But my pardon is already sealed. My reception at Stoke I shall never forget. On that supposition, it evinced a superiority of mind which might call forth admiration, as her other qualities inspire the most ardent love. There were some little traits which can never be effaced from my mind. But I will discourage all such reflections. This is the last time I shall fatigue you with such a theme.*

The thoughts of your absence make me feel a blank in my existence. Yes, my inestimable friend, we shall meet again; the Atlantic shall not long part us. Tho' I opposed the West India project, do not imagine that after your mind was unalterably fixed that I would have declined to accompany you. On several accounts you have made a better choice. But should circumstances require any change of arrangement, depend always on my services. I will fly to join you on any spot of the globe. . . .

Pray, when your spirits will permit, get Kœnig to write out your metaphysical speculations. In case of accident, there should be more than one copy. If one were transmitted to me I would foster it with paternal care.

I may write again before you start. My prayers and wishes will attend you on the voyage. Farewell.

* Sarah Wedgwood had many suitors, some quite in middle life, but she died unmarried. A grand-niece who remembers her in her old age tells me she never can have been beautiful. She was an able and a very generous woman, spent little on herself, and gave away nearly the whole of her fortune in charity.

CHAPTER VII

THE WEST INDIES—A FAILURE

1800

On one of the last days of February 1800, Tom Wedgwood sailed for the West Indies, hoping that some months in the tropics might better his health. It was practically the first separation of the two brothers, and how deeply the feelings of both were stirred by it appears from a letter of Josiah written a few days later.

Josiah Wedgwood to Tom Wedgwood

GUNVILLE,
February 28, 1800.

My dear Tom,—

I cannot resist the temptation of employing my first moment of leisure to unburden my heart in writing to you. The distance that separates us, the affecting circumstances under which we parted, our former inseparable life and perfect friendship, unite to deepen the emotion with which I think of you, and give an importance and solemnity that is new to my communication with you. I did not know till now how dearly I love you, nor do you know with what deep regret I forbore to accompany you. It was a subject I could not talk to you upon, though I was perpetually desirous to make you acquainted with all my feelings upon it. I could not without necessity leave my wife and children, and I believed that I ought not, yet my

resolution was not taken without a mixture of self-reproach.
But I repeat the promise I made to you at Falmouth. I have
not yet been able to think of you with dry eyes, but a little
time will harden me. It is not so necessary for me to see you,
as to know that you are well and happy. Nothing can be
more disinterested than the love I bear you. I know that my
wife and children could alone render me happy, but I see with
the most heartfelt concern that your admirable qualifications
are rendered ineffectual for your happiness and your fame by
your miserable health. But I have a full conviction that your
constitution is strong and elastic, and that your present
experiment bids fair to remove the derangement of your
machine. I look forward with hope and joy to our meeting
again, and I am sure the seeing you again well and vigorous
will be a moment of the purest happiness I can feel.

Perhaps this may be the last time I shall write to you in this
strain. If it should for a time revive your sorrow, it cannot
long injure your tranquillity to be told that I love you, esteem
you, and admire you, truly and deeply.

I took possession of this place this morning with very different
feelings from those I should have had if we had been together.
. . . The last waggon load from Upcott came about an hour
after me. . . .

This place will be exceedingly pleasant in summer. It is
now very cold with a frost and east wind.

I have written to Gregory Watt* to send me a copying
machine, that I may send duplicates by another packet, a
precaution you must not forget. I will send you more copying
paper. I shall curse the French if they take the packet bearing
your first letter. How anxiously will it be expected, and with
what emotion will it be opened and read. We must not expect
to hear from you in less than four months.

Very few of the letters I write afford me any pleasure, but I

* Son of the great inventor. He was an affectionate friend of
Tom and Josiah. Copying machines had lately been invented by
James Watt.

foresee a great pleasure in writing to you all that comes, and just as it comes. There is a pleasure in tender regret for the absence and misfortunes of a person one loves, and corresponding with that person is the complete fruition of it. I feel like Æneas clasping the shade of Creusa. I call up your image, but it is not substantial.

Farewell, dear Tom.

This letter was, so far as the existing Wedgwood papers show, a unique outpouring of feeling on the part of Josiah. The rest of his letters to his brother contain only hints of the sorrow stirred by the continual spectacle of Tom's wrecked life, hardly ever an approach to an expression of his deeper feelings. He was inexpressive in writing as in speech, and his thus breaking through the habitual reserve of years shows how deeply touched he was at this critical moment. His feeling towards his brother was a mixture of compassion, love and admiration. Tom was in truth the great passion of his life.

Tom's letters from the West Indies contain little or nothing that is of extra-personal interest, but they have a pathetic significance as showing the depth of the affection which united him to his family, and the warmth of his gratitude for the never failing sympathy which his sad condition evoked from all his brothers and sisters. His first letter home is a sort of encyclical to the family circle. He seems to have shrunk from writing to any of them individually, feeling how much he owed to all.

Tom Wedgwood to his Family

St. Pierre, Martinique,
April 5th, 1800.

[After referring to the voyage and the circumstances of his arrival]. I staid two days at Barbadoes and gained strength and spirits every moment. . . . The climate, the beauty of the trees and shrubs, the *tout ensemble*, astonished and delighted us all beyond our highest expectations. We came to this place on the 3rd—and found a paradise. I have been for some days in a trance of enjoyment. I am perfectly at a loss how to convey an idea of the exquisite beauty of the scenery. . . . Reconvey me to-morrow by the same intolerable journey to Europe, and I must consider myself as repaid by what I have enjoyed, and by the materials I have laid in for future enjoyment. . . . The near scenery is exquisite, little vallies at the feet of mountains piled on each other in a noble succession, every tree new to the eye, many loaded with brilliant flowers and fruit. Another impression which has not abated is that of a desire to have this astonishing scene disclosed more gradually. The sight aches and the spirit sinks from unceasing excitement. The mind, too full, keeps longing for a moment's respite, for leisure to pursue the various channels, the little bye-streams of those rapid and full currents of thought which pass through it in all directions.

But I will not exhaust myself nor run the risk of disgusting you, for you have not these scenes and feelings present to you to enable you to sympathise in my most imperfect efforts at expression. . . .

To illustrate—we got here in the dark. I rose first in the morning, put my head out of the window—what a picture then lay before me ! I called to King—and we actually embraced each other.

I gain strength very rapidly. . . . If I had no indigestion and headache I should be in heaven. . . .

. I cannot send this off without offering with tears of the

purest love and gratitude, a simple declaration. Believe me then, I am affected in the manner I ought to be by all your kindnesses to me. I know, too, that I must too often have seemed insensible to all their claims, but do not be deceived into this cruel opinion. The languor of illness and a conflict of uneasy sensations never blinded my *observation*, though it prevented any expression of *sentiment*. But I have placed to your credit a thousand tender services which your delicacy in vain attempted to conceal from me. Nothing has more deeply affected me than your mild forbearance with my petulancies and caprices.

But I dare not now proceed in this subject. I dare not indulge in the luxury of those feelings which begin to introduce a disordered agitation. I must add however that I have above made a most unfeigned tender of sentiment to a very numerous band. Let no one who reads this imagine an exclusion. Certainly some individuals have sacrificed more largely to my health and comfort than others. But a *single* enquiry expressed with interest I always consider as an offer and earnest of a host of kind actions. . . .

I cannot write another word.

THOMAS WEDGWOOD.

The exhilaration produced in presence of the glories of tropical scenery did not last long. He thinks at first that he is gaining strength, but that soon turns out to be an illusion; the old pains and physical troubles reappear, and he begins to plan for his return, if there is no sign of real amendment. He tells next to nothing as to what he sees or does. Writing exhausts him, and he cannot waste his little strength upon describing incidents of travel. And there is hardly a word as to the social condition of the people about him, and not a word as to slaves or slave holding.

This is singular when we remember the general set of his ideas, and that the agitation for abolishing the trade by which these islands were supplied with slaves had been going on for many years—and all Wedgwoods were keen abolitionists. But the ceaseless struggle with bodily suffering absorbs him. He is continually speculating on future plans, and as he thinks of these he is always harassed by the thought that his own miseries are spoiling the lives of those who care for him.

The following letter would seem to be his answer to that written by his brother after they parted.

Tom Wedgwood to his brother Josiah

NEVIS,
May 13th, 1800.

MY DEAREST FRIEND,—

I cannot tell you the pleasure your letter gave me. It gave me an assurance of what my conscience and judgment bade me not to be too confident [of], your unabated esteem and affection. . . . Your most welcome assurance brought with it everything which was wanting to complete the charm of that intimate connection which has so long and so happily subsisted between us . . . To the moment of our separation your tenderness and affection were continually on the increase ; I was only apprehensive that even your forbearance and pity might at length be fatigued by the importunate and dismal intercourse of a sick man. I have read your letter a dozen times over. It has inspired me with an increased craving after health. I long so ardently to contribute towards your happiness . . . I cannot endure the idea of being a thorn in your side.

You may judge how welcome your letter was to me when I tell you that I read the receipt to dress a pig three times, merely for the association with your hand-writing. You have never known to what a degree my attachment to you has long risen. When you are with me, I imagine myself an exile from home, longing, as I always do most burningly, for your society. I then exultingly bless myself that you are present to me. . . . You are my great repository, magazine, reservoir of agreeable associations and lively feelings. You are for ever present to my memory, and the chief consolation of absence and a most tedious illness. I often cannot help yielding to the illusion of our mutual affection being *carried forward* into a future and a better existence. . . . Whenever those separations which we both lament have been about to take place, I have always contrived to spend every moment which remained to me in your company. If you have been called from me for a few hours I feel as if robbed of some vital energy, &c. &c., for this strain is endless. Be for ever assured that you *and your wife* are objects of my most perfect love and esteem—your children are most dear to me. Oh God! that I had force to display my own character—to act, in any degree, as I feel. I should not then be making professions. But I am so blasted by my cruel Fates, so crippled and cramped in every energy of mind and body, that with all those qualities for which you give me credit, I am absolutely inferior to the veriest imbecile that eats, drinks, and sleeps away life. But patience, patience—I am determined to live as long as Nature permits, I must therefore humbly submit and patiently bear the evils of existence— Farewell.

My birds are singing on all sides of me—oranges by thousands close to the house—a supper on land-crabs *in prospetto*— and yet I crave for that desart spot, dear, dear Gunville.

His first letter home (*supra*, p. 89), had arrived in England about June 4. Part of its contents must have been communicated by Josiah to Coleridge, who writes as follows :

S. T. Coleridge to Josiah Wedgwood

BRISTOL,
Thursday, June 12, 1800.

MY DEAR SIR,—

Enclosed is £20 . . .

I had heard such pleasing accounts of your dear brother, accounts exaggerated at second hand by the joy of the narrators, that T. Wedgwood's own statement came on me as a disappointment. Still, however, Broxham must have seen a great difference or he *could* not have written as he did. God in heaven bless him ! Your letter to me, that is, the account in your letter, made the tears roll down Poole's face. . . .

Old Mrs. Poole is, I am afraid, dying. . . .*

The doubts as to how Tom Wedgwood was faring were soon set at rest. Poole was surprised one evening at Stowey by receiving the following note :

Tom Wedgwood to T. Poole and S. T. Coleridge

BRIDGEWATER,
Tuesday, 6 *o'clock.*
(Probably *June* 24, 1800.)

MY DEAR FRIENDS,—

It is with the utmost reluctance that I pass so near you without a personal salutation. Accept this, however, such as it is—may it carry to Stowey as warm as it leaves my heart.

You are no doubt much surprised at my return. I have soon convinced myself that a stay in the West Indies would not benefit my health—for many reasons which I cannot now

---

* The omitted sentences refer to Coleridge's fruitless house-hunting about Porlock, and to his intention to try for a house in the Lake country.

enter upon.   I am now hurrying to Cote, to inquire after my
friends ; and my fatigue, joined to anxiety, prevents my making
any round in my journey, or I would surely see you at Stowey.
Let me hear from you.   It will delight me to have a good
account of you and yours, particularly your excellent mother.

Ever yours most cordially,

T. WEDGWOOD.

This must have been scribbled off while he was
changing horses at Bridgewater on his way from Falmouth to Bristol.   The meeting at Cote cannot have
been a happy one.   The West Indies scheme, planned
with much thought and trouble, had failed.   Yet he
had moments when he could fancy himself really re-
covering.   Six weeks later we find him riding to
London from Christchurch, where he had been staying
with his brother Jos.

Writing from a roadside inn he says (August 15,
1800) :

How often have I wished you jogging at my side, to enjoy
what I have done, of air and scenery, and to witness and sympathise in my rapid progress in convalescence.   But for the
many cruel disappointments already experienced, I might now
indulge a hope of regaining my lost health and strength.   I
dare not cherish the viper idea.   If they are restored to me,
God knows they will be welcome—if not, I mean not to sink
lower from disappointment.   I rode 5 hours yesterday and have
ridden, by 11 to-day, 28 miles without any fatigue. . . . Slept
in an alehouse last night—never lay better.   Avoid great inns
—hot, dear, noisy.   You'll hear of me by calling at the single
houses, and in the " pleasant villages." . . .

Believe me,

le plus devoué des êtres humains,

T. W.

HOUSE AT EASTBURY PARK (1902)

T. Wedgwood's Residence

For this and the other views at Grenville the author is indebted to the Editors of "Photography"

And this is followed by a light-hearted letter talking of prospective shooting in the New Forest, and matters incidental to starting life at Gunville. Possibly the sea voyages and the stay in the tropics had made him stronger for the time. During this autumn and the succeeding winter he had continual alternations of what seemed like recovery followed by heart-sickening relapses. It was apparently in the latter part of the year 1800 that he was making his photographic experiments, and there can be little doubt that the persistent recurrence of these periods of illness and suffering was what prevented his following up his discovery. The following extracts from letters of this time show his variable condition :

Tom Wedgwood to his brother Josiah

27 *August*, 1800.
[Travelling from London to Gunville.]

I am gradually fallen these last few days into the *status quo ante iter*. Henceforth I never will entertain, or at least communicate to others, these sanguine anticipations of returning health.

Tom to Josiah and others at Gunville

WHITE HART INN.
[Salisbury, *November* 12 or 13, 1800.]

MY DEAREST FRIENDS,—
I cannot dismiss Samuel without a word to say that I am all the better for the ride hither. . . . I will write on my arrival in town, and as soon after as I am encouraged to do so by any favourable change in my health. I am secure at least from disappointment, for I dare not cherish a hope on the subject. . . .

Once more adieu ! It is in vain for me to repine at the cruel persecution which has soon again forced me from all I hold dear in life. In entering into new scenes I must strive to forget what I leave behind me. . . .

Josiah Wedgwood to Tom Wedgwood

GUNVILLE,
November 13, 1800.

MY DEAR TOM,—

. . . It is useless to repine, and your separation from us was evidently necessary, yet I cannot refrain from assuring you how heartily I sympathise with you. My heart is full, and if it would do either of us good I could cry like a child. But no more of this. . . .

Josiah to Tom Wedgwood

GUNVILLE,
February 6, 1801.

MY DEAREST BROTHER,—

Your letter has excited the most painful feelings in my heart, and I know not what to write, for I have no other topic of consolation than the truest affection and the warmest sympathy, and in your state of health and feeling that is nothing. . . . I cannot deny that every failure renders your situation more cheerless, but I cannot and will not give up my hopes that time will ameliorate your fate. . . . I will not despair of a brother so dear to my heart. . . .

Josiah to Tom Wedgwood

18*th February*, 1801.

MY DEAR TOM,—   . . .

. . . I do not know what to think about your design of staying at home. . . . I can conceive the efforts it must cost you to refrain from giving yourself up to languor and despond-

ency. This consideration ought to reconcile you to the occasional uneasiness that may be excited by our observing your
sufferings.

To a man in this condition any regular work was
of course impossible; and yet in the early part of this
winter (1800–1801), he seems to have been able to see
a great deal of society of a friendly kind. He set up
a temporary abode in the building in York Street,
St. James's Square, in which were the London show-
rooms of the Etruria firm,* and there gave frequent
bachelor parties. Among the relations and friends
whom he was seeing at this time we find the names of
Mackintosh (then making his way at the bar and living
with his wife, Josiah's sister-in-law, in Serle Street,
Lincoln's Inn), Godwin, Leslie, the brothers John and
James Tobin, Gregory Watt (son of the great engineer),
Richard ("Conversation") Sharp, and many more.
He was often, too, at a social club which had been
founded by Mackintosh, and met at a tavern in the
Strand. It had grown out of a dinner-party at
Mackintosh's house, at which Sharp, " Bobus " Smith
(brother of Sydney), Rogers, and John Allen of Cresselly were present, and Bobus had christened it the
" King of Clubs." Tom Campbell the poet describes
it, perhaps a little too magnificently, as a "gathering-
place of brilliant talkers, dedicated to the meetings
of the reigning wits of London," and a " lineal

---

* The building on the east side of the southern end of the street.
It afterwards became a chapel. Mr. Stopford Brooke preached there
for many years.

G

descendant of the Johnson, Burke, and Goldsmith society." *

About this time (November 1800) an incident occurred which threatened to bring a cloud over the friendship between Poole and the Wedgwoods. This was what may be called a quasi-proposal of marriage made by Poole to Catharine Wedgwood, the elder of the two unmarried sisters. After a visit to Gunville he wrote to Josiah Wedgwood, saying : " I have ventured to write to Miss Wedgwood to request her to enter into a correspondence with me, by which she shall know me as I am." The correspondence, he explains, would be " merely a mutual communication of sentiments on such subjects as may occur to us—if you do not blame me you will be my friend, . . . and when I say this I address the same to Mr. T. Wedgwood, on whose unbounded affection shown to me I rely." This of course practically amounted to a proposal, though Poole seems to have persuaded himself it did not. Josiah, writing to Tom, who had left Gunville, describes the answer he gave Poole as "friendly on my part, not uncivil, but peremptory on C.'s, and C.'s

---

* By this he can only mean that it was a club of the old eighteenth-century type, like the one founded by Reynolds. The Johnsonian club exists still ; the " King of. Clubs" lasted till 1824. Here is a glimpse of one of its meetings from a letter of T. W. to Jos. W., December 5, 1800 : " A very pleasant day on Saturday at the club. But it was rather noisy owing to some uproarious visitors, and, as Mackintosh says, afforded a very bad specimen of their meetings. I had a little conversation with Sharp, B. Smith, and Scarlett, but much less than I wished, my neighbour Pearson engrossed me too much. Among the members then or later were Lord Holland, Lord Lansdowne, Henry Brougham, Porson, Romilly, Dumont (of Geneva), Ricardo, and Hallam.

refusal enforced by my approbation of its propriety."
It does not appear that Catharine wrote herself to
Poole. He having asked Josiah to help him, she would
naturally be glad to leave to her brother the disagreeable task of sending an answer.

Poole accepted the rebuff in the most angelic spirit.
He explains, not very successfully, why he wrote as he
did; he cannot quite see why his request was unreason-
able, but the answer is so decided that he takes it as
absolutely final. "I was stunned by it, though I do
not know why; . . . I stood looking at it for an
hour. . . . I submit to it, and assure you, from
its peremptory nature, that I am perfectly satisfied."
The refusal, it is clear, was Miss Wedgwood's, not
her brothers' doing. But it is also clear that Josiah
and Tom took it ill that Poole should have ventured
to think of marrying their sister. Josiah thought it
necessary—why, it is not easy to see—to "enforce"
her refusal by showing his approval of it. And Tom
writes to him: "I am concerned and surprised at
Poole's presumption." Tom, we may be sure, did
not say anything like this to Poole himself (for Poole
"heartily thanks him" for his letter on the subject);
but why should he think it a "presumption"? According to the ordinary ideas of social rank, there
was no such immense gap between Poole and the
Wedgwoods, sons and daughters of a man who had
started from a very modest position. Poole puts it
fairly when he says: "I knew that Miss W. was
among the heads of the class of society in which I filled
a middle station.", If the brothers objected to the
courtship on the ground of difference of social rank

it was an odd attitude to be taken up by philosophical
radicals bound by their creed to despise all such con-
ventional prejudices.   But we need not attribute their
surprise and displeasure to what we now call "snobbism."
Another explanation is quite simple.   All the accounts
of Poole represent him as a man of a decidedly rough
type.   He was a farmer and a tanner, and had the
manners of his class, though far above it, and above most
men of any class, in knowledge and intelligence.   One
of his relatives in a younger generation tells us (T. P.
ii. 312) that "his clownish exterior, and rough, imperious manner, with his very disagreeable voice, spoilt
by snuff, made a strange contrast with his great mental
cultivation and excess in sensibility and tenderness of
heart.   I suppose," she adds, "in his republican
days he cultivated clownishness just as he left off
powder."   This helps us to understand how Kitty was
quite decided against marrying him, and how her
brothers thought it out of the question.   The letters
show he was not all surprised at · their attitude.
"Though," he says, "I have not lost your friendship,
I cannot but be apprehensive that your affection for me
may be diminished by an action which you must with-
-out doubt consider as a *witless presumption*."   This
apprehension weighed much upon his mind, but the
attachment between him and them does not appear to
have been sensibly lessened ; though, naturally, there
remained for a time a certain awkwardness.   This
appears when there is a question of his meeting Kitty
at Gunville a year or so later.   His letters on the subject are excellent in taste, tone, and temper ; his

language is somewhat apologetic, perhaps a little too argumentative, modest, and yet dignified.*

---

* Had Poole's overture led to a marriage, it would have been a suitable one as regards ages. Poole was then thirty-five and Kitty twenty-six. She was rich, but he was not poor. He was sufficiently well off to be able to lead a life of leisure if he chose. There is an interesting comment on the incident in a letter written nearly half a century later by Fanny Allen, sister of Mrs. John and Mrs. Josiah Wedgwood, who was at this time a girl of eighteen. "I have been deep in the letters of the family for these ten days. Poor Tom's letters are very melancholy and touching, and some of Jos's answers very beautiful. What two men they were ! . . . Tom Poole's letters are interesting ; I never cease regretting that Kitty did not accept him. How different would have been her life to that absurd and ridiculous attachment which bound her to Miss M——. Among the mass of letters his are among the most affectionate, and from the most healthful mind." (F. Allen to S. E. Wedgwood, daughter of Josiah, October 3, 1847—Darwin MSS.) Miss M—— was a philanthropical lady of advanced views, an early specimen of the "strong-minded" type. Fanny Allen was a clever and capable old lady, but perhaps it should be added that she was an inveterate match-maker, and so would be inclined, *à priori*, to take the Poole side in the matter. Kitty Wedgwood died, unmarried, in the year 1823. Family tradition represents her as an interesting and able woman. She had the family taciturnity. Bessy Wedgwood (Mrs. Josiah) says, "the more I know her, the more I admire her character." Dr. Robert Darwin, her brother-in-law, used to say of her that she was the only woman he ever knew who thought for herself in matters of religion.

CHAPTER VIII

COLERIDGE AT GRETA HALL—TRAVEL PLANS
1800—1802

It was in July 1800 that Coleridge made his move to Keswick, which became for a time his settled home, and for the rest of this year he and the Wedgwoods seem not to have met. His letters to Josiah during this time include but slight references to Tom Wedgwood, but are interesting in other ways.

S. T. Coleridge to Josiah Wedgwood

Thursday, July 24, 1800.

My dear Sir,—

I found your letter on my arrival at Grasmere, namely, on June 29, since which time to the present, with the exception of the last few days, I have been more unwell than I have ever been since I left school. For many days I was forced to keep my bed, and when released from that worst incarceration, I suffered most grievously from a brace of swollen Eyelids, and a head into which on the least agitation the blood felt as rushing in and flowing back again like the raking of the Tide on a coast of loose stones. However, thank God ! I am now coming about again.

That Tom receives such pleasure from natural scenery strikes me as it does you ; the total incapability which I have found in myself to associate any but the most languid feelings with the God-like objects which have surrounded me lately, and the nauseous efforts to *impress* my admiration into the service of nature, has given me a sympathy with his former state of health which I never before could have had. I wish from the bottom of my soul that he may be enjoying similar pleasures with those which I am now enjoying with all that newness of sensation, that voluptuous correspondence of the blood and flesh about me with breeze and sun-heat, which makes convalescence more than repay me for disease.

I parted from Poole with pain and dejection. For him and for myself in him. I should have given Stowey a decisive preference ; it was likewise so conveniently situated that I was in the *way* of almost all whom I love and esteem. But there was no suitable house, and no prospect of a suitable house. Add to this Poole's determination to spend a year or two on the continent in case of a peace and his mother's death. God in heaven bless her ! I am sure she will not live long.

This is the first day of my arrival at Keswick. My house is roomy, situated on an eminence a furlong from the Town ; before it an *enormous* Garden, more than two-thirds of which is rented as a garden for sale articles, but the walks, &c., are ours most completely. Behind the house are shrubberies, and a declivity planted with flourishing trees of 15 years' growth or so, at the bottom of which is a most delightful shaded walk by the River Greta, a quarter of a mile in length. The room in which I sit commands from one window the Bassenthwaite Lake, woods, and mountains ; from the opposite, the Derwent-water and fantastic mountains of Borrowdale ; and straight before me is a wilderness of mountains, catching and streaming lights or shadows at all times. Behind the house and entering into all our views is Skiddaw.

My acquaintance here are pleasant, and at some distance is Sir Guilfrid Lawson's seat with a very large and expensive library, to which I have every reason to hope that I shall have free access. But when I have been settled here a few days longer, I will write you a minute account of my situation.

Wordsworth lives 12 miles distant; in about a year's time he will probably settle at Keswick likewise. It is no small advantage here that for two-thirds of the year we are in complete retirement. The other third is alive and swarms with Tourists of all shapes and sizes and characters. It is the very place I would recommend to a novellist or farce-writer. Besides, at that time of the year there is always hope that a friend may be among the number, and miscellaneous crowd, whom this place attracts. So much for Keswick at present.

Have you seen my translation of the Wallenstein? It is a dull heavy play; but I entertain hopes, that you will think the language for the greater part natural and good common-sense English; to which excellence if I can lay fair claim in any work of poetry or prose, I shall be a very singular writer at least. I am now working at my introduction to the life of Lessing, which I trust will be in the press before Christmas;—that is, the Introduction, which will be published first, I believe. I shall write again in a few days. Respects to Mrs. W. God bless you and

S. T. COLERIDGE.

S. T. Coleridge to Josiah Wedgwood

KESWICK,
November 1, 1800.

MY DEAR SIR,—

I would fain believe that the experiment which your Brother has made in the West Indies is not wholly a discouraging one. If a warm climate did nothing but only prevented him from getting worse, it surely evidenced *some* power; and perhaps a climate equally favourable in a country of more various interest, Italy or the South of France, may tempt your Brother to make a longer trial. If (disciplining myself into *silent* chearfulness) I could be of any comfort to him by being his companion and attendant for two or three months, on the supposition that he should wish to travel and was at a loss for a companion more fit, I would go with him with a willing affection. You will easily see, my dear friend, that I say this only to increase the range of your Brother's choice—for even in *chusing* there is some pleasure.

There happen frequently little odd coincidences in time, that recall momentary faith in the notion of sympathies acting in absence. I heard of your Brother's Return, for the first time, on Monday last (the day on which your letter is dated) from Stoddart. Had it rained on my naked skin I could not have felt more strangely. The three or 400 miles that are between us seemed converted into a moral distance ; and I knew that the whole of this silence I was myself accountable for ; for I ended my last letter by promising to follow it with a second and longer one before you could answer the first. But immediately on my arrival in this country I undertook to finish a poem which I had begun, entitled " Christabel," for a second volume of the Lyrical Ballads. I tried to perform my promise ; but the deep unutterable Disgust which I had suffered in the translation of that accursed Wallenstein seemed to have stricken me with barrenness, for I tried and tried, and nothing would come of it. I desisted with a deeper dejection than I am willing to remember. The wind from Skiddaw and Borrowdale was often as loud as wind need be ; and many a walk in the clouds on the mountains did I take ; but all would not do, till one day I dined out at the house of a neighbouring clergyman and somehow or other drank so much wine, that I found some effort and dexterity requisite to balance myself on the hither edge of sobriety. The next day my verse-making faculties returned to me, and I proceeded successfully ; till my poem grew so long and in Wordsworth's opinion so impressive, that he rejected it from his volume as disproportionate both in size and merit, and as discordant in its character.* In the mean time I had gotten

* " Christabel " was first printed, unfinished (Parts 1 and 2 only), in 1816. All his life, at intervals, Coleridge talked or dreamed about completing it. Mr. Dykes Campbell, in a note of four pages (" Poetical Works," 601, *sqq.*), brings together, with a fulness of

myself entangled in the old Sorites of the old Sophist, Procrastination. I had suffered my necessary businesses to accumulate
so terribly, that I neglected to write to any one, till the Pain I
suffered from not writing made me waste as many hours in
dreaming about it as would have sufficed for the Letter-writing
of half a life. But there is something beside Time requisite
for the writing of a Letter, at least with me. My situation here
is indeed a delightful situation; but I feel what I have lost—
feel it deeply; it recurs more often and more painfully than I
had anticipated; indeed, so much so that I scarcely ever feel
myself impelled, that is to say, *pleasurably* impelled to write to
Poole. I used to feel myself more at home in his great windy
Parlour than in my own cottage. We were well suited to each
other—my animal spirits corrected his inclinations to melancholy; and there was something both in his understanding and
in his affections so healthy and manly, that my mind freshened
in his company, and my ideas and habits of thinking acquired
day after day more of substance and reality. Indeed, indeed,
my dear sir, with tears in my eyes, with all my heart and soul
I wish it were as easy for us to meet as it was when you lived
at Upcott. Yet when I revise the step I have taken, I know
not how I could have acted otherwise than I did. Everything
I promise myself in this country has answered far beyond my
expectations. The room in which I write commands six distinct Landscapes; the two Lakes, the Vale, the River, and
Mountains, and Mists, and Clouds and Sunshine, make endless
combinations, as if heaven and earth were for ever talking to
each other. Often when in a deep study, I have walked to
the window and remained there *looking without seeing*; all at once

---

knowledge which was all his own, a mass of particulars as to the
wonderful poem, and much that was said and written by Coleridge
on the subject, including a "final utterance" quoted from *Table
Talk* under date July 1833: "The reason for my not finishing
'Christabel' is not that I don't know how to do it—for I have,
as I always had, the whole plan entire from beginning to end in my
mind; but I fear I could not carry on with equal success the execution of the idea, an extremely subtle and difficult one."

the lake of Keswick and the fantastic mountains of Borrowdale at the head of it have entered into my mind with a suddenness as if I had been snatched out of Cheapside and placed for the first time on the spot where I stood; and that is a delightful feeling, these Fits and Trances of *Novelty* received from a long known Object. The river Greta flows behind our house, roaring like an untamed son of the Hills; then winds round and *glides* away in the front, so that we live in a peninsula. But besides this etherial eye feeding, we have *very* substantial conveniences. We are close to the town, where we have respectable and neighbourly acquaintance, and a sensible and truly excellent medical man. Our garden is part of a large nursery garden, which is the same to us and as private as if the whole had been our own; in this too we have delightful walks without passing our garden gate. My landlord, who lives in the Sister House (for the two Houses are built so as to look like one great one), is a modest and kind man, of a singular character. By the severest economy he has raised himself from a carrier into the possession of a comfortable independence. He was always very fond of reading, and has collected nearly 500 volumes, of our most esteemed modern writers, such as Gibbon, Hume, Johnson, &c. &c. His habits of economy and simplicity remain with him, and yet so very disinterested a man I scarcely ever knew. Lately, when I wished to settle with him about the Rent of our House, he appeared much affected, told me that my living near him, and the having so much of Hartley's* company were so great comforts to him and his housekeeper, that he had no children to provide for, and did not mean to marry; and in short, that he did not want any rent at all from me. This of course I laughed him out of; but he absolutely refused to receive any rent for the first half-year, under the pretext that the house was not completely furnished. Hartley quite lives at the house, and it is as you may suppose, no small joy to my wife to have a

---

* His eldest boy, now four years old. All accounts represent him as a singularly charming child.

good affectionate motherly woman divided from her only by a wall. Eighteen miles from our house lives Sir Guilfrid Lawson, who has a princely library, chiefly of Natural History, a kind and generous, but weak and ostentatious sort of man, who has been abundantly civil to me.   Among other raree shows, he keeps a wild beast or two, with some eagles, &c.   The master of the beasts at the Exeter 'Change, sent him down a large Bear— with it a long letter of directions concerning the food, &c., of the animal, and many solicitations respecting other agreeable Quadrupeds which he was *desirous* to send the Baronet at a moderate price, concluding in this manner: "And remain your honour's most devoted humble servant, J.P.   Permit me, Sir Guilfrid, to send you a Buffalo and a Rhinoceros."   As neat a postscript as I ever heard—the tradesmanlike coolness with which these pretty little animals occurred to him just at the finishing of his letter ! !   You will in the course of three weeks see the Letters on the rise and condition of the German Boors. I found it convenient to make up a volume out of my journeys, &c., in North Germany; and the Letters (your name of course erased) are in the Printer's Hands.   I was so weary of transcribing and *composing*, that when I found those more carefully written than the rest, I even sent them off as they were.

Poor Alfred !   I have not seen it in print.   Charles Lamb wrote me the following account of it : " I have just received from Cottle a magnificent Copy of his Guinea Alfred !   Four and 20 books, to read in the Dog Days.   I got as far as the mad monk the first day, and fainted.   Mr. Cottle's Genius strongly points him to the very simple *Pastoral*, but his inclinations divert him perpetually from his calling.   He imitates Southey as Rowe did Shakespeare, with his ' Good morrow to you, good Master Lieutenant ! '   Instead of ' *a* man,' *a* woman,' ' *a* daughter,' he constantly writes ' one, a man,' ' one, a woman,' ' one, his daughter ' ; instead of ' *the* King,' 'the Hero,' he constantly writes " He, the King,' 'He, the Hero'—two flowers of rhetoric palpably from the Joan.   But Mr. Cottle soars a higher pitch, and when he *is* original, it is in a most original way indeed. His terrific scenes are indefatigable. Serpents, Asps, Spiders, Ghosts, Dead Bodies, and Staircases made of NOTHING, with Adders' Tongues for Bannisters— my God ! what a Brain he must have ! he puts as many Plums in his Pudding as my Grandmother used to do ; and then his emerging from Hell's Horrors into Light, and Treading of this Earth for 23 Books together !—C. L."

My *littlest* one is a very stout boy indeed : he is christened by the name of " *Derwent,*" a sort of sneaking affection, you see, for the poetical and the novellish which I disguise to myself under the show that my Brothers had so many Children, John's, James', George's, &c. &c., that a handsome Christian-like name was not to be had except by encroaching on the names of my little Nephews. If you are at Gunville at Christmas, I hold out hopes to myself that I shall be able to pass a week with you then. I mentioned to you at Upcott a kind of comedy that I had *committed*—to writing, in part. This is in the wind.

Wordsworth's second volume of the Ly. Ball. will, I hope and almost believe, afford you as unmingled pleasure as is in the nature of a collection of very various poems to afford to one individual mind. Sheridan has sent to *him* too, requesting him to write a tragedy for Drury Lane. But W. will not be diverted by anything from the prosecution of his great work.

I shall request permission to draw upon you shortly for 20£ ; but if it be in the least inconvenient to you, I pray you, tell me so ; for I *can* draw on Longman, who in less than a month will owe me 60£, though I would rather not do it.

Southey's *Thalaba,* in twelve books, is going to the Press. I hear his *Madoc* is to be *nonum-in-annum'd.* Besides these, I have heard of four other Epic Poems—all in Quarto ! A happy age this for tossing off an Epic or two !

Remember me with great affection to your Brother; and present my kindest respects to Mrs. Wedgewood. Your late Governess wanted one thing which, where there is health, is I think indispensable to the moral character of a young person, a light and cheerful Heart. She interested me a good deal; she appears to me to have been injured by going out of the common way without any of that imagination, which, if it be a Jack O' Lanthorn to lead us out of that way, is however at the same time a Torch to light us whither we are going.

A whole essay might be written on the danger of *thinking* without Images. God bless you, my dear sir, and him who is with grateful and affectionate esteem,

Yours ever,
S. T. Coleridge.

S. T. Coleridge to Josiah Wedgwood

November 12, 1800.
[Postmark: Keswick.]

My dear Sir,—

I received your kind letter, with the 20£. My eyes are in such a state of inflammation that I might as well write blind-fold; they are so blood-red that I should make a very good personification of Murder. I have had Leaches twice, and have now a blister behind my right Ear. How I caught the cold, in the first instance, I can scarcely guess; but I improved it to its present glorious state by taking long walks all the mornings, spite of the wind, and writing late at night, while my eyes were weak.

I have made some rather curious observations on the rising up of Spectra in the eye, in its inflamed state, and their influence on Ideas, &c., but I cannot *see* to make myself intelligible to you. Present my kindest remembrance to Mrs. W. and your brother. Pray did you ever pay any particular attention to the first time of your little ones smiling and laughing? Both I and Mrs. C. have carefully watched our little one, and noted down all the circumstances, &c., under which he smiled, and under which he laughed, for the first six times; nor have we remitted our attention; but I have not been able to derive the least confirmation of Hartley's or Darwin's Theory.

You say most truly, my dear sir, that a *Pursuit* is necessary. *Pursuit*, I say, for even praiseworthy Employment, merely for good, or general good, is not sufficient for happiness, is not fit for man.

God bless you, my dear sir, and your sincerely affectionate friend,

S T. COLERIDGE.

P.S.—I cannot at present make out how I stand in pecuniary way; but I believe that I have anticipated on the next year to the amount of 30 or 40 pound, probably more.

A main interest of Tom Wedgwood's life was metaphysical and psychological speculation, and he seems to have been specially occupied with these subjects in the year 1801. In March of that year he is described as deep in "Time, Space, and Motion," and later he was discussing his theories with Mackintosh and making apparently some kind of effort to put them in a definite shape. Of this there will be more to be said in a later chapter. For the rest, his life in this and the succeeding years might be described in words we find him using to Poole: "I am just the same as last Christmas, eternally racking my brains for some plausible scheme of action, and subject every day to fits of the greatest despondency." The "plausible schemes of action" at home alternated with plans of travel abroad which were equally failures. In July 1801, for example, he crosses the Channel to begin a tour, but a few weeks later he is feeling too depressed to go on, and flies back to England. Again, in May 1802, he has been consulting Cline, with no effective result; he has a "loathing of going abroad," but is "unable to

come to any practicable scheme of living in England."
He starts off on a tour which is to take him to Vienna
and then to Italy for the winter. At Paris he has a
pleasant time with Sharp and other friends. He
spends hours daily among the ancient marbles in the
Louvre, is enthusiastic about " a new Diana supposed
to be by the same hand as the Belvedere Apollo," and
about a young French Sculptor whose " manner is very
much that of Michael Angelo." Also he has discovered, after infinite trouble, a delightful travelling
companion, a young musical composer, Acerbi. Then
comes the inevitable breakdown. " My strength and
spirits have entirely failed me, and I am forced home
by the same demon that drove me thence." *

A month or two later he is going to take a farm in
hand, near Gunville, and work it through a factotum,
" so that I shall have something going on about me. I
shall fit up a good room, . . . shall perhaps place
some companionable musical person there, and so spend
many hours a day with him. . . . But this is all a new
scheme, and judging of it by its predecessors, will be
extinct before this letter reaches you at Geneva." †

The time of closest intimacy between Tom Wedgwood and Coleridge was the latter part of this year,
1802. They were together continuously for more than
two months. It was a sad time in the life of Coleridge. His estrangement from his wife was increasing,

---

* To Poole, June 27, 1802.
† To Poole, August 29, 1802.

ENTRANCE TO EASTBURY PARK (1902)

VILLAGE OF TARRANT GUNVILLE (1902)

and so was his habit of opium-eating, which was to bring him in a few years to that state which he himself described as a "pitiable slavery." This had begun, apparently, about a year earlier, and it was as yet hardly known to his most intimate friends. The Wordsworths seem not to have been yet aware of it. To this there is no open reference in his letters to the Wedgwoods ; of the home trouble there is, alas ! too much.

The following letter would appear to refer to one from Wedgwood mooting some scheme for their travelling together. Such schemes, and the ceaseless search for a companion for the sick man in his wanderings, make up a great part of the Wedgwood correspondence.

S. T. Coleridge to Tom Wedgwood
(*Address :* Eastbury, Blandford.)
Greta Hall, Keswick,
October 20, 1802.

My dear Sir,—

This is my birthday, my thirtieth. It will not appear wonderful to you therefore, when I tell you that before the arrival of your letter I had been thinking with a great weight of different feelings concerning you and your dear Brother. For I have good reason to believe that I should not now have been alive, if in addition to other miseries I had had immediate poverty pressing upon me. I will never again remain silent so long. It has not been altogether Indolence or my habit of Procrastination which have kept me from writing, but an eager wish, I may truly say a Thirst of Spirit, to have something honourable to tell you of myself. At present I must be content to tell you something cheerful. My Health is very much better. I am stronger in every respect, and am not injured by study or the act of sitting at my writing Desk. But my eyes

H

suffer if at any time I have been intemperate in the use of Candle light. This account supposes another, namely, that my mind is calm, and more at ease. My dear sir, when I was last with you at Stowey, my heart was often full, and I could scarcely keep from communicating to you the tale of my distresses, but how could I add to your depression, when you were low? Or how interrupt, or cast a shade on your good spirits, that were so rare and so precious to you? I found no comfort except in the driest speculations. In the *Ode to Dejection** which you were pleased with, these lines, in the original, followed the line " My shaping spirit of Imagination : "

> " For not to think of what I needs must feel,
> But to be still and patient, all I can,
> And haply by abstruse Research to steal
> From my own Nature all the natural man—

---

* "Dejection, an Ode," was printed in the *Morning Post* of October 4, 1802, where probably Wedgwood had just seen it. It was written in the previous April. The passage referred to runs as follows :

> There was a time when, though my path was rough,
> This joy within me dallied with distress,
> And all misfortunes were but as the stuff
> Whence Fancy made me dreams of happiness ;
> For hope grew round me, like the twining vine,
> And fruits, and foliage, not my own, seemed mine.
> But now afflictions bow me down to earth ;
> Nor care I that they rob me of my mirth ;
> But oh ! each visitation
> Suspends what Nature gave me at my birth
> My shaping spirit of Imagination.
> For not to think of what I needs must feel, &c.

"No sadder cry from the depths," says Mr. Dykes Campbell, "was ever uttered, even by Coleridge. Health was gone, and with it both the natural joy which had been his in rich abundance, and that rarer kind which, as he tells us, dwells only with the pure. Nor was this all, for he discovered that he had lost control of his most precious endowment, his 'shaping spirit of imagination.' He felt that poetically he was dead, and that if not dead spiritually, he had lost his spiritual identity."

This was my sole resource, my only plan,
And that which suits a part infects the whole,
And now is almost grown the Temper* of my soul."

I give you these lines for the spirit and not for the poetry.†

*   *   *   *   *   .

But better days are arrived, and are still to come. I have
had visitations of Hope, that I may yet be something of which
those who love me may be proud.

I cannot write that without recalling dear Poole. I have
heard twice, and written twice, and I fear that by a strange
fatality, one of the Letters will have missed him. Leslie was
here some time ago. I was very much pleased with him.

And now I will tell you what I am doing. I dedicate three
days in the week to the *Morning Post*, and shall hereafter write,
for the far greater part, such things only as will be of as permanent interest as anything I can hope to write ; and you will
shortly see a little Essay of mine justifying the writing in a
Newspaper.

My comparison of the French with the Roman Empire was
very favourably received. The Poetry which I have sent has
been merely the emptying out of my Desk. The Epigrams
are wretched indeed, but they answered Stuart's purpose better
than better things. I ought not to have given any signature
to them whatsoever. I never dreamt of acknowledging either
them or the "Ode to the Rain." As to feeble expressions and
unpolished lines, there is the rub ! Indeed, my dear sir, I do
value your opinion very highly. I should think your judgment
on the sentiment, the imagery, the flow of a poem decisive ; at
least if it differed from my own, and after frequent considera-

---

* Mr. Dykes Campbell, quoting this letter (" Poetical Works,"
p. 628), gives this word as " temple," misled, apparently, by one of
Cottle's silly alterations of what Coleridge wrote. In his print of
the poem (founded on the issue of 1829), it appears as " habit."

† Here follows an outpour on the subject of his home troubles.

tion mine remained different, it would leave me at least perplexed. For you are a perfect electrometer in these things ; but in point of poetic diction, I am not so well satisfied that you do not require a certain *aloofness* from the language of real life, which I think deadly to poetry.

Very shortly, however, I shall present you from the Press with my opinions in full on the subject of Style both in prose and verse ; and I am confident of one thing, that I shall convince you that I have thought much and patiently on the subject and that I understand the whole strength of my Antagonist's Cause. For I am now busy on the subject, and shall in a very few weeks go to Press with a volume on the prose writings of Hall, Milton and Taylor ; and shall immediately follow it up with an Essay on the writings of Dr. Johnson and Gibbon. And in these two volumes I flatter myself I shall present a fair History of English Prose.* If my life and health remain, and I do but write half as much and as regularly as I have done during the last six weeks, these will be finished by January next; and I shall then put together my memorandum book on the subject of Poetry. In both I have endeavoured sedulously to state the Facts and the Differences clearly and acutely ; and my reasons for the preference of one style and another are secondary to this. Of this be assured, that I will never give anything to the world in propriâ personâ, in my own name, which I have not tormented with the File. I sometimes suspect that my foul copy would often appear to general readers more polished than my fair copy. Many of the feeble and colloquial expressions have been industriously substituted for others which struck me as artificial, and not standing the test ; as being neither the language of passion, nor distinct conceptions.

---

* All this, and what follows, as to literary work must be treated as merely visionary. Confusion between things done and things which he dreamed of doing was habitual with Coleridge. He "spawned plans like a herring," as Southey tells him in a letter of about this time (Southey's "Life," ii. 190). See D.C. p. 251, on such visions.

Dear sir, indulge me with looking still further on to my literary life. I have since my twentieth year meditated an heroic poem on the Siege of Jerusalem by Titus. This is the Pride and the Stronghold of my Hope. But I never think of it except in my best moods. The work, to which I dedicate the ensuing years of my life, is one which highly pleased Leslie in prospective, and my paper will not let me prattle to you about it. I have written what you most wished me to write, all about myself.

Our climate is inclement, and our houses not as compact as they might be; but it is a stirring climate, and the worse the weather, the more unceasingly entertaining are my Study Windows; and the month that is to come is the Glory of the year with us. A very warm Bedroom I can promise you, and, one that at the same time commands our finest Lake and Mountain view. If Leslie could not go abroad with you, and I could in any way mould my manners and habits to suit you, I should of all things like to be your companion. Good nature, an affectionate disposition, and so thorough a sympathy with the nature of your complaint that I should feel no pain, not the most momentary, at being told by you what your feelings required at the time in which they required it—this I should bring with me. But I need not say that you may say to me, "You don't suit me," without inflicting the least mortification. Of course this letter is for your Brother as for you; but I shall write to him soon. God bless you, and

S. T. COLERIDGE.

In answer to this letter Tom Wedgwood must have replied by a proposal that Coleridge should at once join him, doubtless at Bristol.

Coleridge is evidently ready, if not anxious, to leave his home, and he writes as if he thought his absence would be a long one.

S. T. Coleridge to Tom Wedgwood

KESWICK,
Wednesday, Nov. 3, 1802.

DEAR WEDGWOOD,—

It is now two hours since I received your letter ; and after the necessary consultation, Mrs. Coleridge herself is fully of opinion that to lose Time is merely to lose Spirits. Accordingly, I have resolved not to look the children in the Face (the parting from whom .is the only downright Bitter in the thing), but to take a chaise to morning morning, half past four for Penrith, and go to London by to-morrow's Mail. Of course I shall be in London (God permitting) on Saturday morning. I shall rest that day, and the next, and proceed to Bristol by the Monday night's mail. At Bristol I will go to Cote, and there wait your coming. If the family be not·at home, I shall beg a Bed at Dr. Beddoes's, or at least leave word where I am. At all events, barring serious Illness, serious Fractures, and the et cetera of serious *Unforeseens,* I shall be at Bristol, Tuesday, Noon, Nov. 9th.

You are aware, that my whole knowledge of French does not extend beyond the power of limping slowly, not without a Dictionary Crutch, thro' an easy French Book : and that as to Pronunciation, all my Organs of Speech, from the bottom of the Larynx to the Edge of my Lips, are utterly and naturally Anti-gallican. If only I shall have been any Comfort, any Alleviation to you, I shall feel myself at ease ; and whether you go abroad or no, while I remain with you, it will greatly contribute to my comfort, if I know you will have no hesitation, nor pain, in telling me what you wish me to do or not to do.

I regard it among the Blessings of my Life, that I have never lived among men whom I regarded as my artificial superiors: that all the respect I have at any time paid has been wholly to supposed Goodness, or Talent. The consequence has been that I have no alarms of Pride ; no cheval de frise of Independence. I have always lived among equals.

It never occurs to me, even for a moment, that I am otherwise. If I have quarrelled with men, it has been as Brothers or School-fellows quarrel. How little any man can give me, or take from me, save in matters of kindness and esteem, is not so much a Thought, or Conviction with me, or even a distinct Feeling, as it is my very Nature. Much as I dislike all formal Declarations of this kind, I have deemed it well to say this. I have as strong feelings of Gratitude as any man. Shame upon me, if in the sickness and the sorrow which I have had, and which have been kept unaggravated and supportable by your kindness and your Brother's—shame upon me if I did not feel a kindness, not unmixed with reverence, towards you both. But yet I never should have had my present Impulses to be with you, and this confidence that I may become an occasional comfort to you, if independently of all gratitude, I did not thoroughly esteem you ; and if I did not appear to myself to *understand* the nature of your sufferings ; and within the last year, in some slight degree to have *felt*, myself, something of the same.

Forgive me, my dear sir, if I have said too much. It is better to write it than to say it ; and I am anxious in the event of our travelling together that you should yourself be at ease with me, even as you would with a younger Brother, to whom from his childhood you had been in the habit of saying, " Do this, Col." or " don't do that."

I have been writing fast, lest I should be too late for the Post, forgetting that I am myself going with the Mail, and of course had better send the letter from London with the intelligence of my safe arrival there. Till then, all good be with us.

S. T. COLERIDGE.

Penrith, Thursday morning.

If this letter reaches you without any further writing, you will understand by it that all the places in the Mail are engaged, and that I must wait a day—but this will make no difference in my arrival at Bristol.

CHAPTER IX

SOUTH WALES AND CRESSELLY WITH COLERIDGE
1802

THE two friends had made plans, apparently, for a journey on the Continent, but these were adjourned. Tom Wedgwood's schemes varied from day to day, and the project of the moment was a tour in South Wales.

Tom Wedgwood to Tom Poole *

BATH,
Nov. 11, 1802.

MY DEAR FRIEND,—

I received yours from Paris a day or two since. It is in vain for me to seek for expressions to convey what I feel and have long felt towards you for your unwearied attentions to my comfort. Once for all, be assured that I am as much alive to services like yours as human being can be.

I am now on my road to Cote House, where Coleridge, who is like another comforting spirit to me, gives me the meeting from the Bath. We then proceed to South Wales, where I shall shoot for a fortnight or so, having sent a man and seven dogs before me. Our plan is then to come and see how comfortable we can make ourselves in your new house at Stowey.

* * * * *

For about three weeks, I was much better and stronger than I

---

* Wedgwood MSS., one of many letters given to Josiah by Poole.

have been for some years—and infinitely more cheerful. I
seconded this kindly effort of Nature by every possible exertion
of my own—I lived in the fields—shooting, walking, &c. I
took a farm and wholly abandoned myself to active and cheerful prospects. In the midst of this occupation, as if by some
vile incantation, I was without warning suddenly tumbled into
the lowest condition, and left to contemplate the ruin of all
my projects like the visions of a dream—so completely possessed
by languor and despondency that I was unable even to conceive
how it can ever have entered into my existence to cherish the
views and feelings which had so recently made up my whole
being. I am now a little recovered, but my mind is still shaken
and sore from its fall. Pray write to me at Cote House and
believe me ever most faithfully Yours,

T. W.

The journey into South Wales was mainly a visit to
Cresselly, the country house of John Bartlett Allen,
father of Tom's two sisters-in-law, Jane and Elizabeth
Wedgwood. On the way thither, Coleridge writes
thus to his wife :

S. T. Coleridge to his Wife

St. Clear, Carmarthen,

16 *Nov.* 1802.

My dear Love,—

*   *   *   *   *

The inn, the *Blue Boar*, is the most comfortable little public
house I was ever in, Miss S. Wedgwood (Tom's youngest sister)
left us this morning for Cresselly, Mr. Allen's seat (the Miss
Wedgwood's father), fifteen miles from this place, and T.
Wedgwood is gone out cock-shooting, in high glee and spirits.
He is very much better than I expected to have found him ;
he says the thought of my coming, and my really coming so
immediately, has sent a new life into him. He will be out all
the mornings. The evenings we chat, discuss, or I read to

him. To me he is a delightful and instructive companion. He possesses the *finest*, the *subtlest* mind and taste I have ever yet met with. His mind resembles that miniature in my "Three Graves":

> A small blue sun ! and it has got
> 　A perfect glory too !
> Ten thousand hairs of colour'd light,
> Make up a glory gay and bright,
> 　Round that small orb so blue ! *

*　　　*　　　*　　　*　　　*

My dear love ! I have said nothing of Italy, for I am as much in the dark as when I left Keswick, indeed much more: For I now doubt very much whether we shall go or no. [Then follows more as to the utter uncertainty of all Wedgwood's schemes of travel.] †

I must subscribe myself in haste (the mail is waiting) your dear husband,

S. T. Coleridge.

A few days after this letter was written the travellers

---

* The exact point of the comparison of Tom Wedgwood's mind to the "small blue sun" is not very evident. The quotation of the context may make it clearer. The scene in the poem is an arbour-like nook in a woody dell, wherein three people are resting and talking on a sunny morning :

> The sun peeps through the close thick leaves,
> 　See, dearest Ellen ! See !
> 'Tis in the leaves, a little sun,
> 　No bigger than your 'ee ;
> A small blue sun, and it has got
> 　A perfect glory too !
> Ten thousand hairs of colour'd light," &c.

I imagine that the simile is meant to emphasise, as it were, his underlining the words "*subtlest*," "*finest*." "A small blue sun" became in later editions "a tiny sun."

† The whole letter is printed in Mr. E. H. Coleridge's selection of S. T. C.'s letters, p. 410. It begins with an interesting comparison between the Vale of Usk, "nineteen miles of delightful country," and "our Vale of Keswick"

were at Cresselly, and they remained there or in its neighbourhood for about a month, Wedgwood taking occasional trips for shooting, while Coleridge stayed with the Allens. Cresselly is a country house and estate near Narbeth in Pembrokeshire, a few miles inland from Tenby.

Writing to Poole on December 17, Coleridge tells him that he is very happy here, and that they have

plenty of music and plenty of cream. For at Cresselly (I mention it as a remarkable circumstance, it being the only place I was ever at in which it was not otherwise) *though* they have a dairy, and *though* they have plenty of milk, they are not at all stingy of it. In all other houses where cows are kept, you may drink six shillings worth of wine a day, and welcome, but use three pennyworth of cream, and O Lord ! the feelings of the household.

These sarcasms, according to a note put by Poole on the letter, were aimed at the dairymaid at Stowey, who thought Coleridge made too free with her clouted cream, or at himself.*

That Coleridge was happy at Cresselly is no wonder. Besides the good cream, there was the good company of the daughters of the house. The eldest of them, who was the presiding lady (the squire's wife having died long before), was Jessie Allen, then aged twenty-five, a woman of rare intelligence and singularly beautiful character, sympathetic, warm-hearted, responsive ; in moral qualities the counterpart of her sister Bessy, the universally beloved wife of Josiah Wedgwood. She

---

* T. P., ii. 101.

afterwards, in middle age, became the wife of Sismondi
the historian.   The next sister, Emma, was a person of
more ordinary type, an affectionate and kindly woman.
The youngest of the group, Frances, always spoken of
as Fanny Allen, was in her twenty-first year.   She
lived to be ninety-three, dying in 1875; and was
known to the multitudinous Wedgwood-Allen-Darwin
cousinhood of the next two generations as one of the
cleverest and most entertaining of old ladies.   Her
talk, like her letters, was full of piquancy and point,
and in the early bloom of twenty-one she must have
been a very attractive creature.   Through her, as it
happens, we have some slight reminiscences of this
visit of Tom Wedgwood and Coleridge to Cresselly.
In her old age, sixty-nine years later, she dictated to
her niece, Elizabeth Wedgwood, a few sentences of
" Recollections of Tom Wedgwood."*   These run as
follows :

Fanny says there was a great charm in Uncle Tom's manner ;
it was gracious and elegant, but it was more the charm of his
character which made it so interesting.   His ill health made
him felt to be apart, but in everything he said there was sympathy and great sensibility, and from his not talking much he
was a very keen observer, and his fine taste was easily shocked.
But he judged calmly and sweetly.   When he arrived at
Cresselly, they were all set down to dinner before Mr. Allen,
who was a great invalid, came in ; and Fanny says she never
can forget the beauty of his manner when he rose and took

---

* The paper is endorsed " written by Sarah Eliz. Wedgwood,
eldest daughter of J. W. of Maer, whilst staying with Miss F. Allen
at Tenby in Dec. 1871."   It was found among Mrs. Charles Darwin's
papers.

Mr. Allen's hand with so much respect and feeling. Mr. Allen said afterwards he had never seen so fine a manner. After T. W. left Cresselly he wrote a letter to Sarah * [Wedgwood] speaking of them all with so much delicate affection and of his feeling towards them as sisters, that Fanny regretted never to have seen the letter again.

One day at Cresselly Mr. Coleridge was saying something about the Ten Commandments which T. W. thought would shock Mr. Allen, and he tapped him [Coleridge] on the arm and took him out of the room and stopped him.

Once in London there was a party, and Uncle Tom among them, to see a picture of Christ by Leonardo da Vinci. Dugald Stewart was of the party, and said, "You are all looking at that head—I cannot keep my eyes from the head of Mr. Wedgwood (who was looking intently at the picture); it is the finest head I ever saw." †

Another day at Cresselly, Coleridge, who was fond of reading MS. poems of Wordsworth's, asked Fanny whether she liked poetry, and when she said she did, came and sat by her on the sofa, and began to read the *Leechgatherer*. When he came to the passage, now I believe omitted, about his skin being so old and dry that the leeches wouldn't stick, it set Fanny a-laughing. That frightened her, and she got into a convulsive fit of laughter that shook Coleridge, who was sitting close to her, looking very angry. He put up his MS., saying he ought to ask her pardon, for perhaps to a person who had not genius (Fanny cannot exactly remember the expression) the poem might seem absurd. F. sat in a dreadful fright, everybody looking amazed, Sarah looking angry; and she almost expected

---

* Tom's sister, who had accompanied him and Coleridge into South Wales.

† I find in a letter written by Fanny Allen to the same niece in the fifties an allusion to the "effect that Tom's appearance and manner had on Mackintosh's 'set,' as they were called, the winter he left for India—Sydney Smith was almost awed." Dugald Stewart (d. 1828) was the Edinburgh Professor who had already become famous through his writings on mental and moral philosophy.

her father would turn her out of the room, but Uncle Tom
came to her rescue. "Well, Coleridge, one must confess that
it is not quite a subject for a poem." * Coleridge did not forgive
Fanny for some days, putting by his reading aloud if she came
in. But afterwards he was very good friends with her, and
one day in particular gave her all his history, saying, amongst
other things, "and there I had the misfortune to meet with my
wife."

The two friends seem to have lingered on at Cresselly in a state of complete indecision as to schemes
of further travel. "God knows what I can do," Tom
writes to his brother Josiah, "Coleridge is all kindness to me, and in prodigious favour here. . . . He
takes great pains to make himself pleasant. He is
willing, indeed desirous, to accompany me to any part
of the globe."

Both men were eager to get into a warm climate.
Italy, Teneriffe, Madeira, were talked of in turn.
Then Tom imagines another scheme. "A Mr. Luff,
a friend of Coll's in the North, a young man, formerly of fashion, now in distress, with a pretty little
wife, five years married and no children; he is mad

---

* The poem known in the Wordsworth household as the "Leechgatherer" was first published in 1807, under the title "Resolution
and Independence." Neither in that nor any later edition is there
anything as to the old man's skin or the leeches not sticking.
Dorothy Wordsworth's diary shows that she made two copies of
the poem for Coleridge, one on May 9, 1802, and one on July 5,
1802. In this same year Coleridge sent Sir George Beaumont a
copy, presumably made from one of Dorothy's, it is not known
which; but that copy does not contain the passage in question.
Knight's edition of the Poems, 1896, ii. 12.) Possibly it appeared
the copy made by Dorothy in May, and Coleridge may have
been reading from that.

after field sports, of the best possible dispositions—I
think to form a trio for a year and run wild."

This plan takes them at once to the Lake country,
for Luff's abode is at Patterdale, and on Christmas
Eve we find them calling at Wordsworth's cottage at
Grasmere on their way to Keswick, which they reach
the same day.*   Of this passing visit to Wordsworth
I find a trace in a letter written by the poet to
Josiah Wedgwood after Tom's death. " When your
brother," he says, " entered the room where I am now
writing, about four years ago, I was quite heart-stricken ;
he was deplorably changed, which was painful to see ;
but his calm and dignified manner, united with his tall
person and beautiful face, produced in me an impression
of sublimity beyond what I ever experienced from the
appearance of any other human being." †

These remarkable expressions, used by a man not
given to extravagance of language, show that Wedgwood's personal appearance must have been excep-
tionally striking ; and they agree, it will be seen, with
Fanny Allen's anecdote as to his meeting with Dugald
Stewart and with her remarks as to his dignified bearing when at Cresselly.

Tom's first letter from Coleridge's abode at Keswick
shows that he had again fallen back into a terrible depth
of despondency.

---

* Here Coleridge finds his new-born daughter, Sara, who had
appeared on the preceding day.

† Written in September 1806. The letter is given in a short
account of Tom's life which Josiah drew up for the information of
Mackintosh. In the words "deplorably changed" Wordsworth is
probably recalling Tom's visit to him at Alfoxden (ante, p.52).

Tom Wedgwood to his brother Josiah

GRETA HALL,
25 *Dec.*, 1802.

. . . If that fail [a plan of settling in Wales, one of various schemes for fighting his disease] I will neither distress myself nor my friends by continuing a vain struggle with Nature, but in complete resignation yield to her an existence which she will not allow to be anything but a burden to myself, and a perpetual source of anxiety to all around me. I feel a comfort from this resolution which sustains me in my most gloomy moments—I see a termination of my sufferings. . . . For God's sake understand me aright. I have for more than ten years made every possible effort to recover my health and spirits. In that time I have suffered more than I have ever told and more than can easily be conceived. I am not at all advanced. --My patience is gone. I do not become inured to suffering, and I am determined, after one or two more efforts, to relieve myself from all further effort, and to minister such stimuli as shall diminish the tediousness and misery of my life to a bearable degree, and take my chance for the consequences. If for a moment you could enter into my feelings, you would not be inclined to controvert my resolve. Would to God I could devote my life to your happiness, instead of thus for ever disturbing it !

This letter is headed "Read this by yourself," and is marked "Private." Another following it is in the same strain :

" . . . Shall I add that if the feelings of others were not involved in my decision, I should instantly resort to that final scheme which would bring immediate ease into my mind, by calmly yielding to that power which has baffled as much foresight, courage, and temperance as would have ensured a victory in 99 cases in a hundred ? If I am to continue yet much longer on this earth, I must at all events be separated from all my best friends, the sensation which wrings my soul."

To these despairful utterances Josiah's answer was * :

Josiah Wedgwood to his brother Tom

ETRURIA,
Dec. 31, 1802.

MY DEAR TOM,

I got yours of the 25th only to-day. . . . Your situation fills me with anguish, and I feel it with the more bitterness, having no consolation to offer you, nor any expedient for your relief to point out. Would to God you could show me how I can alleviate your sufferings, for I love you with my heart and soul. If the expression of your feelings afford you the slightest relief, do not refrain from it from any apprehension of giving me pain. I feel your pains, and shall think myself despicable if ever I cease to feel them, but my temper is cheerful, and I am in no danger of being permanently affected. I do not wish you to exhaust yourself by writing long letters, but I beg to hear often from you.

---

* This is a half-sheet bearing no signature. It may have been a draft only.

CHAPTER X

ULLESWATER—TO GENEVA AND FLIGHT HOME

1803

THE new year found Tom in a pleasant resting-place, the cottage of the Luffs at the head of Ulleswater, "embarked," as he says,* "on a new scheme, not of any great promise, but at any rate a temporary relief to a most painful state of irresolution and despondency." His description of his hosts shows them as good affectionate people, doing anything they can to make the sick man's life tolerable. Their cottage is in a delightful spot, a hundred yards from the lake. Behind it are the lower slopes of Helvellyn, in front the great mass of Place Fell, rising on the opposite side of the lake. The garden is washed by the streamlet from Glen Ridding. He is only nine miles away from the Wordsworths, whom he hopes to see not seldom, for he already feels that the society of the cottage "would be dull diet without occasional seasoning"; but there is a "tremendous mountain" [Grisedale Pass] between him and Dove Cottage. He is on the "most cordial terms of intimacy and good understanding" with the Luffs. The lady is a "little being of a simple but kindly nature, extremely limited in

---

* To Josiah Wedgwood, January 1, 1803.

general information " but with " sense of the right sort. Her steadiness of character has rescued her husband from perdition." They are living in this remote spot, partly for fishing and other sport, partly because " Luff has still some debts, and does not wish to have it much known where he is." *

Here Wedgwood thinks to fix himself, at least for a time, after having persuaded these kind people, with some difficulty, to let him share their housekeeping expenses. But as the winter advances he craves for a warmer climate, and is still planning schemes of southern travel. If his strength permits he " may probably induce Luff to go too, as a sporting companion, with Coleridge for conversation."

Coleridge, writing to him from Greta Hall on January 9, develops this wild scheme in his usual optimistic fashion :

In some part of Italy or Sicily which we both liked, I would look out for two houses. Wordsworth and his family would take one, and I the other, and then you might have a home either with me, or if you thought of Mr. and Mrs. Luff under this modification, one of your own ; and in either case you would have neighbours, and so return to England when the home-sickness pressed heavy upon you,

and so on. We hear no more of this visionary project. It is in the letter just mentioned† that Coleridge gives an often-quoted and striking description of a ride over Kirkstone Pass in the face of a furious

---

* They were familiar friends of Wordsworth and his sister.

† Printed in full in Mr. E. H. Coleridge's " Letters of. S. T. C." p. 417. It is the only one of the poet's letters to T. Wedgwood which appears in that collection.

storm, telling how at the top he met a man who had dismounted, not being able to keep on his horse, and who said to him with much feeling : " Oh ! Sir, it is a perilous buffeting." Wedgwood's reply, asking why he ventured to go on in the face of such weather, evoked the following remarkable letter :

S. T. Coleridge to Tom Wedgwood

[*Address* . C. Luff's, Esq , Glenridden, Ulleswater.]
Friday night, Jan. 14, 1803.
[*No postmark : evidently sent from* Greta Hall, Keswick.]

Dear Friend,—

I was glad at heart to receive your letter (which came to me on Thursday morning), and still more gladdened by the reading of it. The exceeding kindness which it breathed was literally medicinal to me ; and I firmly believe, cured me of a nervous rheumatism in my head and teeth. I daresay that you mixed up the scolding and the affection, the acid and the oil, very compleatly at Patterdale ; but by the time it came to Keswick, the oil was atop.

You ask, in God's name, why I did not return when I saw the state of the weather ? The true reason is simple, though it may be somewhat strange—the thought never once entered my head. The cause of this I suppose to be that (I do not remember it at least) I never once in my whole life turned back in fear of the weather. Prudence is a plant, of which I no doubt possess some valuable specimens, but they are always in my hothouse, never out of the glasses, and least of all things would endure the climate of the mountains. In simple earnest, 1 never find myself alone with the embracement of rocks and hills, a traveller up an alpine road, but my spirit courses, drives, and eddies, like a Leaf in Autumn ; a wild activity, of thoughts, imaginations, feelings, and impulses of motion, rises up from within me ; a sort of *bottom-wind*, that blows to no point of the compass, comes from I know not whence, but agitates the whole of me ; my whole being is filled with waves that roll and stumble, one this way, and one that way, like things that have no common master. I think that my soul must have pre-existed in the body of a Chamois-chaser ; the simple image of the old object has been obliterated ; but the feelings, and impulsive habits, and incipient actions are in me, and the old scenery awakens them. The further I ascend from animated Nature, from men, and cattle, and the common birds of the woods and fields, the greater becomes in me the Intensity of the feeling of life. Life seems to me then a universal spirit, that neither has, nor can have, an opposite. " God is everywhere," I have exclaimed, " and works everywhere, and where is there room for death ? " In these moments it has been my creed, that Death exists only because Ideas exist ; that life is limitless Sensation ; that Death is a child of the organic senses, chiefly of the Sight ; that Feelings die by flowing into the mould of the Intellect, and becoming ideas ; and that Ideas passing forth into action reinstate themselves again in the world of Life. And I do believe that truth lies enveloped in these loose generalisations. I do not think it possible that any bodily pains could eat out the love and joy, that is so substantially part of me, towards hills, and rocks, and steep waters ; and I have had some Trial.

On Tuesday I was uncommonly well all the morning, and eat an excellent dinner ; but playing too long and too rompingly with Hartley and Derwent, I was very unwell that evening. On Wednesday I was well, and after dinner wrapped myself up warm, and walked with Sarah Hutchinson* to Lodore. I never beheld anything more impressive than the wild outline of the black masses of mountain over Lodore [here he gives a rough sketch of the mountain outline] to the Gorge of Borrowdale, seen through the bare Twigs of a grove of

---

* Sister of Mrs. Wordsworth. Lodore is the cataract near the Borrowdale end of Derwentwater.

Birch Trees, through which the road passes ; and on emerging from the grove a red planet (so very red that I never saw a star so red, being clear and bright at the same time) stood on the edge of the point where I have put an asterisk ; it seemed to have sky behind it ; it *started*, as it were, from the Heaven, like an eye-ball of Fire. I wished aloud for you to have been with me at that moment.

The walk appeared to have done me good, but I had a wretched Night; had shocking pains in my head, occiput, and teeth, and found in the morning that I had two blood-shot eyes. But almost immediately after the receipt and perusal of your letter the pains left me, and I have bettered to this hour ; and am now indeed as well as usual, saving that my left eye is very much blood-shot. It is a sort of duty with me to be particular respecting facts that relate to my health. I am myself not at all dispirited. I have retained a good sound appetite through the whole of it, without any craving after exhilarants or narcotics ; and I have got well, as in a moment. Rapid recovery is constitutional with me ; but the two former circumstances I can with certainty refer to the system of Diet, abstinence from vegetables, wine, spirits, and beer, which I have adopted by your advice.

I have no dread or anxiety respecting any fatigue which either of us is likely to undergo, even in continental Travelling. Many a healthy man would have been layed up with such a Bout of thorough wet and intense cold at the same time as I had at Kirkstone. Would to God that also for your sake I were a stronger man ; but I have strong wishes to be with you, and love your society ; and receiving much comfort from you, and believing that I receive likewise much improvement, I find a delight (very great, my dear friend ! indeed it is), when I have reason to imagine that I am in return an alleviation of your destinies, and a comfort to you. I have no fears ; and am ready to leave home at a two days' warning. For myself I should say two hours ; but bustle and hurry might disorder Mrs. Coleridge, She and the three children are quite well.

I grieve that there is a lowring in politics. The *Moniteur* contains almost daily some bitter abuse of our ministers and parliament, and in London there is great anxiety and omening. I have dreaded war from the time that the disastrous fortunes of the expedition of Saint Domingo,* under Le Clerc, was known in France.† . . .

I remain, my dear Wedgewood, with most affectionate esteem and grateful attachment,

Your sincere friend,
S. T. COLERIDGE.

A month later, Coleridge is with Poole at Stowey, and Tom at Cote House. The scheme for their travelling together forms the burden of several more letters, but doubts and hesitations increase as the weeks go on.

S. T. Coleridge to Tom Wedgwood

[*Address :* COTE HOUSE, BRISTOL.]

STOWEY,

Thursday night ‡ : *Feb.* 10, 1803.

. . . You bid Poole not reply to your letter. Dear Friend, I *could* not, if I had wished it. Only with regard to myself and my accompanying you, let me say this much. My health is not worse than it was in the North ; indeed it is much better. I

---

* The expedition sent by Buonaparte to enforce the re-establishment of slavery in the island.   Only about 2000 out of 35,000 lived to return to France.   It was then that Toussaint l'Ouverture, "most unhappy man of men," was seized and carried off to die in a French dungeon.

† What follows is as to errands, shoppings, &c., with an invitation to Greta Hall.

‡ I think it needless to print another letter he writes on this same date to Tom Wedgwood at Cote. . It is without interest, except that it refers to a request made by Coleridge to Captain John Wordsworth (the poet's brother) to get from India some " bang " for Wedgwood's use.

have no fears. But if you feel that my health being what you know it to be, the inconveniences of my being with you will be greater than the advantages, feel no reluctance in telling me so. It is so entirely an affair of spirits, that the conclusion must be made by you, not in your reason, but purely in your Spirits and Feelings. Sorry indeed should I be to know that you had gone abroad with one to whom you were comparatively indifferent. Sorry if there should be no one with you, who could with fellow-feeling and general like-mindedness, yield you sympathy in your sunshiny moments. Dear Wedgewood! my heart swells within me as it were. I have no other wish to accompany you than what arises immediately from my personal attachment to you, and a deep sense in my own heart, that let us be as dejected as we will, a week together cannot pass in which a mind like yours would not feel the want of affection, or be wholly torpid to its pleasurable influences. I cannot bear to think of your going abroad with a mere travelling companion ; with one at all influenced by salary, or personal conveniences. You will not suspect me of flattering you, but indeed, dear Wedgewood, you are too good and too valuable a man to deserve to receive attendance from a hireling, even for a month together, in your present state.

If I do not go with you, I shall stay in England only such time as may be necessary for me to raise the travelling money, and go immediately to the south of France. I shall probably cross the Pyrenees to Bilboa, see the country of Biscay, and cross the north of Spain to Perpignan, and so on to the north of Italy, and pass my next winter at Nice. I have every reason to believe that I can live, even as a traveller, as cheap as I can in England. [Here are some lines as to a commission of Josiah's for buying some malt.]

God bless you! I will repeat no professions, even, in the subscription of a Letter. You know me, and that is my serious simple wish that in everything respecting me you would think altogether of yourself, and nothing of me ; and be assured that no Resolve of yours, however suddenly adopted, or however nakedly communicated, will give me any pain, any at least arising from my own Bearings.

Your's ever

S. T. COLERIDGE.

P.S.—I have been so overwhelmed that I have said nothing of Poole. What indeed can or ought I to say? You know what his feelings are, even to men whom he loves and esteems far less than you. He is deeply affected.

Perhaps Leslie would accompany you.

S. T. Coleridge to Tom Wedgwood

[*Address:* COTE HOUSE, BRISTOL.]

POOLE'S,

Thursday, February 17, 1803.

MY DEAR WEDGEWOOD,—

I do not know that I have anything to say that justifies me in troubling you with the Postage and Perusal of this scrawl. I received a short and kind letter from Josiah last night. He is named the sheriff [of Dorset]. Poole, who has received a very kind invitation from your Brother in a letter of last Monday, and which was repeated in last night's letter, goes with me, I hope, in the full persuasion that you will be there before he is under the necessity of returning home. He has settled both his might-have-been-lawsuits in a perfectly pleasant way, exactly to his own wish. He bids me say, what there is no occasion of saying, with what anxious affection his Thoughts follow you. Poole is a very, very good man. I like even his incorrigibility in little faults and deficiencies; it looks like a wise determination of Nature " to let well alone."

Are you not laying out a scheme which will throw your Travelling in Italy into an unpleasant and unwholesome part of the year? From all I can gather, you ought to leave this country in the first days of April at the latest. But no doubt you know these things better than I. If I do not go with you, it is very probable that we shall meet somewhere or other; at

all events you will know where I am, and I can come to you
if you wish it. And if I go with you, there will be this
Advantage, that you may drop me where you like, if you should
meet any Frenchman, Italian, or Swiss, whom you liked, and
who would be pleasant and profitable to you. But this we can
discuss at Gunville.

As to Mackintosh, I never doubted that he *means* to fulfil
his engagements with you ; but he is one of those weak-moraled
men, with whom the meaning to do a thing means nothing.*
He promises with his whole Heart, but there is always a little
speck of cold felt at the core that transubstantiates the whole
resolve into a Lie, even in his own consciousness. But what I
most fear is that he will in some way or other embroider himself upon your Thoughts ; but you, no doubt, will see the
Proof Sheets, and will prevent this from extending to the injury
of your meaning. Would to Heaven it were done ! I may
with strictest truth say, that I have *thirsted* for its appearance.

I remain in comfortable Health. Warm rooms, an old
Friend, and Tranquillity, are specifics for my complaints.
With all my ups and downs I have a deal of joyous feeling,
that I would with gladness give a good part of to you, my
dear Friend ! God grant that Spring may come to you with
healing on her wings !

My respectful remembrances to your Brother, and Mrs. J.
Wedgewood.

I desire Mrs. J. Wedgewood, when she writes to Crescelly,
to remember me with affection to Miss Allen, and Fanny and
Emma ; and to say how often I think with pleasure on them
and the weeks I passed in their society. When you come to
Gunville, please not to forget my Pens. Poole and I quarrel
once a day about them.

---

* This and what follows refers to Mackintosh's undertaking to
put into shape Wedgwood's philosophical speculations, a promise
which was not fulfilled. But that Coleridge of all men should com-
plain of any one else as being " one with whom the meaning to
do a thing means nothing "—— ! !

God bless you, my dear Wedgewood!

I remain with most affectionate esteem and regular attachment and good wishes.

Your's ever,
S. T. COLERIDGE.

The messages to the Cresselly sisters, and allusions in other letters, give the impression that Coleridge made good friends among the Allen ladies. That Tom's near relations, however, did not all sympathise with him in his admiration for the poet is shown by a letter from his sister Kitty which must have been written about this time. It is interesting as giving a cool estimate of the man as he appeared to an intelligent, though matter-of-fact bystander. Some of her criticism was certainly of a kind not very easy to answer.

Kitty Wedgwood to Tom Wedgwood

[*No date—endorsed* COTE, 1803.]

*   *   *   *   *

We shall do everything to make your bed-room warm and Mr. Coleridge's comfortable, though it cannot be smart, as he must ascend to the tower. I don't know whether we shall ever agree in our sentiments respecting this gentleman, but I hope if we do not that we may agree to differ. I certainly felt no scruples of conscience in joining the attack at Cresselly. I have never seen enough of him to overcome the first disagreeable impression of his accent and exterior. I confess, too, that in what I have seen and heard of Mr. Coleridge there is in my opinion too great a parade of superior feeling; and an excessive goodness and sensibility is put too forward, which gives an appearance, at least, of conceit, and excites suspicion that it is acting; as real sensibility never endeavours to excite notice. I will tell you sincerely my opinion of him, whether it is well or ill founded. He appears to be an uncomfortable husband, and very negligent, of the worldly interest at least, of his children; leaving them in case of his death to be provided for by his friends is a scheme more worthy of his desultory habits than of his talents. I think a sturdy independent spirit is so very admirable that, to be extremely candid, I have never recovered his so willingly consenting to be so much obliged to even you. You see I have not much to say, but 'tis the impression I have of his thinking himself much better than the world in general that inclines one to look more closely into his own life and conduct; and as his judgments of others are not inclined to the favourable side, he does not from his own conduct claim lenity.

I am almost afraid to let you see this letter, but it does as clearly as I can express contain my present opinion of Mr. Coleridge. I think I am not so rivetted to this opinion but that I can change, if upon seeing more of him he gives me sufficient grounds. That I shall ever think him very agreeable I do not imagine. I agree with you in some parts of your character entirely, and of the others I cannot judge. I think it would have been strange if he had not been very civil and obliging at Cresselly where he was so hospitably received— I question whether Emma will celebrate his politeness*—I hope this subject is very interesting—otherwise you will be very much tired, but I was glad to state quite plainly and sincerely my opinion.

At length the plan of joint travel, a hopeless one at the best, for two sick men of such abnormal tempers as Coleridge and Wedgwood, finally collapsed when, on

---

* I find nothing in the letters to explain this doubt. Emma Allen was the one plain figure in the group, and though an intelligent woman, was not nearly so agreeable as her sisters; but one would not like to think this made Coleridge less polite to her than to the rest. What " the attack " was there is nothing to show.

the top of all other difficulties, came imminent threat-
enings of renewed war with France.   But Tom found
a companion, an artist named Underwood, and on
March 25, 1803, crossed to Calais.   At that moment
his countrymen were all flying home.   A few days
previously Buonaparte had personally insulted Lord
Whitworth, our Ambassador, at an official reception at
the Tuileries, and the general belief was that war was
inevitable.   On April 16 we find Tom at Paris, and a
fortnight later he is at Geneva, planning moves to
warmer regions; but, alas! with scarce a hope of any
betterment.   "Nothing," he says, "can be more hopeless than my situation."   He shrinks from returning,
and yet all other schemes seem impracticable.   He tells
his brother his troubles, blaming himself for doing so.
"The repugnance I feel at again distressing you with
my almost hopeless case, *believe me*, is most extreme."
He lingered at Geneva very nearly too long, and only
just escaped being caught and made a *détenu* under
Buonaparte's iniquitous decree.   On May 6, he is in
fear of "the Calais passage being shut."   He must
have left a day or two later, and got to Paris just as
the English Ambassador was leaving it.   He crossed
the Channel on the very day of the declaration of war,
May 16; and on the 22nd Buonaparte ordered the
arrest of all English residents and travellers.   His
travelling companion, Underwood, who had stayed in
France with intent to pursue his art studies, had the
bad luck to be caught,* and was a *détenu* for at least two

---

* Wedgwood did all he could to obtain his release, but without
avail, and sent him supplies of money.   His letters give one an

years, if not for another nine, till the end of the war.

---

idea of the amount of undeserved suffering caused by the decree. For a long time he was unable to learn whether his old mother was dead or alive. It took about two months to get letters from England, as they had to go round by Sweden. Without Wedgwood's help he would have been nearly starved. The latest of his letters, a very sad one, is dated April 3, 1805 (three months before Wedgwood's death). The First Consul's abominable act, which was a violation of all rules of war, made about ten thousand English families miserable in this way. It is curious that the Whig pro-Buona-partists should have forgotten all this when they inveighed against the cruelty of keeping their hero at Longwood, where he was living in one of the most delightful climates in the world, and with twelve thousand a year wherewith to get himself any luxury he might fancy.

CHAPTER XI

CONTINUED STRUGGLE FOR HEALTH—INVASION ALARMS AND VOLUNTEERING

1803—1804

WEDGWOOD's malady, whatever it was, had evidently been advancing, and from 1803 onwards to his death two years later the burden of his letters to his brother is an increasing hopelessness: "If I recrossed the Channel it has only been to seize the last possibility of staving off a little longer that termination which nature seems determined to force upon me." But he still kept struggling on. In the summer of this year he was trying to make out something of a life for himself in London. His main abode was the house of the Wedgwood firm in York Street, St. James's, but he was often at the chambers of John Hensleigh Allen (brother-in-law of his two brothers) in the Temple. In July he says: "I am almost living with Tobin in Barnard's Inn"; and later he is "messing with Tobin" for a month.*

* This Tobin I understand to be John, the solicitor and dramatist, brother to the James who was an intimate friend of Tom's, as he was also of the Wordsworths. James was the "dear brother Jem" who figures in the first edition of "We are seven,"

"A simple child, dear brother Jem,
    Who lightly draws its breath," &c.

See the Fenwick note to the poem, where Wordsworth tells how

Among his chief associates at this time were two new acquaintances with whom he quickly became intimate, Richard ("Conversation") Sharp and Thomas Campbell the poet. Every mention of Sharp shows him as one of the most sympathetic and helpful of friends—"He is devoted to my service," " out-doing all former kindnesses," &c. Campbell was then a young man of twenty-six at the outset of his literary career. " The Pleasures of Hope" had appeared in 1799. To him Tom Wedgwood was strongly attracted, and the feeling was warmly returned. A letter of Campbell's to his great friend Dr. Currie gives us a curiously expressed record of the impression made upon him by Wedgwood. After enlarging on a singular kind of feeling which, when he is in a certain mood, prevents his writing to Currie with perfect ease and frankness, he says :

The mischief is, I respect you ; I am afraid of prattling to you, and for fear of that I can say nothing. Worse than this, I have another fault of true English temperament. When the world crosses me . . . or when I have a slight headache or derangement of stomach, the duty of *propriety*, and above all in correspondence, stares me in the face like a gorgon. . . . Every motion of my mind grows cramped and ungraceful. I lose confidence in myself and the world. . . . I thought this malady of metempsychosis peculiar to one unhappy being. . . . If I had observed symptoms of it in others, it was in some bad characters whom I did not like myself for resembling. But I found it lately, by the confession of a candid and worthy man, in one who is more than my fellow-creature in this failing, as he has it even worse than myself ; I have even been

James Tobin entreated him to cancel it—" for if published it will make you everlastingly ridiculous."

reconciled to it from seeing it the concomitant of a mind perhaps the finest I ever met with. The person I speak of is Thom. Wedgwood, the son of the potter, of whom you may have heard, as he is known to literary people. We have been sometime well acquainted ; and from finding him a man above par, I was fond of his conversation. We met one day, both in a cold and cramped metempsychosis, with bad health, and I was crossed with my love affair ; and our conversation got upon this subject. . . . I cannot help noticing poor Wedgwood —a strange and wonderful being. Full of goodness, benevo-lence, with a mind stored with ideas, with metaphysics the most exquisitely fine I ever heard delivered, a man of wonder-ful talents, a tact of taste acute beyond description—with even good nature and mild manners, he is not happy. I thought till I saw him, that happiness was to be defeated by no other circumstances than weakness, vice, or an uncommanded temper.*

Still meditating foreign travel, Tom Wedgwood tried to get Campbell to accompany him, but had to give up the idea, as he found that Campbell was on the point of marrying. He calls this " a cruel disappoint-ment." He then thought of Hazlitt. The vivid account of Hazlitt given by Coleridge in the follow-ing letter was evidently an answer to some inquiry made by Tom in this view.†

---

* Beattie's " Life of Campbell," i. 46. I know of nothing to explain why Campbell should apply the Greek term for the trans-migration of souls to the kind of mental malaise which he describes as common to Tom Wedgwood and himself.

† William Hazlitt (b. 1778, d. 1830) was at this time twenty-five years old, seven years younger than Tom Wedgwood. He was trying portrait-painting for a livelihood, and had not yet done any literary work.

S. T. Coleridge to Tom Wedgwood

(At Mr. Allen's Chambers, Inner Temple.)

GRETA HALL, KESWICK,

September 16, *Friday* [1803].

MY DEAR WEDGWOOD,—

I reached home on yesterday noon, and it was not a Post Day. William Hazlitt is a thinking, observant, original man, of great power as a Painter of Character-Portraits, and far more in the manner of the old Painters than any living Artist, but the objects must be *before* him ; he has no imaginative memory. So much for his Intellectuals. His manners are to 99 in 100 singularly repulsive ; brow-hanging, shoe-contemplative, strange. Sharp seemed to like him ; but Sharp saw him only for half an hour, and that walking. He is, I verily believe, kindly-natured ; is very fond of, attentive to, and patient with children ; but he is jealous, gloomy, and of an irritable Pride. With all this, there is much good in him. He is disinterested ; an enthusiastic lover of the great men who have been before us; he says things that are his own, in a way of his own ; and though from habitual Shyness, and the outside and bearskin at least, of misanthropy, he is strangely confused and dark in his conversation, and delivers himself of almost all his conceptions with a Forceps, yet he says more than any man I ever knew (yourself only excepted) that is his own in a way of his own ; and oftentimes when he has warmed his mind, and the synovial juice has come out and spread over his joints, he will gallop for half an hour together with real eloquence. He sends well-headed and well-feathered Thoughts straight forwards to the mark with a Twang of the Bowstring. If you could recommend him as a portrait-painter, I should be glad. To be your Companion he is, in my opinion, utterly unfit. His own Health is fitful.

I have written, as I ought to do, to you most freely, *imo ex corde ;* you know me, both head and heart, and will make what deductions your reasons will dictate to you.* I can think of no other person. What wonder? For the last years I have been shy of all mere acquaintance.

> " To live beloved is all I need,
> And when I love, I love indeed."

I never had any ambition , and now, I trust, I have almost as little vanity.

For 5 months past my mind has been strangely shut up. I have taken the paper with the intention to write to you many times ; but it has been all one blank Feeling, one blank idealess Feeling. I had nothing to say,—I could say nothing. How dearly I love you, my very Dreams make known to me. I will not trouble you with the gloomy tale of my Health. While I am awake, by patience, employment, effort of mind, and walking, I can keep the fiend at arm's length, but the Night is my Hell ! sleep my tormenting Angel. Three nights out of four I fall asleep struggling to lie awake ; and my frequent night-screams have almost made me a nuisance in my own House. Dreams with me are no Shadows, but the very substances and foot-thick calamities of my Life. / Beddoes, who has been to me ever a very kind man, suspects that my stomach " brews vinegar." I am careful of my Diet. The supercarbonated kals does me no service, nor magnesia, neither have I any head-ach. But I am grown hysterical. Meantime my looks and strength have improved. I myself fully believe it to be either atonic, hypo-chondriacal Gout, or a scrophulous affection of the Mesenteric

---

* Cottle's version of this sentence may be quoted to show what utter nonsense his reckless editing makes of what Coleridge wrote : " I have written as I ought to do : to you most freely. You know me, both head and heart, and I will make what deductions your reasons may dictate to me." A sentence a few lines higher up is similarly travestied out of all recognition. Here Cottle, not understanding Coleridge's odd anatomical metaphor, calmly cuts it out, and puts in a patchwork of his own : " . . . When he has wearied his mind, and the juice is come out, and spread over his spirits, he will gallop, &c."

Glands. In the hope of drawing the Gout, if Gout it should be, into my feet, I walked, previously to my getting into the Coach at Perth, 263 miles in eight Days, with no unpleasant fatigue ; * and if I could do you any service by coming to town, and there were no Coaches, I would undertake to be with you, on foot, in 7 days. I must have strength somewhere ; my head is indefatigably strong ; my limbs too are strong ; but [here he launches into a wild description of his bodily troubles.]

All my family are well. Southey, his wife, and Mrs. Lovell are with us. He has lost his little girl, the unexpected gift of a long marriage ; and stricken to the heart is come hither for such poor comforts as my society can afford him.

To diversify this dusky letter, I will write an Epitaph, which I composed in my sleep for myself, while dreaming that I was dying. To the best of my recollection I have not altered a word. Your's dear Wedgwood, and of all that are dear to you at Gunville, gratefully and most affectionately,

S. T. Coleridge.

Epitaph.

" Here sleeps at length poor Col. and without screaming,
   Who died, as he had always liv'd, a dreaming :
   Shot dead, while sleeping, by the Gout within,
   Alone, and all unknown, at E'nbro' in an inn."

It was on Tuesday night last, at the Black Bull, Edinburgh.

Before Wedgwood received this letter he had put aside, for a time at least, the scheme of travel which prompted the inquiry about Hazlitt, and was immersed

---

* This alludes to his solitary wanderings in the Highlands after leaving Wordsworth and his sister in the middle of the Scotch tour described in Dorothy's delightful " Recollections," He left them on the plea of being unwell, but the real reason must have been that being with them interfered with his taking laudanum.

in another project, one of the oddest of the many
plans by which, when all regular doctoring had failed
to do anything for him, he sought to circumvent his
mysterious malady. The beginning and end of this
may be told in a few sentences from his letters to Poole
and to his brother.

"(11 Sept. 1803) . . . going to take a house in town by the
week. My plan is to busy myself in the little practical concerns of housekeeping. I have a friend who will be with me.

(17 Sept.) I am fairly embarked in my scheme, having
just made the beds and explained my intentions to Frederic,
and [with] a louis bribe to a discreet silence. His room is
now fitting up as my kitchen. I am going to York Street for
stores. At one I return to cook our dinner. If I can only
escape those horrible lownesses, I shall certainly adhere to this
new plan of life. As to making life pleasant on the whole, I
have no such expectation. I aim only at making it tolerable.
Send Frederic's flute by waggon.

(19 Sept.) I persevere in my plan—have cooked two dinners
and made beds, &c. &c. . . I like the plan better than I expected,
and find that living with one person will furnish as much work
as I shall ever want, including washing and ironing. Aslet
certainly will not do for that person. His temper is bad.

(23 Sept.) I experienced a most cruel mortification yesterday. After nine days steady perseverance, I found myself so
low and so languid that I was obliged to get Frederic to finish
the cooking of the dinner, washing, &c. Cooking I resign for
ever ; it deprives me of all stomach for my dinner. I am so
harassed by fever, tho' I have lived on fish for the last fortnight,
that I am afraid I must desist from labour for a while. I am
frightened at the prospect before me.

(28 Sept.) So extremely feeble I can't prosecute my labours,
which, when cookery is excluded, are indeed insufficient in
quantity. . . .

And so he turns to other plans. He is "impatient to quit London," and thinks at one time of getting some additions made to a farmhouse near Gunville, where Luff and his wife can come and companionise him ; then of "running up a room" for himself with a "minute Kitchen" on his Eastbury estate.

In the autumn of 1803 all England was in a ferment in the expectation of a French invasion. Napoleon's "Army of England" was encamped at Boulogne, with the flotilla of transports ready to carry 100,000 men across those few miles of sea at the first fair wind. The country was fully roused, and able-bodied men of all ranks were being enrolled as volunteers. Even Tom Wedgwood, sick as he was, fancied at moments that he might do some kind of service. "If it lasts," he says (October 3), speaking of a slight improvement in his health, "I seriously mean to offer myself for garrison service on the coast, but last night I found myself unable to get off my chair, and for the time abandoned the idea of ramming a cannon." But he could not rest without doing something towards the defence of the country. "As my health," he wrote to Poole, "will not allow me to serve in person, it is my duty to serve by my purse. I have, therefore, made an offer to Government to raise a Company of volunteers and clothe them at my expense."

Poole, then in London for his Poor Law work, helped him to arrange this at the War Office. He learnt that about Patterdale and the Lakes, where he had stayed with the Luffs, the men were eager to volunteer; but that money was wanted for the needful expenses. He therefore, with Luff's aid, formed a Company of eighty men from among the "statesmen" of the district, clothing and arming them as riflemen. The cost of doing this, including pay for twenty days exercise, which he gave the men while they were "supernumeraries," before Government allowed them the regular pay of volunteers, came to about £800. Luff, who had been in the army, was put at their head, and proved a most zealous organiser and commander. The Company decided on taking the name of its founder, and it was known as "Wedgwood's Mountaineers." They "exercised through the first winter," says Josiah Wedgwood, "often mid-leg deep in snow, many of them walking ten miles to the field." All the accounts go to show that they were a splendid set of men. An inspecting officer tells them he shall "report them as not only fit for immediate service, but perfectly equal to being brigaded with any regiment of the line, and to be sent on the most arduous duty." That they were grateful for Wedgwood's help is testified by a letter dated "Ulcatrow Moor," signed by "John Sutton and John Robinson Lieutenants," and addressed to "Charles Luff Esq., Captain Wedgwood Loyal Mountaineers," wherein they request him to "represent to our most worthy patron Mr. Wedgwood our sincere and grateful acknowledgements for the Honour, and in this county unexampled favour, he has conferred on us, by putting us in a state to serve our King and Country, where every Hand and stout Heart should join; but without this favour we had been left, like too many others, unable though

willing to join our brother Soldgers." In a letter of
Luff's to Tom Wedgwood we have an animated account
of a field-day held, in the next summer (May 1804),
at and about Gowbarrow Park :

A very severe day it was, but an excellent dinner of Beef
and plumb pudding, to which 120 sat down, recruited their
exhausted strength. What would I not have given to have
had you on the spot ! [Wedgwood was ill in Dorsetshire.]
The gratitude of the men was unbounded. William Wordsworth dined with us on the lawn before the house,* and declared
it to be the most interesting day he ever witnessed, such as he
should long remember ; and said he almost envied you your
feelings on the occasion.

We may imagine how the poet would be stirred by
that scene when we remember that it was he who, in
those memorable sonnets of 1803, had given voice to
the emotions aroused by that great national crisis.

" No parleying now !   In Britain is one breath ;
We are all with you now from shore to shore ;
Ye Men of Kent, 'tis victory or death."

The Wedgwood letters of 1803 reflect the anxieties
which must have disturbed hundreds of households,
especially those near the coasts, during that memorable

---

* The house here mentioned is presumably that known as "Lyulph's
Tower," on the beautiful slope just above that bit of the Ulleswater
shore which is familiar to all Wordsworth-lovers as the scene of the
Daffodils.
"The Wedgwood Mountaineers" continued to exist till long
after the fear of an invasion had passed away with the victory of
Trafalgar. Up till 1812 Josiah Wedgwood, as Tom's executor,
continued to provide Luff's captain's pay, and find money for other
expenses in connection with the corps.

autumn. Tom, who is in London, and hears all kinds of speculations as to when and where the French may land, is naturally thinking of his mother and sisters at Eastbury and his brother's family at Gunville, only a few miles from the coast of Dorset. Jos has " ordered a tilt for his wagon," in case of having to move in bad weather, and is packing up some of the most important things, but his old mother is averse to moving, and Bess is unwilling to send the children away.

Tom Wedgwood to Josiah Wedgwood

TEMPLE,
Oct. 10, 1803.

DEAR JOS,—

It seems to be the general opinion that the French will land somewhere or other. Now your family is on the coast ; have you anticipated deliberately all the circumstances immediately arising from a landing in your neighbourhood ? I am afraid there would be a great deal of distress, great difficulty of removal. Your horses would be pressed for service. Might it not be wise, in so awful a moment of danger, for your family and my mother's to retire to the centre and most secure part of the island ? Or at any rate, to make immediate and complete arrangements for removal, such as packing valuables, etc., and perhaps to occupy Cote House for the next critical month. For as Pitt said at Margate :—*Expect the French every dark night.* Don't suppose that I write in a moment of excessive alarm ; I have heard the subject a good deal canvassed lately, and I am convinced that some of the stoutest hearts in the Island are apprehensive about the event. I have made enquiries about the measures of removal, and as far as I can foresee, there will be amazing confusion the moment the landing of the French in any neighbourhood is proclaimed. Sounding the alarm is no doubt very unpleasant : but a balance must be struck.

Tom's urgency was intelligible, considering that Gunville was only some three or four hours' march from Poole Harbour. Gloucestershire was a much safer place for non-combatants. George III., we may remember, had at this time made all arrangements for the Queen and Princesses moving from Windsor, at a few hours' notice, to the Palace of his friend Bishop Hurd, at Worcester. Weekly rehearsals were going on at Boulogne of the embarkation of the troops, and Pitt, now Warden of the Cinque Ports, was "riding up and down the coast of Kent" looking after the 3000 volunteers of the Walmer district. The prospect of seeing the French on English soil was serious enough, though some still maintain that the "Armée d'Angleterre" was more or less of a sham, and that Napoleon's real object was a great move across the Rhine.*

Kitty Wedgwood to her brother Tom

EASTBURY,
Oct. [*about* 16th (?), 1803].

*   *   *   *   *

We are just returned from Lymington, and I own I was glad to be at home again without any alarm from the enemy. The day after, we had a slight one, which seemed to arise from the Blandford Volunteers being ordered to Poole. . . . We feel quite unsettled from having a doubt whether we will not retire

---

* Which hardly agrees with Napoleon's having had a medal struck with the legend : " *Descente en Angleterre : frappé à Londres en MDCCCIV.*" (A copy of this medal may be seen at Boulogne, and Earl Stanhope has one at Chevening.) Some of the plans imagined in France for transporting the troops seem to have been simply insane. Mr. Rose's recent "Life of Napoleon" gives a picture of a new kind of ship which, according to the figures given, would have a deck area of many acres.

into the interior for the winter. . . . I really think that we shall feel more anxiety thinking every morning that perhaps Dorsetshire is all in confusion. What I most fear is that in very bad weather we should really be obliged to go, and my mother would perhaps suffer from want of accommodation on the road ; besides, the hurry and confusion of the scene—or even travelling in very cold weather is a great risk for her. She is not in the least alarmed, and I believe would dislike the thoughts of removing ; but we shall certainly consider whether we had not better. Jos will not be here in case of danger [being High Sheriff of the county] and it would be one anxiety the less for him.

*   *   *   *   *

Tom Wedgwood to Josiah Wedgwood

TEMPLE,

Oct. 17, *Monday*, 1803.

DEAR JOS,—

I am afraid I shall hardly get you a guinea, as Howorth does not receive any in York St., nor can any be got at our bank.* I had begun a little store before I received yours, and have yet only amassed eight. I had no thoughts of your leaving the county, and am very glad you are so well prepared for quitting at a moment's notice.

*   *   *   *   *

I sent the Birds to Mack's also as he has company to-day. He says he shall begin *Time and Space* tomorrow, and has invited me to join in the attack, *which I totally decline.*†

Tom Wedgwood to Josiah Wedgwood

HENRIETTA ST.,

Oct. 18, 1803.

I don't know what to say about their continuing in Dorsetshire. I am afraid my mother's want of apprehension of

---

* John Wedgwood's bank in Pall Mall. Howorth is the cashier at the York Street show-rooms.

† See p. 157.

danger is derived from a very inadequate consideration of it. Mackintosh thinks a landing will certainly be effected, as the attack will probably be made at many points. Now, as Kitty says, a forced march in mid-winter happening when she may be indisposed might be very distressing. I should think Cote House tolerably secure, and [they] will much easier move forward into the interior.

*　　*　　*　　*　　*

Pray prepare Bess and all about you for the horrors that are almost inevitable. Bess writes with too much composure for a woman who may, even probably, find herself a widow in a week. My repugnance to inactivity increases with my strength ; but I am still utterly unable to enter into any corps.

*　　*　　*　　*　　*

Howorth has a friend who has promised him 20 guineas— these shall be saved for you, and a few more he has collected. What say you to a little bullion, or gold grains ? It is now at £4 1s. 8d. the ounce. I shall get a few ounces.

*　　*　　*　　*　　*

Tom's view prevailed, and before long his mother and sisters moved to John's house at Cote, near Bristol. There, too, we find Tom himself in November, reading the second edition of Malthus on Population, and corresponding with military people in London, and with Lord Lowther the Lord Lieutenant of Westmoreland, about his volunteer corps. Volunteering is the great business of the moment. Jos is distracted between his duties as Captain of a Staffordshire corps, formed from the Etruria works, and as High Sheriff of Dorset ; but as " there are now 230,000 enrolled " —this was when the population of England was about a fourth of its present amount—he thinks there is " no great necessity for more."

The family event of that winter was the departure of Mackintosh, with his wife and children, for India. He had just been made Recorder of Bombay, and there was a large muster in London of the Wedgwood-Allen families, and of intimate friends, the Sydney Smiths, the Horners, and many more, to bid them farewell. Some time before this Mackintosh had agreed to write an essay expounding Tom Wedgwood's philosophical views, about which they had had much discussion, orally and in writing, and the following letter, written about two years before this time, would seem to imply that he had made some kind of beginning of the task.

Tom Wedgwood to Sir James Mackintosh.

YORK STREET,

December 11*th*, 1801.

DEAR MACKINTOSH,—

If I was called upon to declare the action which required the most good nature and self sacrifice and which originated in the purest disinterestedness, I should not hesitate an instant to cite your kind attempts to relieve me from my distressing perplexities. I cannot sufficiently admire the kindness of the offer nor the unwearied patience of the execution.

I feel considerably embarrassed in proceeding with the subject of my letter. Don't imagine that I feel any repugnance to lying under so great an obligation to you ; but in employing your time and talents, I am using a fund which is the peculiar property of your family. You have already had the satisfaction of a completely generous action ; it is my part to prevent the interests of your family suffering from its consequences. Take then without scruple in its behalf the retainer on the other side. I cannot write more at present—so extend your good nature to giving me credit for wishing to treat your feelings with all possible tenderness, and believe me your ever obliged and sincere friend,

THOS. WEDGWOOD.

Cheque for £100 sent herewith.

But Mackintosh's departure for India practically put an end to this design; though, as we see from the following letter, he seems to have fancied that he would be able to accomplish it in what he characteristically calls the "long and undisturbed leisure" of his judicial life at Bombay.

Sir James Mackintosh to Tom Wedgwood

17, DOVER STREET,
26th Dec., 1803.

DEAR WEDGWOOD,—

Will you have the patience to read beyond the first line when I begin by telling you that our MS. is in the drawer of my library table on board the Winchelsea, for the present inaccessible to human hand or eye.

I began in November, not only with the most honest intention but with the most anxious and ardent wish, to execute our project. I sat down at least ten mornings to do it. I was constantly interrupted—I was annoyed not merely by the bustle of preparation but sometimes by anxieties of so painful a kind that they left no quiet for Philosophy. Leisure I could command, but tranquillity, which I found equally necessary, was not so easily to be had. It would not have been difficult to have written something but I could not bring my conscience to do injustice to speculations which I estimate so very highly. Under these circumstances, after many ineffectual attempts I resolved, at the risk of your displeasure, to send the MSS. on board ship that I might apply the long and undisturbed leisure of Bombay to the undertaking. I did this without consulting you, because I was fearful that justly resenting my past in- fidelity and distrusting my future faith you might have recalled your MSS., which I should have very severely regretted. The first moment after my books are placed on their shelves shall be devoted to Time and Space.

They are in the same drawer and will share the same fate with all the MSS. I have in the world on Metaphysics Morals and Politics. When I have finished them I shall print a dozen copies at Bombay for the sake of security and easy transmission to Europe.

Great as my faults have been with respect to your philosophy, they are still more in appearance than they are in reality, and though I do not know whether with your present knowledge you can forgive me, I think I should be certain of your pardon if I could communicate to you the whole succession of incidents which have frustrated my intention.

All here join in kindest good wishes to your party, and I am

Dear Wedgwood

Your's most affectionately

JAMES MACKINTOSH.

Of the gathering of friends and relatives to see the last of the Mackintoshes we have pleasant glimpses in some lively letters of Fanny Allen to her sister Bessy in the country. The merriment of Sydney Smith helped to brighten the "sadness of farewells," and we hear of amusing dinner-table discussions as to the comparative virtues of the Allen sisters, and of his, Sydney Smith's, final pronouncement on that interesting point.

Fanny Allen to her sister Bessy (Mrs. Josiah Wedgwood).

11 Jan. 1804. "Sydney Smith was in his highest spirits, and pleased me particularly by talking of my sisters in the way I wish to hear them talked of, as the very first of women. 'I cannot tell you,' he told me, 'how much I admire and like all your sisters, but I think that Mrs. Jos Wedgwood surpasses you all.' "

25 Jan. 1804. "I kept back [in the previous letter] part of the good things he said of you. Mackintosh, Kitty, and I dined with the Smiths on Sunday last, and I have scarcely ever passed a merrier day. The company, as usual, were Sharp, Rogers, Horner, and Boddington. . . . You were again the subject of a very warm eulogium from more of the gentlemen than S. S. It was a very humorous dispute—I will not detail it to you because of your unbelief. But Sydney put an end to that part of it which treated of the different degrees of dependence they could place in you and my other sisters in case of any emergency, by declaring he would rely on your kindness to nurse him during a fever, and Jenny's *only in a toothache*. This was unanswerable and unanswered."

The beginning of another year found Tom Wedgwood still in a condition which seemed to be quickly passing into a state of despair. His most frequent mood, henceforward, is that reflected in the following letters.

Tom Wedgwood to Josiah Wedgwood

COTE,
Jany. 10, 1804.

* * * * * *

I have endured pangs and torments such as none can conceive who have never been in like circumstances. These nothing shall lead me to renew. As far as the coldest prudence

can procure me peace, I will have it. I am now endeavouring
to habituate myself to my near exit without dismay, to separate
all idea of melancholy and repugnance from an event which
may put an end to intolerable sensations, to suppress all regret
of the hopes and pleasures to which my qualifications, if I know
myself at all, might have been expected to lead me. Vanity
may influence my opinion, but I have no concealment with
you ; as far as I know other men and can examine myself, I
feel very certain that at the age of fifteen I held out more
promise, and united a greater variety of talent, a more ardent
longing after all that is beautiful and good, in morals, things,
and art, than any young man I have ever met with. That this
should all perish and come to nothing, I should regret in the
liveliest manner in another—and I certainly do still more in
my own person. But I feel that I have now made every
possible effort to save myself, and I do not harass myself with
any further plans. I am interrupted—this is a subject on
which I could write folios, but there is no harm in being
stopped.

Tom Wedgwood to Josiah Wedgwood

Cote,
Jany. 23, 1804.

Dear Jos,—

*   *   *   *   *

I find myself every day more and more unable to combat
with my disorder, and I am convinced of the necessity of
keeping my room if not my bed. I cannot think of entering
on this melancholy scheme at this place—it would entirely
destroy the comfort of the little society here. I propose
returning with you to Gunville, and making the North room
as noise-proof as we can. I need not expatiate to you on the
extreme repugnance I feel at introducing myself and all my
attendant gloom in the midst of a prosperous family like yours,
but it is my fate in this life to cast a gloom around me. The
pains I have taken and the sacrifices I have made to prevent it

L

are the only consolation and excuse I have left.   What other alternative is left me ?

*   *   *   *   *

Though I cannot sit up, nor longer bear to be present a lifeless unparticipating thing in living scenes—yet I know from several trials, that my sufferings in the seasoning to this self-entombment, are to be very acute.   There may be times, and frequently, when I may require your company and patient attendance.   God only knows the horrors which low spirits sometimes produce.   At those times solitude is insupportable.

*   *   *   *   *

I feel that my plan has nothing definite—if it had, I could not bring myself to state it.   It is an act of resignation to a consuming disorder against which I have kept up a fight of twelve years.   I shall no longer think of health, but administer every present comfort—and I imagine this process will give such an advantage to my implacable foe, that his complete triumph and mine, no less a one, in his victory, must be hastened. Perhaps you will send your horses from Bath—the chaise will meet you when you write to have it.   My mother and sisters bore the communication as I could wish—with feeling and composure.   My kindest love to Bess.   I stop because my powers and paper are exhausted—or I could converse with you for a month without a stop.

These are terrible letters, for a man only in his thirty-second year. Josiah's reply to them is, as always, deeply sympathetic, though he can only bid his brother struggle on. The one bright spot in this story of a wrecked life is the unwearying kindness with which the sick man's relatives and friends strove to do all that was possible to mitigate his sufferings. Outside his family, Poole, perhaps, was the most devoted of his friends, always on the alert to seek some way of cheering or helping him under the constant struggle. Coleridge's affection for him must have been deep and lasting, whatever we may think of the over-effusive manner of its expression. And there are signs that from various less intimate associates, Sharp, Campbell, and others, he met with much real sympathy and kindness. Josiah's devotion to his brother Tom was an absorbing passion, and was Tom's greatest solace. "I find" (he says to Josiah, Nov. 4, 1804), "that yourself and Sally always move me most to think of a love more than mortal, which cannot flourish in this chilling world, and must survive it. Your deep affection, and Sally's angelic kindness, give a certain value to life in its most trying moments." In a letter of this year Sally had said to him: "I have sometimes feared I must have appeared insensible to your sufferings, when my taciturnity has really been owing partly to the family infirmity." The affectionate terms on which he stood with Bessy Wedgwood are shown in the following letter, while her reply is significant of the warm and sympathetic nature which made her perhaps the best beloved member of that united family:

Tom Wedgwood to Mrs. Josiah Wedgwood

Cote,

[*Dated, in another hand, Feb.* 17, 1804].

My dear Bess,—

Pray come—and stay as long as you can. Don't imagine for a moment that you can ever be in my way. I look upon you as no half-sister. I have even felt towards you as sister in full, with all rights and privileges, and, also, with a claim on you for duties and attentions as such. After ten years intimacy

I am less inclined than ever to love you by halves. You must not judge always of my feelings towards you by my manners and exterior. These are under the control of sufferings greater than you have ever imagined them—and my temper is nearly gone in the general wreck. I cannot now write more, nor is there to you any occasion. Everybody finds you all kindness, and the deficiencies in kindness and respect at times from me have been forgotten and forgiven by you before I had either forgotten or forgiven them myself.

Ever your's most affectly,

T. W.

Mrs. Josiah Wedgwood to Tom Wedgwood

GUNVILLE,

Feby. 20, 1804.

MY DEAR TOM,—

I was more gratified than you can imagine by the few kind lines I received from you yesterday, made doubly valuable by the inconvenience (to use the lightest expression) with which you write at present. It was impossible for a moment to doubt of your kindness, but a real want of self-confidence makes it soothing and delightful to me to receive so touching an assurance of it, and I thank you from the bottom of my heart. I cannot enter into the sympathy with which I consider your sufferings, it is deep and sincere, nor would anything I think, in this world, make me so happy as to see you restored to health and enjoyment. I wished very much to have gone with Jos to Cote, but I am deterred by the uncertainty I am in as to poor Kitty's movements at Ryde,* as I believe the wind is entirely against their sailing, and if it continues in a settled point I should not wonder if she were to come here. She has also been so very anxious to see some of us, that I am afraid of putting it out of my power to go there if I find that I cannot resist her affectionate entreaties.

---

* Lady Mackintosh is just sailing from Spithead for Bombay.

A sentence in a letter of Bessy Wedgwood to her husband well shows the feeling which this warm-hearted and unselfish woman had for her sorely afflicted brother-in-law. Such an absorbing attachment as that of Josiah to Tom might have made some wives jealous, and she seems to have had a fear —it was, of course, quite groundless—that Jos might imagine this possibility in her case. "I am very glad," she says, "that you acquit me of all jealousy with respect to dear Tom. I really deserve it, for there are no sacrifices I would not make to be of any use to him compatible with my other duties."* The situation had its difficulties, and it must have needed her unalterable sweetness of character and tact to avoid friction. Tom, for one thing, made the Gunville nursery a field of philosophical study, observing and recording the doings of its little inhabitants as material for working out his various psychological and educational theories. If little Bess was out of temper, or Joe disobedient to his governess, he would note the incident as illustrating some principle of child-training, and perhaps propound a plan for correcting the infant's evil tendencies, based on the principles of Locke, Hartley, or Rousseau. An uncle given to these pursuits must have been at times a troublesome guest, and family tradition tells us that even the sweet-tempered Bessie sometimes found Tom's frequent incursions into her nursery embarrassing.

---

* Letter of September 1, 1800 (Darwin MSS.).

CHAPTER XII

THE LAST YEAR

1804—1805

COLERIDGE and Tom Wedgwood never met, apparently, after their parting at Patterdale in January 1803. Coleridge came to London in January 1804, bent on making a voyage to a warm climate for the sake of his health. He writes thus from the office in Westminster where Poole was carrying on his statistical poor-law work.

Coleridge to Tom Wedgwood

(*Address*: COTE HOUSE, BRISTOL.)

16, ABINGDON STREET,
WESTMINSTER,
Wednesday afternoon,
[25 *Jan.*] 1804.

MY DEAR FRIEND,—.

Some divines hold that with God to think and to create are one and the same act. If to think and even to compose had been the same as to write with me, I should have written as much too much as I have now written too little. The whole Truth of the matter is that I have been very, very ill; your letter remained four days unread, I was so ill. What effect it had upon me I cannot express by words; it lay under my pillow day after day. I should have written 20 times, but as it often and often happens with me, my heart was too full and I had so much to say that I said nothing. I never received a delight that lasted longer upon me, " brooded on my mind and made it pregnant," than the six last sentences of your Letter, which I cannot apologize for not having answered, for I should be canting calumnies against myself, for for the last six or seven weeks I have both thought and felt more concerning you, and relatively to you, than of all other men put together. Somehow or other, whatever plan I determined to adopt, my fancy, good-natured Pandar of our wishes, always linked you on to it ; or I made it your Plan, and linked myself on.

I left my home December 20, 1803, intending to stay a day and a half at Grasmere, and then to walk to Kendal, whither I had sent all my Cloaths and Viatica ; from thence to go to London, and to see whether or no I could arrange my pecuniary matters so as leaving Mrs. Coleridge all that was necessary to her comforts, to go myself to Madeira, having a persuasion strong as the life within me, that one winter spent in a really warm, genial climate, would compleatly restore me. Wordsworth had, as I may truly say, *forced* on me a hundred Pound, in the event of my going to Madeira ; and Stuart had kindly offered to befriend me ; and during the days and affrightful nights of my disease, when my Limbs were swoln and my stomach refused to retain the food taken in in sorrow, then I looked with pleasure on the scheme. But as soon as dry frosty weather came, or the rains and damps passed off, and I was filled with elastic Health from Crown to Sole, then the Thought of the weight of pecuniary Obligation, having hitherto given no positive proof that I was a fit moral object of so much exertion from so many people, revisited me.

But I have broken off my story. I stayed at Grasmere a month, ¾ths of the time bed-ridden ; and deeply do I feel the enthusiastic kindness of Wordsworth's Wife and Sister, who sate up by me, one or the other, in order to awaken me at the first symptoms of distressful Feeling ; and even when they went to rest, continued often and often to weep and watch for me even in their dreams. I left them, Saturday, Jan. 14th, and have spent a very pleasant week at Dr. Crompton's, at Liverpool, and arrived at Poole's lodgings last night, at 8 o'clock.

Though my right hand is so much swoln that I can scarcely keep my pen steady between my Thumb and Forefinger, yet my Stomach is easy, and my Breathing comfortable ; and I am eager to hope all good things of my health ; and that gained, I have a cheering, and I trust prideless confidence that I shall make an active perseverant use of the faculties and acquirements that have been entrusted to my keeping, and a fair trial of their Heighth, Depth, and Width. Indeed I look back on the last four months with honest Pride, seeing how much I have done, with what steady attachment of mind to the same subject, and under what vexations and sorrows from without, and amid what inward sufferings. So much of myself. When I know more, I will tell you more.

I find you are still at Cote, and Poole tells me you talk of Jamaica as a summer excursion. If it were not for the Voyage, I would that you would go to Madeira, for from the Hour I get on board the vessel to the time that I once more feel England beneath my feet, I am as certain as past and unvarying experience can make me, that I shall be in Health, in high Health ; and then I am sure, not only that I should be a comfort to you, but that I should be so without Diminution of my activity or professional usefulness. Briefly, dear Wedgwood ! I truly and at heart love you, and of course it must add to my deeper and moral happiness to be with you, if I can be either assistance or alleviation. If I find myself so well that I defer my Madeira Plan, I shall then go forthwith to Devonshire to see my aged mother once more before she dies, and stay two or three months with my Brothers. But wherever I am, I never suffer a day (except when I am travelling) to pass without doing something.

Poole made me promise that I would leave one side for him, and preciously I have remembered it. God bless him ! He looks so worshipful in his office, among his Clerks, that it would give you a few minutes' good spirits at least to look in upon him. I pray you as soon as you can command your pen, give me half a score Lines, and now that I am *loose*, say whether or no I can be any good to you.

S. T. COLERIDGE.

This letter, I imagine, crossed one from Tom in which he told Coleridge of his despairful resolve to shut himself up at Gunville and to give up struggling with his disease. This Coleridge answers in a strain of passionate protest :

S. T. Coleridge to Tom Wedgwood

(*Address:* COTE HOUSE, BRISTOL.)

16 ABINGDON STREET,

WESTMINSTER,

Satuiday, Jan. 28, 1804.

MY DEAR FRIEND,—

It is idle for me to say to you, that my Heart and very soul ache with the dull pain of one struck down and stunned. I write to you, for my letter cannot give you unmixed Pain, and I would fain say a few words to dissuade you. What good can possibly come of your plan ? Will not the very chairs and furniture of your room be shortly more, far more intolerable to you than new and changing objects! more insufferable Reflectors of Pain and Wearisomeness of Spirit? Oh, most certainly they will! You *must hope*, my dearest Wedgwood ; you must act as if you hoped! Despair itself has but that advice to give you. Have you ever thought of trying large doses of opium in a hot climate, with a diet of grapes, and the fruits of the climate ?

Is it impossible that by drinking freely you might at last produce *Gout*, and that a violent Pain and Inflammations in the extremities might produce new trains of motion and feeling in your stomach, and the organs connected with the stomach, known and unknown? Worse than what you have decreed for yourself cannot well happen. Say but a word, and I will come to you, will be with you, will go with you—to Malta—to Madeira—to Jamaica, or (of the climate of which and its strange effects I have heard wonders, true or not) to Egypt.

At all events, and at the worst, even if you do attempt to realize the scheme of going to and remaining at Gunville, for God's sake, my dear dear friend! do keep up a correspondence with one or more ; or if it were possible for you, with several. I know by a little what your sufferings are ; and that to shut the eyes and stop up the ears is to give one's self up to storm and darkness and the lurid forms and horrors of a Dream. Poole goes off to-night, but I shall send this Letter by the Post.

I scarce know why—it is a feeling I have and hardly understand—I could not endure to live if I had not a firm Faith that the Life within you will pass forth out of the Furnace : for that you have borne what you have borne, and so acted beneath such Pressure, constitutes you an awful moral Being. I am not ashamed to pray aloud for you.

Your most affectionate Friend,

S. T. COLERIDGE.

Poole will call on you some time before Dinner on Monday, for an hour, unless he hear from you a wish to the contrary, addressed to him at Mr. King's, No. 12 Redcliffe Parade.

Eight weeks after this Coleridge was leaving England for Malta. Two or three days before his departure he writes thus :

S. T. Coleridge to Tom Wedgwood

[*No date: Postmark* 24 *Mch,* 1804.]

MY DEAR FRIEND,—

Though fearful of breaking in upon you, after what you have written to me, I could not have left England without having written both to you and your Brother. I received your letter at the very moment I received a note from Sharp inform- ing [me] that I must instantly secure a place in the Ports- mouth Mail for Tuesday, and if I could not, that I must do so in the Light Coach for Tuesday early morning.

I am agitated by many things, and only write now because you desired an answer by return of Post. I have been dan- gerously ill, but the illness is going about, and not connected with my immediate ill health, however it may be with my general Constitution. It was the cholera morbus. But for a series of the merest accidents I should have been seized in the Streets, in a bitter East wind with cold rain ; at all events have walked through it struggling with the seizure—it was Sunday night—and have suffered it at Tobin's, Tobin sleeping out at Woolwich, no fire, no wine or spirit, or medicine of any kind, and no human Being within call. But luckily—perhaps the occasion would better suit the word providentially—Tuffin took me home with him. After the first painful Fit

[Here he describes the attack.]

*   *   *   *   *

· But however this is rather a History of the past than of the present. I have now only enough for memento, and already on Wednesday I considered myself in clear sunshine, out of the Shadow of the Wings of the Destroying Angel. What else relates to myself I will write on Monday.

Would to heaven you were going with me to Malta, if it were not for the voyage ! For all other things I could make the passage with an unwavering mind, not without chearings of Hope. Let me mention one thing. Lord Cadogan was brought to absolute Despair and Hatred of Life by a Stomach Complaint, being now an old man. The symptoms, as stated to me, were strikingly like yours, considering the enormous difference of the two characters; the same flitting Fevers, dire costiveness with Diarrhœa, Dejection, compelled Changes, &c. He was advised to reduce lean Beef to a pure jelly by Papin's digester, with as little water as would secure it from burning, and of this to take half a wine glass from 10 to 14 times a day; this and nothing else. He did so. Sir George Beaumont saw within a few weeks a letter from Lord C. to Lord St. Asaph, in which he states the circumstance, his perseverance in it, rapid amelioration, and final recovery. "I am now," he says, "in real good Health; as good, and in as chearful spirits as ever I was when a young man." Mingay, the medical man of Thetford, was his attendant. I could give you all particulars.

May God bless you, even *here*,

S. T. Coleridge.

This is the latest letter of Coleridge among the Wedgwood papers. He did not return to England till after Tom Wedgwood's death. When in Malta he wrote but little to any friends or relations, and probably not at all to Tom or his brother.

The rest of the year 1804 shows no lightening of the gloom which is the dominant note of Tom Wedgwood's letters. He was now resorting to opium as a relief from his sufferings, but to what extent or how continuously he took it is not clear. "The quantity not exceeding four grains often proves," he says, "wholly insufficient to produce any tolerable exhilaration." At times the language in which he describes his sufferings (to his brother Josiah) is such as might well suggest a doubt of his complete sanity, as when he says "the nature of my miseries is too shocking for communication"; but the tone of other letters dealing with affairs of ordinary life shows, I think, that there was no definitely mental disturbance. A frequent topic in the family correspondence of this time was "the disordered state of John's affairs." John had not the faculty of keeping his expenditure within his income, and his chronic state of embarrassment was a constant source of anxiety to his brothers and sisters. In a letter of May 1804, to Josiah, Tom discusses this matter, and does so in a thoroughly rational way. It is the letter of a man in complete command of his faculties. He proposes to lend his brother "some thousands," in order to "bring his affairs completely round." He thinks John "should abandon Cote, and perhaps might be induced to live at Etruria." "Jane has given up all hope of his ever regulating his expenditure." *

It was at this time Leslie brought out the book embodying the results of the investigations which the annuity given him by Tom Wedgwood had enabled him to carry on for some seven years past at his home in Fifeshire. It appeared under the title of "An Inquiry into Heat and Electricity," and it established his position as a natural philosopher. In a letter of March (1804) he had sent Wedgwood a draft of the dedication, written in his usual portentously ornate style, asking, "What alteration do you wish?" This inquiry seems to have remained unanswered, as in another letter Leslie alludes to Wedgwood's having, "with uncommon delicacy," declined to read the draft. In the dedication as printed, he refers vaguely to being under obligation to Wedgwood, but does not mention the annuity or make any allusion to money help.†

---

* John Wedgwood gave up Cote House shortly after this. He had a great love of planting and gardening, and was the founder, or had most to do with the founding, of the Royal Horticultural Society. His name appears still on the Society's papers. He died in the year 1844.

† Nor, strange to say, is there a word about it in the Memoir

As the year (1804) went on he was again, notwithstanding all previous disappointments, making plans of
travel ; and this always involved finding a travelling
companion.   The discovering of a suitable person was
a matter of infinite trouble, the difficulties always
attending companionship in travel being aggravated
in this case by his sad condition, and his more or less
fastidious tastes.   He was a great lover of music, and
himself a player on the violin and flute.   He generally
tried to find some one who was accomplished in that
art, while having enough knowledge and intelligence
to afford the chance of rational conversation.   So the
problem was a complicated one.   At one time he seems
to have thought of getting a lady to travel with him.
This idea, however, the discreet Josiah did not think
one to be encouraged.

Josiah to Tom Wedgwood

(*Address :* COTE HOUSE, BRISTOL.)

MAER,*

July 19, 1804.

MY DEAR TOM,—

Susan [Darwin, their sister] does not at present recollect
any female at all likely to answer your purpose except a young
woman that has lived as nurse and companion with Miss

(Edinb., 1838) by Macvey Napier, who knew Leslie intimately, and
"had the advantage" (he says) "of all the information possessed by
the family." Napier represents him (p. 14 of the Memoir) as living
during these years on the fruits of his own work, which shows that
the biographer knew nothing of the annuity, though it was the thing
that had determined Leslie's career.

* A country house a few miles from the Potteries, which Josiah
had lately bought, and which ultimately became the home of his
family till the death of his widow in 1846.

Pannell, and has in that situation learnt French and some other accomplishments. She has left Miss P. on some quarrel, but Miss P. is endeavouring to get her again. If she should not go to Miss P. I imagine she would not be likely to consent to accompany you, as indeed I think no young person can with safety do. Her brothers are bringing up to the Church; she left Miss P. on account of some slight, real or supposed; and I should suppose she or her family would be very scrupulous as to appearances and character. I will make what enquiry I can, and I understand that you mean male or female. As to Dugard [a doctor at Shrewsbury] I believe there is no chance of his quitting his present prospects.

Would not a change of place be useful to you now? Susan will in all probability leave us in a week and we can keep the house tolerably quiet and give you a quiet bedroom. My mother remains very well. Susan as usual. All unite in love to Jane and you.

Your affectionate,

J. W.

P.S.—The Etruria were inspected with the Hanley and Lane End Volunteers yesterday who have been on permanent duty. I think we are in no respect worse than them, and in steady orderly conduct and keeping our arms in order very far their superiors. Col. Broughton said he had seen no volunteers with their arms so well taken care of as ours.

Nothing more was heard, apparently, of the lady-companion scheme. During the most of this year Tom divided his time between Gunville, Eastbury, and Cote; but in the first days of October he set off for Westmoreland to stay with the Luffs, partly that he might see how his corps of " Loyal Volunteers " was getting on with its training. When there " he wrote " (says his brother) " an address to the Company, pointing out the advantages and necessity of strict discipline, but was too ill to speak it to them, and Captain Luff had to read it for him." On this visit to Patterdale he is again smitten with the beauty of the lovely land of lakes and mountains, and has dreams of making it his place of abode. "This country is heavenly beautiful, I would buy here if I could have a day's health a week."

One of the sweetest nooks in that delightful region is a little farm, called Bleawick, close to the head of Ulleswater; a homestead surrounded by a few acres of pasture sloping to the water's edge, sheltered from east winds by the overhanging mass of Place Fell, and looking across at Glen Ridding and the crests of Helvellyn. This little place, which is as charming now as it must have been in 1804, was then for sale, and Tom seems to have tried to buy it. He writes to Jos (November 5) putting to him a case of conscience. A friend is after it, "but while he is shilly-shallying, other purchasers may carry it off." Is he bound, he asks, to let Mr. A. go on with the negotiation without having a try for it himself? The project, however, came to nothing. Meanwhile, he found the home of the kind Luffs a welcome retreat, and he was generous in helping them in their poverty. He lent them, which must have meant giving them, several hundred pounds.

This is but one of many instances which occur in the letters testifying to his liberality in assisting friends and others in trouble. Basil Montagu and Godwin were among those whom he helped. In one of his letters to Godwin he prefaces a gift of £100 by some admirable reasons for *not* giving it :

I have no opinion of the good, upon the whole, resulting from great facility in the opulent in yielding to requests of the needy. I have no doubt that it is best that every one should anticipate with certainty the pinch and pressure of distress from indulging in indolence, or even from misfortune. It is this, certainly, which quickens the little wit that man is ordinarily endowed with and calls out all his energies. And were it removed by the idea that the rich held funds for the distressed, I am convinced that not only half the industry of the country would be. destroyed, but also that misfortunes would be doubled in quantity. I confess to you I have always a doubt of the value of any donation or loan at the same time.

But after this exposition of perfectly sound principles, which we may guess would not particularly please the philosopher, he explains how strong is his natural desire to give relief to suffering, and how in Godwin's case he can't resist the impulse, and so he sends him the hundred pounds.*⟧

⟦Another friend whom we find him helping more than once was Campbell, the poet. A letter from him appealing for a loan of £100 discloses a singular excuse for the request. A lady who had lent Campbell £100, and "is since mad," is publishing accounts of his "baseness, dishonesty, and ingratitude," calumnies which it is "not easy for him to refute," the debt being real. So he asks Wedgwood for £100 to relieve him from. this objectionable woman. "This letter," he says, "is, I must own, a thunderbolt of. indelicacy," a phrase which is explained by his alluding to a note.

---

* Letter of April 25, 1804: Kegan Paul's "Godwin," ii. 125. A year later (K. P., ii. 141) we find another "loan" in progress.

for £100 which Wedgwood him sent him a year previously. Wedgwood lent him the money. But Campbell was not a borrower of the Godwin type, and three months later he repaid it " with a heart full of gratitude."

It was in July 1805, that Tom Wedgwood's poor broken life came to an end. It had been long apparent that his struggle for health was a hopeless one. But he never gave it up. He again planned a voyage to the West Indies, had secured a companion, was on the point of leaving Gunville to embark, when the mortal stroke came, suddenly and painlessly. Here is the letter in which his affectionate sister-in-law sent the news to her relatives at Cresselly.

Mrs. Jos. Wedgwood to her sister Emma Allen

GUNVILLE,
Wednesday, July 10, 1805.

MY DEAR EMMA,—

John [their brother] arrived yesterday to carry away our Fan from me, which is a great damper to the pleasure his company always gives me. [Here she breaks off.]

Friday ye 12th.—I was writing to you on Wednesday morning, when all the agreeable feelings with which I sat down to the employment, were cruelly dampt by the sad intelligence that poor Tom was so ill that there was no hope of his recovery. He had not been worse than usual, and we thought him rather better, from the custom he had taken up of going out every day with Jos in the gig; but on Monday I think he got a little chilled, which brought on much internal pain, and left him weak. On Tuesday night Joe parted with him with an engagement as usual to go and breakfast at Wood Gates, but at midnight he rang his bell, and told his servant to give him something, for he was very weak, but not ill. He told him also to come in in two hours time, and see how he was, and to call Jos at 5. The servant did so, and found him as he thought sleeping, but in fact he was then without any sign of sense except that he still breathed. When Jos came he also thought him sleeping, and sat down an hour and half beside him, before he discovered that he was not; when he did he became alarmed and sent for Dr. Crawford, who immediately said he was dying. He continued in that state, his head quietly reposing on his arm, till seven in the evening, when he expired without seeming to have suffered the least pain. What a day for poor Jos, watching him dying for 12 hours. They have all had such a preparation for this stroke by the long sufferings he has undergone, that it ought only to be now considered as a relief, though it is grievous just at the time; but I quite feel it a blessing to us and to him that he died now, before he went aboard-ship, rather than to have suffered all the pain of parting and then perhaps to have sunk under the first attack of seasickness, which I now suppose would certainly have been the case. We have prevailed on his mother and sisters to come down here, till they go to Staffordshire, which they now mean to do as soon as they can. On Tuesday will be the Funeral, and we wish them to go before that, as we are so near the Church. He is to be buried in the Vault belonging to this place. He has left his fortune equally between all his brothers and sisters, and he has left a discretionary fund in Jos's hands to supply the generous purposes that his death would otherwise have cut short, to assist a great number who have often felt his bounty before. He has also left a Memorandum with Jos that Edward Drewe *

---

* Caroline Allen, a sister of Mrs. Jos. and Mrs. John Wedgwood, married Edward Drewe, Rector of Broadhembury, near Honiton. One of her daughters (Georgina) married Baron Alderson, and was the mother of the late Marchioness of Salisbury; another was wife of the first Lord Gifford.

is to have £20, Caroline £20 as a remembrance from him, and each of their daughters a hundred a piece. This Caroline does not yet know, as I did not hear it till to-day; but I am more gratified at it than I can express, as I know it will give Caroline so much pleasure to have been remembered by him. Indeed the more I think of him the more his character rises in my opinion; he really was too good for this world. Such a crowd of feelings and remembrances fill my mind while I am recalling all his past kindnesses to me and mine, and to all his acquaintance, that I feel myself quite unfit to make his panegyric, but I trust my children will ever remember him with veneration as an honour to the family to which he belonged. I have been writing to Kitty Mackintosh, as the fleet is not yet sailed, and to others; and I feel nervous and shaken, so if I write incoherently you must excuse it.

Ever yours,
E. W.

Such a death could be thought of by his friends only as a happy release. Twenty years of childhood and youth, and fourteen of struggle with disease, made up the whole of his life of thirty-four years. Though he himself never quite despaired, there could have been no real hope of betterment. The struggle might conceivably have been prolonged, but we cannot imagine him regaining the power of effective work. "As to your poor brother's death," wrote Sydney Smith to Jos Wedgwood, "it is difficult to know in what light to consider it. It is painful to lose such a man, but who would have wished to preserve him at such a price of misery and pain? He will not easily be forgotten. I know no man who appears to have made such an impression upon his friends."

TARRANT GUNVILLE CHURCH (1902)
Burial-place of T. Wedgwood

A few years after Tom Wedgwood's death, a re-markable description of his character and powers, but without a mention of his name, was appended by Coleridge to one of his Essays in "The Friend." The passage is as follows—it has no formal heading or introduction:

A lady once asked me if I believed in ghosts and apparitions. I answered with truth and simplicity: No, madam! I have seen far too many myself. I have indeed a whole memorandum book filled with records of these phænomena, many of them interesting as facts and data for psychology, and affording some valuable materials for a theory of perception and its dependence on the memory and imagination. *In omnem actum perceptionis imaginatio influit efficienter;* says Wolff. But he is no more, who would have realised this idea: who had already established the foundations and the law of the theory; and for whom I had so often found a pleasure and a comfort, even during the wretched and restless nights of sickness, in watching and in-stantly recording these experiences of the world within us, of the *gemina natura, quæ fit et facit, et creat et creatur!* He is gone, my friend; my munificent co-patron, and not less the benefactor of my intellect!—He who, beyond all other men known to me, added a fine and ever-wakeful sense of beauty to the most patient accuracy in experimental philosophy and the profounder researches of metaphysical science; he who united all the play and spring of fancy with the subtlest dis-crimination and an inexorable judgment; and who controlled an almost painful exquisiteness of taste by a warmth of heart, which in the practical relations of life made allowances for faults as quickly as the moral taste detected them; a warmth of heart, which was indeed noble and pre-eminent, for alas! the genial feelings of health contributed no spark toward it. Of these qualities I may speak, for they belonged to all man-kind. The higher virtues, that were blessings to his friends, and the still higher that resided in and for his own soul, are

themes for the energies of solitude, for the awfulness of prayer!—
virtues exercised in the barrenness and desolation of his animal
being; while he thirsted with the full stream at his lips, and
yet with unwearied goodness poured out so all around him,
like the master of a feast among his kindred in the day of
his own gladness! Were it but for the remembrance of him
alone and of his lot here below, the disbelief in a future state
would sadden the earth around me, and blight the very grass in
the field.*

Part of the thought that inspired these moving
words is to be found in a letter of Coleridge, written
some years earlier, to his and Wedgwood's friend
Richard Sharp :

Of our common friends, my dear Sir, I flatter myself that
you and I should agree in fixing on T. Wedgwood and on
Wordsworth as genuine Philosophers, for I have often said (and
no wonder, since not a day passes but the conviction of the
truth of it is renewed in me, and with this conviction the

---

* "The Friend," vol. i. p. 249 (ed. 1818). In this reprint the name
of Wedgwood is not given ; and I suppose it was not in the original.
It appears in a footnote in the edition of 1850, vol. i. p. 190. "The
Friend " first appeared in June 1809, and was described in its title as
"A Literary, Moral, and Political Paper, excluding Personal and
Party Politics and the Events of the Day. Conducted by S. T. Coleridge, of Grasmere, Westmoreland. Price, each number One Shilling.
Penrith : Printed and Published by J. Brown and will be delivered
free of expense by post throughout the kingdom to Subscribers." It
ceased to appear in 1810. Its early death was not surprising. Coleridge and J. Brown lived 28 miles apart, with Kirkstone Pass between
them. The proofs travelled to and fro, sometimes by the weekly
post, sometimes by the carrier, and sometimes by a casual post-chaise.
Coleridge was habitually late with his "copy," and the interval
between the issues varied from one to seven weeks But the
papers published in this absurd fashion contained some of his most
characteristic utterances; and in its book form "The Friend "
had, as the century went on, a lasting influence on the thought of
the time.

accompanying esteem and love), often have I said that T. Wedgwood's faults impress me with veneration for his moral and intellectual character more than almost any other man's virtues; for under circumstances like this, to have a fault only in that degree is, I doubt not, in the eye of God, to possess a high virtue. Who does not prize the retreat of Moreau more than all the straw-blaze of Napoleon's victories? And then to make it (as Wedgwood really does) a sort of crime even to think of his faults by so many virtues retained, cultivated and preserved in growth and blossom, n a climate where now the gusts so rise and eddy, that deeply rooted must *that* be which is not snatched up and made a plaything of by them—and, now, " the parching air burns frore."

W. Wordsworth does not excite that almost painfully profound moral admiration which the sense of the exceeding difficulty of a given virtue can alone call forth, and which, therefore, I feel exclusively towards T. Wedgwood.*

Another expression of Coleridge's feeling as to his dead friend appears in a letter written in 1809, about four years later, to Sir Humphrey Davy, just after he had heard of the death of Beddoes. After expressing his deep attachment to Beddoes and the emotion with which he heard of his death, he says, "The death of T. Wedgwood pulled hard at my heart ; I am sure no week of my life—almost I might have said scarce a day [has passed] in which I have not been made either sad or thoughtful by the recollection. . . . There are two things which I exceedingly wished, and in both

---

* Letters of S. T. C., p. 448. An estimate of Wordsworth's character follows. " 'The parching air burns frore," is from Milton's description of the icy region of Hell in " Paradise Lost," Book ii.

have been disappointed : to have written the Life and prepared the Psychological Remains of my revered friend and benefactor, T. W. : and to have been intrusted with the biography, etc., of Dr. B." *

---

* "Fragmentary Remains, &c., of Sir H. Davy," by John Davy, M.D., 1858, pp. 108, 110.

CHAPTER XIII

THE PHOTOGRAPHIC WORK

OF Wedgwood's photographic work we know hardly any more than is discoverable from the "Account" in the Journal of the Royal Institution for 1802.

It was evidently only an episode in his life. In his letters I find no allusion to it; nor do I find anything in his handwriting relating to his experiments in physics, save only the "Memorandum" of 1792 as to his giving up experimenting (*ante*, p. 21). But in a letter of November 18, 1800, written by Leslie in London to Wedgwood at Gunville, there is a sentence which presumably refers to the photographic work. "A few days ago I left at York Street an object-glass and some thin cylinders for the solar microscope, and half a dozen bits of painted glass which will, I think, suit you. I have more pieces, which you may have at any time." This makes it probable that Wedgwood's photographic experiments, in which coloured glasses and the microscope were used, were going on at about that time; and various letters show that he came to town on November 17, 1800, and stayed there till December 8 or later. Another little piece of evidence, however, points to photographic work some ten years earlier than that. During the discussions of 1864–5 on what were called the "Early Photographs" (see

Appendix C.), there was produced at a meeting of the Photographic Society a letter, written by James Watt, apparently in 1790 or 1791, to Josiah Wedgwood, and beginning with the following words: "Dear Sir, I thank you for your instructions as to the Silver Pictures, about which, when at home, I will make some experiments." (The rest of the letter is about a mill at Etruria.) This letter has the date "Thursday" only, but it is described as having been "docketed by Josiah Wedgwood, Jan. 1790," which date Mr. Hensleigh Wedgwood, the owner of the letter, afterwards corrected to 1791.* Tom Wedgwood was certainly working at questions of light and heat during the years preceding 1792, and as nitrate of silver was used in his later experiments we can hardly avoid the inference that the "silver pictures" mentioned by Watt were early photographic attempts. These pictures would naturally excite interest in the Wedgwood circle, and Watt, an intimate family friend, had probably asked for information about them. The question, however, of the exact date of the experiments is of no special interest, there being no doubt

---

* It is not known where this letter of Watt's now is. I quote it from the Report in the Photographic Journal of the meeting of the Society, January 5, 1864. It was obtained by Dr. Diamond, the Secretary, from the late Mr. Hensleigh Wedgwood (son of Josiah), but Dr. Diamond appears not to have returned it. The theory which it was produced to support having been clearly disproved, there would be no special reason for preserving it. There seems to have been some doubt as to its date, for Miss Meteyard ("Group of Englishmen," p. 130) describes it as "docketed 1799." If this was the date, it must have been addressed to the younger Josiah, the father having died 1795. If written in 1790 or 1791 it might have been addressed either to the old or to the young Josiah, but more probably to the father.

as to the date of the first announcement of the process to the world.

This was made in a paper of June 1802, printed in the first volume of the "Journals of the Royal Institution." No name is appended to it, but as Humphrey Davy, then a young man of twenty-three, was at the time Assistant Editor of the Journal, and as the "Account" was included, after his death, in the collected edition of his works, we may take it to have been written by him.

Presumably the experiments were made in the Laboratory of the "Royal Institution." The Institution had been founded three years previously, and it occupied from the first the building in Albemarle Street which is still its home. Josiah Wedgwood (Tom's brother) was one of the first "Proprietors," subscribing a hundred guineas to its funds. Davy became "Assistant Lecturer" there early in 1802. The Wedgwoods had known him when he was an apothecary's apprentice at Penzance, and Tom must have seen much of him when he was employed by Dr. Beddoes in the "Pneumatic Institute" at Bristol.

The second volume of Davy's collected works, edited by his brother (9 vols., 1839–40) is, so far as I know, the only book in which the paper has been reprinted, and the original volume of Journals is to be found in but few libraries. The "Account" has thus been virtually inaccessible to ordinary readers, and one of the motives which prompted the compilation of this Memoir was the wish to put within the reach of all who are interested in the origins of photography the only authentic record of what appears to have been the first essay in the Art. It is to be found at p. 171 of the first volume of the Journals, and is usually said to have been published in June 1802, but no dates are appended to the various papers and reports contained in the volume. A sentence in the preface says: "The first three sheets were published under Count Rumford's direction. Dr. Young was the editor of the next four; and the subsequent parts have been conducted jointly by Dr. Young and Mr. Davy."* The title-page of the volume is as follows:

JOURNALS

OF

THE ROYAL INSTITUTION -

VOLUME I.

LONDON.

Sold at the house of the Institution, Albemarle
Street; by Cadell & Davies, Strand;
Johnson, St. Paul's Churchyard; Longman and
Rees, and H. D. Symonds, Paternoster Row.
1802.

From the Press of the Royal Institution of Great
Britain: W. Savage, Printer.

---

* Fragmentary extracts from the "Account" are, of course, to be found in many books relating to the history of Photography, but when these are examined it becomes evident that they are generally quotations from quotations, that the authors have not seen the complete "Account," and are often only further abridging previous abridgments. The longest extract I have met with is in Robert Hunt's "Researches on Light," 1844. The whole was reprinted (since this was written) in *Photography* for May 1902.

An Account of a method of copying Paintings upon Glass, and of making Profiles, by the agency of Light upon Nitrate of Silver. Invented by T. WEDGWOOD, ESQ. With Observations by H. DAVY.

White paper, or white leather, moistened with solution of nitrate of silver, undergoes no change when kept in a dark place; but on being exposed to the daylight, it speedily changes colour, and after passing through different shades of grey and brown, becomes at length nearly black.

The alterations of colour take place more speedily in proportion as the light is more intense. In the direct beams of the sun, two or three minutes are sufficient to produce the full effect. In the shade, several hours are required, and light transmitted through different coloured glasses acts upon it with different degrees of intensity. Thus it is found that red rays, or the common sunbeams passed through red glass, have very little action upon it: Yellow and green are more efficacious, but blue and violet light produce the most decided and powerful effects.*

---

* The facts above mentioned are analogous to those observed long ago by Scheele, and confirmed by Senebier. Scheele found, that in the prismatic spectrum, the effect produced by the red rays upon silver muriate was very faint, and scarcely to be perceived; whilst it was speedily blackened by the violet rays. Senebier states, that the time required to darken silver muriate by the red rays, is 20 minutes, by the orange 12, by the yellow 5 minutes and 30 seconds,

The consideration of these facts enables us readily to understand the method by which the outlines and shades of paintings on glass may be copied, or profiles of figures procured, by the agency of light. When a white surface, covered with solution of nitrate of silver, is placed behind a painting on glass exposed to the solar light, the rays transmitted through the differently-painted surfaces produce distinct tints of brown or black, sensibly differing in intensity according to the shades of the picture, and where the light is unaltered, the colour of the nitrate becomes deepest.

When the shadow of any figure is thrown upon the prepared surface, the part concealed by it remains white, and the other parts speedily become dark.

For copying paintings on glass, the solution should be applied on leather; and in this case it is more readily acted upon than when paper is used.

After the colour has been fixed upon the leather

---

by the green 37 seconds, by the blue 29 seconds, and by the violet only 15 seconds. "Senebier sur la Lumière," vol. iii p. 199.

Some new experiments have been lately made in relation to this subject, in consequence of the discoveries of Dr. Herschel concerning the invisible heatmaking rays existing in the solar beams, by Dr. Ritter and Böckmann in Germany, and Dr. Wollaston in England.

It has been ascertained, by experiment upon the prismatic spectrum, that no effects are produced upon the muriate of silver by the invisible heatmaking rays which exist on the red side, and which are least refrangible, though it is powerfully and distinctly affected in a space beyond the violet rays out of the visible boundary. See "Annalen der Physik, siebenter Band," 527.—D.

or paper, it cannot be removed by the application of water, or water and soap, and it is in a high degree permanent.

The copy of a painting, or the profile, immediately after being taken, must be kept in some obscure place. It may indeed be examined in the shade, but in this case the exposure should be only for a few minutes; by the light of candles and lamps, as commonly employed, it is not sensibly affected.

No attempts that have been made to prevent the uncoloured part of the copy or profile from being acted upon by light have as yet been successful. They have been covered with a thin coating of fine varnish, but this has not destroyed their susceptibility of becoming coloured; and even after repeated washings, sufficient of the active part of the saline matter will still adhere to the white parts of the leather or paper, to cause them to become dark when exposed to the rays of the sun.

Besides the applications of this method of copying that has just been mentioned, there are many others. And it will be useful for making delineations of all such objects as are possessed of a texture partly opaque and partly transparent. The woody fibres of leaves, and the wings of insects, may be pretty accurately represented by means of it, and in this case, it is only necessary to cause the direct solar light to pass through them, and to receive the shadows upon prepared leather.

When the solar rays are passed through a print and thrown upon prepared paper, the unshaded parts are slowly copied ; but the lights transmitted by the shaded parts are seldom so definite as to form a distinct resemblance of them by producing different intensities of colour.

The images formed by means of a camera obscura have been found too faint to produce, in any moderate time, an effect upon the nitrate of silver. To copy these images was the first object of Mr. Wedgwood in his researches on the subject, and for this purpose he first used the nitrate of silver, which was mentioned to him by a friend, as a substance very sensible to the influence of light ; but all his numerous experiments as to their primary end proved unsuccessful.

In following these processes, I have found, that the images of small objects, produced by means of the solar microscope, may be copied without difficulty on prepared paper. This will probably be a useful application of the method ; that it may be employed successfully, however, it is necessary that the paper be placed at but a small distance from the lens.

With regard to the preparation of the solution, I have found the best proportions those of 1 part of nitrate to about 10 parts of water. In this case, the quantity of the salt applied to the leather or paper will be sufficient to enable it to become tinged, without affecting its composition, or injuring its texture.

In comparing the effects produced by light upon muriate of silver with those produced upon the nitrate, it seemed evident that the muriate was the most susceptible, and both were more readily acted upon when moist than when dry, a fact long ago known. Even in the twilight, the colour of moist muriate of silver spread upon paper slowly changed from white to faint violet; though under similar circumstances no immediate alteration was produced upon the nitrate.

The nitrate, however, from its solubility in water, possesses an advantage over the muriate : though leather or paper may, without much difficulty, be impregnated with the last substance, either by diffusing it through water, and applying it in this form, or by immersing paper moistened with the solution of the nitrate in very diluted muriatic acid.

To those persons not acquainted with the properties of the salts containing oxide of silver, it may be useful to state that they produce a stain of some permanence, even when momentarily applied to the skin, and in employing them for moistening paper or leather, it is necessary to use a pencil of hair, or a brush.

From the impossibility of removing, by washing, the colouring matter of the salts from the parts of the surface of the copy which have not been exposed to light, it is probable that, both in the case of the nitrate and the muriate of silver, a portion of the metallic acid abandons its acid to enter into union with the animal or vegetable substance, so as to form with it an insoluble compound. And, supposing that this happens, it is not improbable, but that substances may be found capable of destroying this compound, either by simple or complicated affinities. Some experiments on this subject have been imagined, and an account of the results of them may possibly appear in a future number of the Journals. Nothing but a method of preventing the unshaded parts of the delineation from being coloured by exposure to the day is wanting, to render the process as useful as it is elegant.

Such is Davy's account. Considered as a piece of exposition, it is clear, but dull, dry, and rigid. It reads as if the writer were trying to say as little as possible, beyond the conveying of the main fact. It is plain that Davy, whatever may have been his scientific aptitudes, was destitute of the scientific imagination. He was describing something which, so far as he knew, and so far as we know, had never before happened. Up to that moment every picture produced by man had been made by the human hand, guided by the human eye.. But here was a picture, or a sort of picture, a representation of an object, which had come into existence by the spontaneous action of natural forces, by a chemical change produced by the action of light. Obviously, one might say, this was a fact behind which lay wonderful possibilities. But to Davy, apparently, no such thought occurred. Now we do not, of course, expect that the discoverer of a hitherto unknown fact should foresee all that is to result from it. When Oersted noticed (in 1819) that a magnetic needle on his table was deflected by an electric current, he had probably no idea that the quivering of that needle meant that some forty years later people would be sending instantaneous messages from Copenhagen to the Antipodes. But one might suppose that to a scientific mind like Davy's it would be self-evident that when an entirely new use of one of the forces of nature is discovered *some* important results are pretty sure to follow. He failed, however, to make that inference. In the title of his paper he suggests two uses only to which the new process may be applied, the making of profiles, and the copying of glass-paintings. As the making of profiles could interest but few people, and only glass-painters could find a use for copying such paintings, he could hardly have chosen a title less likely to arouse attention.* And it is odd that he did not notice the awkward ambiguity of the phrase, which many people would read as meaning the making of copies, on glass, of oil paintings or other paintings. The oversight was probably due to haste, but when taken along with the general tone of the paper, it is significant. Had he felt any real interest in the matter, or thought there was any value

---

* This title always reminds me of Mr. Dick in "David Copperfield." Mrs. Crupp had told him his room at Hungerford market was not big enough to swing a cat in. "But you know Trotwood, I don't want to swing a cat, I never do swing a cat. Therefore, what does that signify to me?" A reader might have said to Davy: "I don't want to copy paintings on glass, so what does that signify to me?"

in the "invention" he would surely have given a few moments' thought to the words which he put at the head of his report.

It is possible, of course, that Wedgwood himself may not have attached any special importance to the experiments, or perceived what great possibilities were opened up by his partial success. But whether this was so it is impossible to say; as not a word of any writing of his on the subject is extant, and we know nothing of the exact circumstances under which the account was drawn up. He was out of England when it appeared in print, and had been constantly moving about since November 1800, the date when Leslie was getting him the coloured glasses, &c. I am inclined to believe that there was probably no time between that date and his departure from England, early in 1802, in which he could have been working at the subject. Probably he left the whole matter, after his experiments of November 1800, in Davy's hands. In any case, it was utterly impossible for him, broken as he was by disease, to pursue the subject himself.

It may seem at first sight strange that the appearance of this Account by Davy should not have stimulated some one conversant with chemistry to attack the problem of finding a means of "preventing the unshaded parts of the delineation from being coloured by exposure to the day"—i.e., of "fixing" the image of the object on the paper. But this is not so surprising when we discover what the "Journal" was. It was not a periodical published in the ordinary way, but a little paper printed from time to time to let the subscribers to the infant institution know what was being done there. It was not announced as appearing at any stated periods, but was to be issued "as often at least as once a fortnight." This announcement, however, was not acted upon. The first number came out in April 1800, but the next not till fourteen months later, and the "Journal" did not live beyond a first volume.* There is nothing to show that Davy's account was ever read at any meeting; and the print of it would have been read, apparently, if read at all, only by the small circle of members and subscribers to the institution, of whom, we may be pretty sure, only a small minority can have been scientific people. For the Royal Institution was in its early years something quite different from what it afterwards became. It was founded in 1799 by Count Rumford, in co-operation with a "Society for Bettering the Condition of the Poor," with the object of providing a place for the exhibition of models of mechanical inventions, and for teaching "the applications of science to the common purposes of life." The chief things exhibited in the "Repository" appear to have been improved cooking appliances, roasters, fireballs, economical grates, brewers' boilers, laundry fittings, ventilators, models of cottages, &c. Thus Davy's paper cannot be said to have been "published," in any effective sense, in the year 1802. Wedgwood was at the time out of the country, and under these circumstances it is no wonder that the record of his first steps towards the creation of a wholly new art should have escaped general notice.

---

* "The Royal Institution, its founders and first professors," by Dr. Bence Jones, 1871.

That Davy did not seriously tackle the problem of fixing the pictures is, I think, evident from the closing sentences of the Account. He contented himself, it would seem, with "*imagining some experiments*" on the subject, the result of which might "possibly" be reported at a future day. Dr. Davy, when he included the Account in the complete edition of his brother's works (1834–1840), added a note saying "recently this method of delineation has been futher cultivated, especially by Mr. Talbot in this country," but said nothing as to Sir Humphrey having done or written anything more as to the silver pictures of 1802. The discoveries of Daguerre and Talbot were then attracting much attention. Dr. Davy was referring to Talbot's "Photogenic Drawing" (which was described in the *Athenæum* of February 9, 1839), and if he had known anything of further researches by his brother in the same direction he would certainly have mentioned them. Indeed a note on p. 14 of Dr. Davy's "Fragmentary Remains, &c., of Sir H. D." (1858) makes it certain that Sir H. did nothing more than is shown in the Account.

Sir William Abney, in his article on photography in the "Encyclopædia Britannica," after describing the Wedgwood process as reported by Davy, says:

"In this method of preparing the paper lies the germ of the silver printing processes which are practised at the present time (1884), and it was only by the recent spread of chemical knowledge that the hiatus was filled up, when hyposulphate of soda, discovered by Chaussier in 1799, or three years before Wedgwood published his paper, was used for making the print permanent."

Mr. Jerome Harrison, in his account of fixing processes, writes as follows : *

"The only thing deplored by Wedgwood and Davy in 1802 was their inability to discover any satisfactory solvent for the salts of silver—the muriate (or, as we should now call it, the chloride) and the nitrate—which they employed."

Mr. Harrison would here seem to imply that Wedgwood and Davy were really working together at the problem in 1802. But I see nothing to show that this was so. I think it is evident that Davy gave the question no serious attention. We do not know when he drew up the Account, or when the experiments were made. He does not describe them ; he merely states their result, and the language of the Account, all through, rather suggests that he is telling an old story. I incline to think that when he printed it he probably had already dismissed the subject from his mind, as one of no particular interest, which it certainly would have been, if it had involved nothing more important than the copying of glass-paintings.

"In 1819," continues Mr. Jerome Harrison, "Sir John Herschel pointed out (in the *Edinburgh Philosophical Journal*) the ready solubility of silver salts in the alkaline hyposulphates. From this time the problem of photography was solved ; but, unfortunately, Niépce, Daguerre, and Talbot seem to have known nothing of the work already done by Davy and by Herschel. In 1839 Daguerre fixed his iodised silver plates by washing them either with ammonia or with a strong solution of common salt. At the same time, too, Talbot used common salt, and also solutions of bromide of potassium and iodide of

---

* "History of Photography" (Trubner 1888), p. 89.

potassium. Immediately Herschel heard of Daguerre's and Talbot's successes in photography (in January 1839), he remembered the substance whose solvent power for silver salts he had announced in 1819 (hyposulphate of soda), and the directions which he gives for its use, in a valuable paper read before the Royal Society on February 20, 1840, have ever since formed the foundation of our ordinary method of fixing photographs on paper."

From these statements of expert authorities I infer that if Davy had tried seriously to find a "fixing" process, there was nothing to hinder his soon discovering one. And this appears to be the view taken by Dr. Eder in his account of Wedgwood's work.

"Wedgwood and Davy had forgotten, or not known, Scheele's important discovery that white chloride of silver is completely dissolved in ammonia, but that when darkened by light it leaves behind a deposit of silver, which is much to be wondered at, considering how widely disseminated were Scheele's writings, of which there was also an English translation. By this a means would have been given of fixing the chloride of silver pictures.*

Dr. Schiendel makes a similar observation :

"It must appear highly remarkable that a chemist of Davy's rank should not have been acquainted with Scheele's weighty discovery that chloride of silver dissolves in ammonia, and that Wedgwood had at his command, in that discovery, a very easily procurable means of making his pictures permanent." †

---

* " Geschichte der Photochemie und Photographie." Dr. Joseph Maria Eder (Halle a. S. 1891).

† "Geschichte der Photographie," 1891, p. 19. I find it, however, difficult to suppose that Wedgwood can have overlooked any material point in Scheele's researches. They are referred to in the Account, and in a letter to Godwin on philosophical subjects (Jan. 14,

The whole story seems to show that in getting Davy's collaboration Wedgwood made an unlucky mistake. The "Account" being practically a record of failure in the critical point as to fixing the pictures, Davy's eminence as a chemist—for he had already made a name, though only at the beginning of his career— would make such failure, or apparent failure, all the more discouraging to future investigators. That in one instance it had this effect appears from a remark made by Fox-Talbot in 1839 when describing his own work.* He there relates how Davy's announcement of what seemed a complete failure had discouraged a scientific friend of his from pursuing the matter; adding that it would have perhaps led himself to consider the attempt as hopeless, if he had not, fortunately, before he read the "Account," discovered a method of fixing the image.   Dr. Eder makes a like remark, though he is in error, as I believe, as to the extent of Davy's efforts, when he says: "The want of any result from the experiments deterred his (Davy's) contemporaries from attempting the solution of a problem on which a scientific man of the first rank had wrecked himself (*gescheitert war*); and thus many years passed before the fixing of silver pictures was discovered."

If these views are sound, we may apparently infer that if Davy had had some little imagination, and had taken any reasonable amount of pains in following up

1797) we find him saying: "This talent" [for philosophical investigation], "if I have it in any degree, I attribute to a spirit of accurate analysis acquired from the writings of Scheele and Bergmann, and practised in the operations of the laboratory."

* *Athenæum*, Jan. 1839, p. 144.

Wedgwood's footsteps, photography would probably have come into existence as a practical art some thirty-five years before the time of Daguerre and Talbot.

A question of some interest in regard to these later inventors is, Was any of their work prompted by a knowledge of Wedgwood's imperfect results? On this point we have little or no positive evidence, but what we do know seems to make it unlikely that they were aware of Wedgwood's work. The first recorded effective photography was undoubtedly that achieved by Nicéphore Niépce, who, at least as early as 1816, thirteen years before the time when he entered into his partnership with Daguerre, was taking, by means of a camera, pictures of outdoor scenes—pictures which might be called "permanent," as compared with the evanescent products of Wedgwood's experiments. The fullest account of his work* gives no hint of his having derived his ideas from any predecessor, and the circumstances were such as to make it extremely unlikely that he had ever read Davy's "Memoir" of 1802. He was not a professed chemist or *savant*, and was living the quietest of lives at Chalon-sur-Saone, some hundreds of miles from Paris. It was in 1813 that he began

---

* Namely, the series of private letters to his brother Claude Niépce given in the biography entitled, " *La verité sur l'invention de la photography : Nicéphore Niépce, sa vie, &c.*," par Victor Fouque. Chalon-sur-Saone, 1867. M. Fouque's narrative, which certainly seems to be borne out by the documents he prints, purports to show that Niépce was the real inventor of the art, having accomplished the most decisive steps before he entered into the partnership under which he and Daguerre agreed to "pool" their knowledge and their results ; and that it was only by a series of dishonest measures that Daguerre contrived to secure to himself the credit of the discovery, and get the art called (for a time) by his own name.

trying to apply to lithography (then a new art in France) the alterative power of sunlight ; and we know how slight was the intercourse between England and France during all that war-time. Daguerre's ideas on photography were mainly derived from Niépce. Arago's Report of 1839 on " Daguerrotypie," though it mentions Davy's " Memoir " as the earliest announcement of a photographic process, gives no hint of this having been known to Daguerre. There is thus no reason to think that either of the two first French photographers took anything from Wedgwood.

Fox-Talbot knew of Wedgwood's experiments, but not, apparently, until after he had himself found a method of fixing the image.*

But though Wedgwood's attempts to produce permanent light-pictures failed to stimulate his contemporaries to pursue the subject, one of his conclusions, at least, seems to have led to an important result nearly forty years later, just at the critical time when the art was reaching the stage of unqualified success. After the publication, in 1839, of the processes of Talbot and of Daguerre, the advance of photography much depended on the question how it might be possible to shorten the time of exposure necessary to secure a picture. In 1841 Talbot patented his " Calotype " process, which reduced the time of exposure

---

* *Ante*, p. 201. The soundness of Fox-Talbot's claim, however, to be an original inventor has been disputed. Werge ("Evolution of Photography," pp. 14; 101) holds to the view that his process, as first announced, did not go beyond Wedgwood's, and that he must have seen Davy's " Memoir." Of the merits of this controversy I know nothing, but the reasons given by Werge for doubting Talbot's statement do not seem to me to have much weight.

to two or three minutes. This was effected by brushing over the sensitive paper with a mixture of gallic acid and nitrate of silver. But in this system, says Mr. Jerome Harrison,* "it is tolerably certain that Talbot had been anticipated by the Rev. J. B. Reade." This was established in a trial (Talbot *v.* Laroche) arising from an attempt to upset Talbot's patent on the ground of "previous discovery." Now Reade's use of the gallic acid had arisen from his noticing Davy's statement that in Wedgwood's process leather was found to be more readily acted upon than paper. In order to repeat Wedgwood's experiment, he had borrowed a pair of light coloured kid gloves from his wife. She, however, objected to lend him a second pair ; " and this " (here I quote his own words) " led me to say, ' Then I will tan paper.' " Reade was at this time (1837) taking photographs of objects by the solar microscope, and employing an artist to copy the images on the screen. To avoid the continued expense of this copying,

"I fell back,"† he says, "but without any sanguine expectations, upon the photographic process adopted by Wedgwood. My fortunate inability to replenish the stock of leather induced me to apply the tannin solution to paper, and thus I had the pleasure of succeeding where Talbot acknowledged that he failed. . . . My old friend, Mr. Andrew Ross, told Mr. Talbot how first of all, by means of the solar microscope, I threw the image of the object on prepared paper, and then, while the

---

* "A History of Photography " (1887), pp. 30, sqq.
† I am abbreviating here his rather rambling account as given by Mr. Werge. Reade, a country clergyman, was an amateur astronomer and microscopist. He died in 1870. (Werge, pp. 15, 16, 90.)

paper was yet wet, washed it over with the infusion of galls, when a sufficiently dense negation was quickly obtained. In the trial (Talbot *v.* Laroche) Mr. Talbot in his cross-examination, and in an almost breathless court, acknowledged that he had received this information from Ross."

This essential detail in Talbot's process thus seems to have come to him, through Reade and Ross, from T. Wedgwood.

CHAPTER XIV

HIS METAPHYSICS AND PSYCHOLOGY

I WILL not here attempt any estimate of Tom Wedgwood's character. His letters reflect clearly enough its moral side, his temper and disposition, but, as the reader will have seen, they tell little or nothing as to his intellectual interests. Pre-occupied as he necessarily was with the ever urgent question of his bodily health, it is hardly strange that, to his nearest and_dearest friends, he could write of hardly anything else. When the great question for every day was whether it was or was not to be passed in misery, any free play of thought on things less personal was scarcely to be looked for. If we had his letters to Coleridge, they might give us a completer knowledge of his mind ; but none of these, so far as I know, are extant.

His first serious efforts, as has been shown, were in the direction of physical science, and I imagine that if he had had ordinary health his best work would have been of that kind. Sir Humphrey Davy's remarkable words: "His opinions were to me a secret treasure, and often enabled me to think rightly when otherwise perhaps I should have thought wrongly," presumably referred to their interchange of ideas on physical problems. But the main drift of his thoughts, after ill-health had forced him to give up experimenting in the laboratory, was in another direction, as is shôwn by the mass of writing which he left behind him. This is, for the most part, a chaotic heap of rough MSS., dealing wholly with one group of subjects, namely, metaphysical and psychological speculation, with excursions into educational and social questions. It seems to have been mainly his talk on these subjects that gave his friends and acquaintances such a high opinion of his powers. And if we are to accept the judgment of Mackintosh, who was then (and is still) thought an authority on the subject, there must have been something distinctively original in his handling of some of the most time-honoured meta- physical problems.* Mackintosh undertook to be the editor of his philosophical speculations, " or," he says, " as I would rather call them, discoveries," and he took with him to India, as we have seen, various MSS. of Tom's, intending to draw up, as he had promised, an exposition of his views.

After Tom's death (in the next year) Mackintosh renewed his promise to Josiah Wedgwood, and it was then settled that the publication should include a Memoir by Coleridge, towards which Poole, Sharp, and others were to assist. But this project came wholly to naught. Whether Mackintosh seriously attempted to do his part is not quite clear. It was hardly possible,

---

* Josiah, telling Poole (in 1800) of his brother's discussions with Mackintosh, writes: " 'The subjects cleared are no less than Time, Space, and Motion; and Mackintosh and Sharp think a meta-physical revolution likely to follow.'" Coleridge, who never liked Mackintosh, receives this news with chilling caution. He thinks it likely Tom has fallen upon some valuable truth, but has " many reasons for being exceedingly suspicious of supposed discoveries in Metaphysics." (T. P., ii. 28–30.)

and if possible would have been scarcely decent, that the judge of an important court at Bombay should find time for dissertations on subtle metaphysical questions—"time," "space," and the everlasting controversy between Intuitionists and Empiricists. So the promise good-naturedly but not wisely made was never redeemed. Nor was anything ever heard of Coleridge's Memoir, save in the way of belated excuses and apologies, with a confused story of papers of his having been lost at Malta or thrown overboard from the ship which was carrying them home.

Tom Wedgwood's speculations in psychology led him on to theories about education. "Child-study" was one of his constant interests, stimulated perhaps by his having subjects of observation always at hand in Josiah's young family. His views hereon, as on human affairs generally, are largely Rousseauistic. The omnipotence of education, philosophically guided, in the formation of character is taken for granted; inheritance and congenital character are ignored; he puts no limit to what may be achieved by appropriate training. Here we have the perfectibilism of Godwin and the pre-French-Revolution philosophers. The great engine of child-management is the Hartleian doctrine of the "association of ideas." This he applies more to the play of the emotions than to purely mental phenomena. We come here and there on entertaining illustrations of the method. They are explained with the utmost seriousness; for though Erasmus Darwin, when Tom Wedgwood was staying with him at the age of eight years, wrote to his father of the boy's "humour," I have not detected the smallest sign of that quality in the mature philosopher. His methods remind us of those of another child of the Revolution, Thomas Day, once so well known in English nurseries by his "Sandford and Merton." Day, in order to cultivate presence of mind in the two orphan girls whom he set about training with the view of choosing one of them, for a wife, used to drop hot sealing-wax on their bare arms, or suddenly fire pistols at their petticoats. Wedgwood, in the course of a disquisition on the same virtue, suggests a similar method of teaching children "how men elude danger and inconvenience by address." "The parent might invite the attack of a fierce bull, stand with perfect composure until the animal be within two or three paces of him, then suddenly open an umbrella, hold his hat before his face, or somehow contrive to amuse and terrify the foe, whilst his child, on the other side of the stile, shall witness his intrepidity, and by degrees practise the same feat himself in company with his parent." This recipe is awkwardly vague on the critical point *how* the parent, while on the bull's side of the stile, is to "amuse or terrify the foe," but Wedgwood kindly provides, for the benefit, no doubt, of less heroic spirits, a less trying variant of the same procedure, in which "a raging turkey cock" does duty for the bull; and he explains at some length the *rationale* of the effect produced on the bull's or the turkey cock's mind by the parent's manœuvres.

Richard Sharp was a remarkably acute critic and much given to philosophical speculation, but what the discoveries were from which he "thought a revolution in metaphysics likely to follow," is a question which I,

o

though I have looked through the box full of Tom's MSS. which has been kept as a family relic for nearly a century, am quite unable to answer. And I doubt whether the best equipped and most industrious of experts in these high matters would be able to extract from them much definite metaphysical doctrine. They are mostly rough note-books and fragmentary essays, or bits of essays, many of them evidently jotted down in a travelling carriage. What they most clearly show is, that Wedgwood had an acute and penetrating mind, and delighted in the minute analysis of mental and psychical processes. The same perseverance which kept him trying for six months to hang a thermometer *in vacuo* here appears in the laborious minuteness with which he dissects little every-day experiences of memory and association. He believed, apparently, that through such minute analysis lies the road, if any road there be, to discovering what is the exact process by which we arrive at a belief in the existence of an external world ; and how emotion, thought, and will (if there be such a thing), are related to the primary facts of sensation. To many people speculation of this kind, the laborious attempt to discover by thinking what thinking *is*, seems something like an eye's trying to look into itself. But however that may be, it does not seem to me likely that any exposition of Tom Wedgwood's metaphysical views, outgrowths of the thought of more than a century ago, could now have any other than a historical interest. In metaphysics, as in other matters, " much has happened since then." To note one point only, Englishmen then had no knowledge of the course of philosophical speculation in Germany. Coleridge's

influence as the "interpreter of Germany to, England "* had not begun. Kant's " Critic of Pure Reason "
appeared in 1781, but as late as about 1816, we find
Dugald Stewart could only read it in a Latin transla-
lation, and "abandoned the undertaking in despair."
I see nothing to show that Wedgwood read or knew
German (though he travelled in the country for some
weeks or more in 1796). (Mackintosh knew nothing
of it till 1804, when he took some lessons from his
children's German governess on his voyage to Bombay.)
Another thing which would necessarily, I conceive,
make Wedgwood's discussion of mental phenomena
out of date is the immense advance since made in our
knowledge of the physiology of the brain and nervous
system.   Not till some five years after his death did
Sir Charles Bell's great discovery of the distinction between sensory and motor nerves become known to the
world.†

For a substantially similar reason his lucubrations

---

* Sir L. Stephen.

† The only bit, so far as I know, of Wedgwood's metaphysical
work which has been printed, is a short article in the third volume
(1817) of the "Journal of Science and the Arts" (edited at the
Royal Institution), entitled "An Enquiry into the origin of our
notion of distance, drawn up from notes left by the late Thomas
Wedgwood, Esq." This, as its vague title shows, is not actually of
Wedgwood's writing. It is a recast of a MS. essay bearing nearly
the same title, with additions taken from another MS. called an
"Essay on Vision," some portions being paraphrases of Wedgwood's
words or additions by the editor. I have not discovered who edited
or arranged this paper. Might it possibly have been done by
Mackintosh? If so one can understand his not wishing to put his
name to a very partial attempt to redeem the promise made so many
years previously. The paper deals with the Berkleyan theory of
vision, but I have not sufficient knowledge of this thorny subject to
venture on a summary of the arguments. It was reprinted in Miss
Meteyard's "Group of Englishmen," 1871.

on education, and matters touching politics and sociology (to use a modern phrase), could scarcely have any interest for a reader of the twentieth century. How long, or how closely, he held to his early Godwinian creed is not clear; but in turning over his MSS. one perceives that his mind is still moving within that same order of ideas. We have the familiar denunciation of the tyranny of custom and convention, and appeals to the "simplicity of nature," with the underlying Rousseauistic implication that the evils of the world, in fact, all its modern polity and civilisation, have come about by way of corruption and depravation of a primitive ideal. The now dominant conception of Evolution has taught us to treat that view of the past not merely as the fantastic vision which probably most of our grandfathers saw it to be, but as a completely topsy-turvy view of the history of the race.

A biographer of Tom Wedgwood, however, when touching the matter of evolution, cannot help remembering that there were links, though only of a personal kind, between him and the genesis of that doctrine. He was often exchanging ideas with old Erasmus Darwin, his sister's father-in-law, in whose speculations (as his grandson was careful to point out) there were foreshadowings of evolution; but we have no reason to think that when reading "Zoonomia," or the notes to the "Botanic Garden," he saw in them any special significance of this kind. It was not till 1809, three and a half years after his death, that there appeared, in his sister's nursery at Shrewsbury, the baby out of whose little brain there was to come, fifty years later, the book which did most to establish

the order of ideas now increasingly dominant in all
regions of thought—ideas, the growth of which has
quietly relegated to the domain of history the systems
of many more notable philosophers than Tom Wedgwood.*

---

* Charles Darwin, Tom's nephew, was born Feb. 12, 1809.
"The Origin of Species by means of Natural Selection," appeared
in Nov. 1859. It is hardly possible to say when the idea of Evolution first began to make an impression on the general world of
thought. "In Memoriam" will serve to remind posterity that it
was in the air some time before Darwin's work became known.
Old people remember the excitement produced, perhaps more in
religious than in scientific circles, by the "Vestiges of Creation" in
1844, which was the work, not of a man of science, but of a clever
"litterateur." In the Life of Tennyson there is a noticeable
letter in which he asks his publisher to get him that book, saying:
"It seems to contain many speculations with which I have been
familiar for years, and on which I have written more than one
poem." A reader in the future, not having in mind the dates,
might naturally think some pages of "In Memoriam" must have
been written after the "Origin," but it was not so. The wonderful
stanzas beginning:

> "Contemplate all this work of time,
>   The giant labouring in his youth,"

and ending with

> "Move upward, working out the beast,
>   And let the ape and tiger die,"

as well as the earlier section, "'So careful of the type?' but no,"
must have taken shape between 1833 and (about) 1840. Darwin
was at that time quite unknown except to a few naturalists and
private friends. He and Tennyson were at Cambridge together, but
did not know each other till the sixties.

APPENDICES

A

AN ALLEGED DISCOVERY OF
PHOTOGRAPHY IN 1727

I CALL Wedgwood the first photographer (adopting a phrase used by more than one writer) because he was, so far as we know, the first person who conceived and put in practice the idea of using the agency of light to obtain a representation of an object ; while to call him the inventor of photography would be inaccurate, inasmuch as he did not fully succeed in his attempt. But two writers of high authority (already mentioned in these pages), Dr. Eder and Herr Schiendel, give the title of "inventor of photography" to John Hermann Schulze, a German university professor who died many years before Wedgwood was born. This they do on the strength of a Memoir by Schulze, describing an experiment whereby he accidentally discovered the darkening effect of light upon silver-salt in or previously to the year 1727. This Memoir, however, shows, not that Schulze did anything or thought of anything to which the word "photographic" can properly be applied, but only that he observed (and was possibly the first to observe) a fact which about a century later became the groundwork of photographic processes.

As Schulze tells his story in an entertaining way, and extracts might give a misleading idea of his drift, I subjoin a translation of the entire Memoir.*

* A paper on this question, including the translation here given was read by me in October 1898 at a " Technical Meeting " of the

It is to be found in the Transactions of the "Cæsarean Academy" for the year 1727. The full title of the volume is, "*Acta Physico-Medica Academiæ Cæsareæ Leopoldino-Carolinæ, Naturæ Curiosorum exhibentia Ephemerides, sive Observationes Historias et Experimenta celeberrimis Germaniæ et exterarum regionum viris habita et communicata.*" Norimbergæ : An. MDCCXXVII.

John Hermann Schulze, born at Kolditz in Saxony in 1687, was a man of considerable note in his time, chiefly as a linguist and philologist, and as a historian of ancient medicine. He was professor of anatomy, and also of Greek and Arabic, at the University of Altdorf in Franconia, and afterwards became professor of Eloquence and Antiquities at Halle. He died in 1744.

"AN OBSERVATION BY MASTER DOCTOR JOHN HENRY SCHULZE. SCOTOPHORUS DISCOVERED INSTEAD OF PHOSPHORUS, OR A CURIOUS EXPERIMENT ON THE EFFECT OF THE SUN'S RAYS." (OBSERVATIO CCXXXIII.)

We often discover by accident what we should hardly have found out by intention or design. In this way, while looking for and working at one thing, I discovered something I could not have hoped for. Whether in communicating the whole story to other inquisitive people, and leaving it to their further discussion, I am doing what is worth the trouble, the benevolent reader will judge for himself. Fair judges will pardon the freedom of my title. My only reason for calling my experiment "scotophoric" is to indicate the darkening effect which it showed me. While the "Bologna stone" receives light from the sun's rays, this mixture of mine is darkened by the sun and

Royal Photographic Society of Great Britain (see the *Photographic Journal* of November 30, 1898). In the discussion which then followed the views expressed by members present agreed with mine.

takes a dusky colour. But I think that the true cause of this darkening is no less deserving of investigation by the natural philosopher than is that of the light which emanates from any of the class of phosphorescents.

It is about two years ago that, while reading various things about phosphorescents, I bethought myself of examining the " Baldwin process." * I happened then to have at hand some *aqua fortis* containing a very small quantity of silver particles, say about as much as is wanted to make the preparation suitable for separating gold from silver. I was using this *aqua fortis* for saturating chalk with it, as one has to do in the Baldwin experiment. I was doing this at an open window, into which the sun was at the time shining very brightly. I was surprised to see that the colour of the surface changed to a dark red, inclining to violet. But I was more surprised to see that the part of the dish not touched by the sun's rays did not at all show that colour.

Seeing this, and considering that it deserved further examination, I put aside the Baldwin experiment, and applied myself to this (as it were) darkness-making experiment, in order to get an explanation of the change of colour. Doubting what plan to follow, I divided the saturated chalk into two parts, one of which I put into a round oblong glass of the kind we commonly use in dispensing liquid medicines. And in order to get the thick mixture more conveniently into the bottle I began to pour in more *aqua fortis*. But as the *aqua fortis* made too much ebullition and began to dissolve the chalk, I added some water to check this action. I then put the glass in a place exposed to the sun's rays. Scarcely a few minutes elapsed when I saw that the glass, on the side touched by the sun, showed a similar colour, namely, dark red verging towards blue. The rest of the mixture I left in the dish exposed to the sun's rays and to light until it dried, and noticed the coloured surface remaining

* Baldwin was the discoverer, about 1677, of a kind of phosphorus, afterwards called by his name, different from the " Bolognian." It was made by dissolving chalk in *aqua fortis*.

so for several days until the stuff was used up in further experiments.

I showed the discovery to friends who visited me, in order to learn their opinions. Some appeared to think the darkened colour was due to heat. To ascertain therefore whether the effect arose from heat, we tried various tests. First we put the glass close enough to a bright fire to make it pretty hot, but in such a position that the part which had not been reached by the sun's rays, and which had none of the colour, fronted the fire. That caused no change of colour, though the glass had become so hot that the hand could hardly bear to touch it.

This is sufficient proof that nothing here was due to heat, so I pass over the other experiments made to this end. But in order to see more clearly, and show others, that the dark colour was induced by the sun's light, not his heat, I shook up the glass, thus mixing up the chalk sediment and the fluid at the top, so completely as to remove all difference of colour. Dividing the liquor (if I may so call the mixture) in this state, I decided to put one bottleful of it in a dark place not exposed to sunlight, and kept another for fresh experiments. I accordingly put [the former] in the sun, tying a thin thread from the mouth to the bottom of the bottle, so as to divide the side exposed to the sun in about the middle, and left it for some hours in a very hot sun, not to be touched or disturbed by any one. When the thread was removed we were delighted to perceive that the part which it had covered showed the same colour as the back of the bottle which no ray of the sun had reached. We tried the same experiment with the same result with horsehair, with human hair, and with an extremely thin silver wire; so that there was no doubt that the change of colour depended wholly on the sun's light, and that heat, even the sun's heat, had had nothing to do with it.

I further instituted experiments in a contrary sense, that is to say, whenever I wished to repeat the experiment, I mixed up the fluid so as to make it of uniform colour, and covered the greater part of the glass with opaque bodies, leaving a small part of it freely accessible to the light. I thus several times wrote words or entire sentences on paper, and after carefully cutting out with a sharp knife the ink-marked parts, stuck the paper, perforated in this way, on the glass by means of wax. Before long the sun's rays, on the side on which they had touched the glass through the apertures in the paper, wrote the words or sentences so accurately and distinctly on the chalk sediment, that many people curious in such matters, but ignorant of the nature of the experiment, were led to attribute the result to all kinds of artifices.

I said that I had kept the dried portion of the saturated chalk. This also, I found, quickly changed its colour whenever it was exposed freely to the sun, and in such a way that nothing could be attributed to the heat, but that the whole change was attributable solely to the light. I mentioned also that I put another bottle of the same material in a dark place. That, whenever I looked at it, kept the same whitish colour, not showing in any part even a trace of change of colour. Just as I have often found a solution of silver made with *aqua fortis* does not get dark in a quite dark place, while when exposed to the sun a dark red colour is induced, verging afterwards towards blue.

I saw that it remained to investigate the cause of the effects described. But I was under the belief that all the results depended on chalk and *aqua fortis* being mixed together, and so began theorising on the effect of light operating on those substances ; for it had wholly escaped me that the *aqua fortis* which I had employed had been altered, or, as we commonly say, " precipitated," by some few particles of silver. It was a happy chance, therefore, that it occurred to me to repeat the same experiments afresh. I had at hand some very penetrating fuming spirit of nitre, such as is used in preparing oil of vitriol. This, in order that it should not quite dissolve the chalk, I diluted with a good deal of water, and thus began to saturate

the chalk. But, though I did this in the brightest sunlight, I
could not in the least see the remarkable change of colour before
observed.   I therefore tried the process with *aqua fortis* as sold
in the chemists' shops. The result was the same as I observed
to follow with the spirit of nitre, and not what I expected.
Whence it came into my mind to remember that the *aqua fortis*
I had first used had produced the phenomena by reason of the
particles of silver in it.

Now, therefore, following up the matter more closely, I
dissolve a portion of silver in *aqua fortis*, weaken the solution
with water, and saturate the chalk as before.   The same phenomena made their appearance, but the colour now showed itself far more distinctly as a larger quantity of silver particles
were immersed in the saturating fluid. I remember, in fact,
that when I repeated the experiment with *aqua fortis* charged
with a sufficient quantity of silver to form a complete solution,
the result was that even the parts of the glass not reached by the
direct rays of the sun soon took a distinctly blackish hue from
the reflected rays. I exposed the same solution, but diluted
with water and with no admixture of chalk, in a window open
to the sun's rays, and found that the dark colour was equally
produced in the fluid.

To make the more sure that the effect described was due to
the sun's light, I put a bottleful of the mixture in such a position
that it received the sun's rays reflected from a plane mirror, and
soon discovered that all the results followed under this condition
just as well as if I had put it to catch the sun directly. I found
at the same time that, to make the experiment with proper
precautions, the mixture in the bottle must be so placed as not
to have behind it any object which can reflect the sun's rays.
I remember I put a glass (of the mixture) at night in a window
which did not get the sun till the afternoon. But there was a
house opposite, which had lately been covered with a coat of
quite white plaster, and this refracted the morning light vividly
into my room. I looked at the bottle in the morning and
detected the usual colour. After this I often placed it so as to

front a brightly sunlit wall, while no part of it was touched immediately by any direct ray. I found that it showed the usual colour, though more slowly than when the light came from the mirror.

My use of powdered chalk was only accidental, since, as I have said, my intention was to prepare some Baldwin's phosphorus. But I think it makes no difference if one prefers to substitute for the chalk some other white substance, such as hartshorn, white magnesia, &c. I have myself used ceruss of lead in the same experiment with nearly the same success. But this seemed inconvenient, as the ceruss both sticks more firmly to the sides of the bottle, and is slower in gravitating to the bottom, and after remaining still a long time mixes less easily with the fluid—a thing which it should do [easily] in order that the induced colour may be removed for the purpose of fresh experiments.

If any one desires to see the effect produced in a few moments, he should concentrate the sun's rays on a bottle full of the mixture by means of a burning-glass; taking care, however, not to put the bottle exactly in the focus, but a little away from it. In this way he will see that even in a moment the colour of the mixture in the bottle will be distinctly darkened.

This is a summary account of a frequently repeated experiment. I should add something as to the cause of the phenomenon if I could satisfy myself with regard to it. We may at any rate take it as demonstrated that the effect of solar light and heat is different from any that can be looked for from a kitchen fire. I have further thought that this experiment of mine might also have a use in helping the testing of minerals or metals, in case one wishes to ascertain whether they include any portion of silver; for these phenomena have so far not been observed to hold in the case of any other metal or mineral when similarly treated. Nor do I despair of its being possible that the experiment should lead the curious investigators of nature to other useful results. On which account I have not hesitated publicly to submit it to the further examination of those more learned than myself.

It seems strange that any one reading this should take it as showing that Schulze was the "discoverer of photography." It is clear that he found out for himself the fact that silver-salt is darkened by sunlight; but there is not a word in his paper which suggests that he had any idea of using this fact so as to get a picture or representation of an object, which is of course the essential idea of photography. Only one practical suggestion occurs to him, the possibility, namely, of the discovery being used to test the presence of silver in an alloy.

Dr. Eder, after describing what Schulze did, quotes in the original Latin the passage describing the cutting out of the paper patterns, and proceeds: "From this account it unquestionably appears that Schulze had not only a thorough knowledge of the sensitiveness to light of silver-salt as early as 1727, but that he also applied it to copying written characters (Schriftzüge zu copiren) by means of sunlight. Accordingly Schulze, a German, must be designated the discoverer of photography (*Erfinder der Photographie*), though he has never once been so called, a fact which may be attributed to the difficulty of getting access to the original sources of information." *

From this it would seem that Dr. Eder rests his view mainly on what he calls Schulze's "copying of written characters." But surely it is straining Schulze's account to say that when he cut out words on a piece of paper, and stuck the paper on the bottle, he was "copying" writings. He had already satisfied himself that the light darkened the mixture, by the device of the thread, and by covering up part of the bottle. The artifice of cutting out the words was simply a more vivid and amusing

---

* "Geschichte der Photochemie und Photographie." Dr. Josef Maria Eder. Halle, 1891. Dr. Eder had already published the substance of this part of his history in *Photographische Correspondenz* for January 1881, No. 207.

way of showing the same fact. If he had had any* idea of applying it to the copying of anything whatever, he would have said so. Evidently no such thought occurred to him. The device of the cut-out words amused him and amused his friends, as a bit of "natural magic." From his lively account we can picture the scene—they are astonished at the mysterious writing, seen *inside* the glass ; he gives the bottle a shake, and the writing vanishes! No wonder that, in the year 1727, the *multi curiosi* made wild guesses as to how the trick was done. Dr. Eder has fallen into the mistake—not a very uncommon one—of reading an old story by the light of current ideas. He sees photography in what was only photochemistry. Priestley, who described Schulze's experiment in a few clear sentences (" History and Present State of Discoveries relating to Vison, Light, and Colours," 1772), and who evidently wrote with the memoir before him, treats it simply as a demonstration of the fact that the silver in the mixture was the cause of the change of colour.

Probably to this notice by Priestley is due the appearance of Schulze's experiment with the paper word-patterns in a book, apparently popular more than a century ago, entitled " Rational Recreations, in which the principles of numbers and Natural Philosophy are elucidated by a series of easy, entertaining and interesting experiments, &c.," by W. Hooper, M.D. (1774). Schulze's name is not mentioned, but " Recreation xliii " (vol. iv. p. 143) runs as follows : " Writing on glass by the rays of the sun. Dissolve chalk in *aqua fortis* to the consistence of milk, and add to that a strong dissolution of silver. Keep this liquor in a glass decanter well stopped, then cut out from a paper the letters you would have appear, and paste the paper on the decanter, which you are to place in the sun, in such a manner that its rays may pass through the spaces cut out of the paper, and fall on the surface of the liquor. The part of the glass through which the rays pass will turn black, and that under the paper will remain white. You must observe not to move the bottle during the time of the operation."

P

Herr Schiendl ("Geschichte der Photographie," Wien, &c., 1891) is even more determined than Dr. Eder to prove that Professor Schulze was the first photographer. "I entirely agree," he says, "with Dr. Eder's view that Schulze especially may be considered the discoverer of photography, for no one before him knew the effect of light (as such) on silver-salts, and he was without dispute the first who made use of the operation of light to produce light-pictures, evanescent though they were, by means of silver-salts through patterns (negatives)." *

Herr Schiendl here gives two reasons for his view, but it is the latter, doubtless, on which he really relies. He can hardly mean that Schulze's discovery of the "light-sensitiveness of silver-salt" in itself made him the discoverer of photography, for that would imply that the discoverer of a fact is also the discoverer of whatever the knowledge of that fact may ultimately lead to. On this principle we might give the discoverer of photography to Porta, who invented the camera obscura three centuries ago; or, with equal reason, to whoever first noticed the fading of a curtain under sunlight. Substantially, Herr Schiendl's point is that Schulze "made use of the operation of light to produce light-pictures." But surely he did not do this. He clearly had no thought of producing a picture. His procedure was the converse of what is represented. He did not use the operation of light to produce the image of the word-pattern, but used the image of the word-pattern to show the operation of light. When he has got the image, or "negative," as Herr Schiendl calls it, by a startling anticipation of the language of a century later, he has no thought of preserving or repeating it. All he does is to destroy it. He shakes the bottle and it vanishes.

But Herr Schiendl cannot get rid of modern photographic ideas. He would seem even to suggest that Schulze tried to "fix" the image. For in a later page, referring to the sun-

---

* "Stencil-patterns" may perhaps represent Herr Schiendl's meaning His words are "um mittelst Silbersalzen durch Schablonen (Negative) Lichtbilder, wenn auch vergangliche, herzustellen."

pictures taken by Thomas Wedgwood, he says : "Schulze similarly produced silhouettes in 1727* on a light-sensitive silver-salt, and could not fix them, any more than Davy and Wedgwood."

Now not only does Schulze give no hint of trying to "fix" the image, but the form of the experiment shows that he could not have had any such idea. The image was on the surface of a liquid or semi-liquid substance—" the liquor," as he calls it—and any disturbance of the stuff at once dissipated the dis- colouration. One is inclined to ask, can Herr Schiendl have read the whole memoir, or only some misleading summary of it ? It is difficult to account for the almost angry language (emphasised by large type) with which he ends the chapter: "The priority, then, of discovery in getting light-pictures from silver-salts belongs indisputably to Schulze, and only an intentional mis-understanding and ignoring of the above adduced facts made it possible to throw doubt on his claim."

In spite of these strong words the extent of Schulze's work is clear. He certainly made a remarkable discovery, namely, the darkening effect of light upon silver-salts, and he did this about half a century before the time of Scheele, who is usually said to have first made known the fact. But more than this he did not do. Seventy years had to pass before Thomas Wedgwood tried to get light-pictures, and did get them, though he failed to fix them ; while more than a century elapsed from the time of Schulze's *Observation*, before Niépce, Daguerre, and Talbot created the art in a practical sense.

---

* Printed " 1737 " (evidently in error).

B

THE STORY OF PROFESSOR CHARLES'S SILHOUETTES

In many accounts of the origin of photography we find reference to a Professor Charles of Paris, who is said to have taken some kind of shadow-pictures or silhouettes of his pupils, as a lecture-room experiment, at some time about the beginning of the last century. The story is very vague, resting only on tradition, and it has been generally put aside by English writers as mythical or unimportant. But French writers treat it more seriously, and it has some interest, as being apparently (if true and assigned to a true date) the only trace of anything that can be represented as photographic work before the time of Wedgwood. I cannot find that any writer on the history of photography has examined it with care, and I will here put together such information about it as I have been able to collect.

First, as to who and what Charles was. There are notices of him in the "Biographie Universelle" (Michaud, Paris, vol. lx, 1836), in the "Biographie des Contemporains" (Levrault, Paris, 1834), and in the "Nouvelle Biographie Universelle" (F. Didot, vol. ix., 1854). His career is also described in an "Eloge Historique" delivered before the French Academy on July 16, 1828, by Baron Fourier, the mathematician, then Perpetual Secretary of the Academy. This is the fullest of the biographical accounts I have found, and from it, mainly, I take the following summary:

Jacques Alexandre César Charles was born at Beaugency, November 12, 1746. He first distinguished himself in literary studies, then cultivated music and the fine arts. He had for a long time a modest clerkship in the Office of the Ministry of Finance. This post being suppressed, he retired with a fair pension and thus got the free disposal of his time. It was when Franklin's discoveries in electricity were astonishing the world. Charles took up natural science, and soon became a successful public lecturer on physics. His lectures, given in the Louvre, drew large and brilliant audiences, and he "had the same success for thirty years." He was celebrated for his striking experiments ; he "aimed at exciting attention by the grandeur and intensity of his results " ; in microscopical experiments he used enormous enlargements ; in lectures on electricity "il foudroyait un animal." Among his hearers were Volta and Franklin. Then came (1783) the Montgolfiers' discovery of ballooning. Charles took a leading part in the early ascents, and it was he who suggested using hydrogen gas to fill the balloon (the method still practised), as an improvement on the Montgolfiers' plan of heating atmospheric air. Fourier gives details of his ascents. He must have been a man of enterprise and courage, for he was actually the first man who ventured to ascend, alone, in a free balloon.* One day he had a curious experience. A man came to see him who professed to have made discoveries in physics and to have proved that certain theories of Sir Isaac Newton were wrong. Charles and his visitor got into a lively discussion ; the visitor became angry, and in a fit of rage drew a sword and rushed at the Professor. Charles was unarmed, but seized his assailant, threw him down and broke his sword. The man fainted and had to be carried home. This fiery person was Marat, afterwards the terrible revolutionary leader. On the famous August 10, 1792, the Tuileries were invaded by the Paris mob, who found their way to Charles's laboratory. He was surrounded by a raging multitude, but

---

* See article Aërostation in " Encyc. Brit."

saved himself by telling them he was the Charles of the balloon ascents, pointing to the car which hung from the ceiling.

Fourier says he cannot give a full enumeration of Charles's many researches. He mentions his " Megascope " and his important experiments on the dilatation of gas. It is by the result of these (" Charles's law ") that his name is still known to students of physics. " To get an idea," says Fourier, " of his work and talents, one should consult the many reports in which he took part." He was " Librarian of the Royal Institute," at what time Fourier does not say. The " Biog. Univ." says he became member of the Academy in 1795, " and then Librarian of the Society." The " Nouvelle Biog. Univ." gives 1785 as the date of his becoming a member of the Academy. The same notice says that he wrote very little, and that in Biot's " Traité de Physique Expérimentale " nearly all his work (presque tous ses travaux) had been transmitted to us. This article mentions various observations of his as to electricity, gases, lightning-conductors, optics, acoustics, &c., but has no reference to the silhouettes, nor can I find in the above work of Biot any allusion to Charles in connection with the effect of light on chemicals.

The " Biog. des Contemporains " (1834) says he wrote little about science—" quelques mémoires imprimés dans les recueils de l'Académie des Sciences," and some mathematical articles in the " Encyclopédie Méthodique," are his only works ; also, that he gave courses of lectures in physics at the Louvre up to the time of the Revolution (" jusqu'à l'époque de la Révolution "). None of the above notices refer to the silhouettes. The earliest mention of these which I have found is that by Arago, in the famous discourse given before the French Academy of Sciences in 1839, on the occasion when, as representative of the scientific commission which had recommended the national grants to Daguerre and to Isidore Niépce, he gave to the world the particulars of the Daguerre-Niépce method. In this address, after referring to previous speculations and discoveries bearing on the subject, Porta's " camera obscura," the attempts of the alchymists, &c., Arago says (I italicise in this and other quotations the more important phrases) :

"Ces applications de la si curieuse propriété du chlorure d'argent, découverte par les anciens alchymistes, semblaient devoir s'être présentées d'elles-mêmes et de bonne heure ; mais ce n'est pas ainsi que procède l'esprit humain. Il nous faudra descendre jusqu'aux *premières années du dix-neuvième siècle* pour trouver les premières traces de l'art photographique. Alors Charles, notre compatriote, se servira, dans ses discours, d'un *papier enduit pour engendrer des silhouettes à l'aide de l'action lumineuse.* Charles *est mort sans décrire la préparation* dont il faisait usage ; et comme, sous peine de tomber dans le plus inextricable confusion, l'historien des sciences ne doit s'appuyer que sur des documents imprimés, authentiques, il est de toute justice de faire remonter *les premières linéaments du nouvel art* à un Mémoire de *Wedgwood*," and he goes on to describe and quote from the account of Wedgwood's discovery published in the *Journal of the Royal Institution* for June 1802.

A later allusion to Charles is found in a tract by Arago, entitled "Le Daguerreotype," printed in vol. vii. of his complete works. This is apparently a reprint of a former publication, but no date or title-page is given to show when the original appeared. From internal evidence, I infer it to have been written at some date near 1850. It is an account of the discoveries of Niépce and Daguerre. In a chapter entitled, "Examen de quelques réclamations de priorité," he discusses the priority-claim made by Fox Talbot, and in this he says : "La première idée de *fixer les images de la chambre obscure ou du microscope solaire* sur certaines substances chimiques, n'appartient ni à M. Daguerre ni à M. Talbot. M. Charles, de l'Académie des Sciences, qui faisait des silhouettes dans ses cours publics, à précédé M. Wedgwood. Les premiers essais de M. Niépce pour perfectionner le procédé de M. Charles ou de M. Wedgwood sont de 1814." In section xv. of this tract Arago says : "Je me suis attaché, dans cette notice, à démontrer que la photographie est une invention complétement française," adding that Talbot has undeniably the credit of a large share in the invention of processes for taking photographs on paper. This variation by Arago of his earlier account is singular. In 1839 he put Charles's experiments in the first years of the last century, and gave no hint of his using the camera. One would like to know what led him afterwards to say Charles " preceded Wedgwood," which must mean did his experiments before 1802, the date of publication of Wedgwood's discovery. One cannot help noticing that the latter statement is in a paper the declared object of which was to show that photography was wholly a French invention. It would have been more satisfactory if he had given some indication of the actual date, instead of the loose phrase, " preceded Wedgwood." But this later account, apart from any question of the date of the experiment, gives a wholly new turn to the story. It would seem to imply that Charles used both the camera and the solar microscope, and also that he tried to " fix " his pictures. The earlier statement merely says he used a prepared paper to make silhouettes. Now, if the " silhouette " of the tradition means, as surely it must, a *shadow*-picture thrown on the paper by the head of the sitter,* Charles could not have used a camera. For with the camera, as we all know, it is not the interception of light, but the light proceeding from the object, that produces the image. On this point Arago's later version seems to be quite unintelligible. And if the tradition he mentioned in 1839 included anything as to the use of a camera, or as to " fixing the image," it was surely most strange that he should then have said nothing as to these important details. The Charles story may be said now to rest upon Arago's statements as to the tradition existing in his time, and it is unlucky that these statements were so lacking in precision. That Arago could be careless even when he was specially bound to be accurate, for his business in 1839 was to set forth the grounds for a grant of public money, is shown by his confusing Tom

---

* See quotation, *infra*, from M. Tissandier.

Wedgwood with his father, the potter. If he had looked at the "Biographie Universelle," it would have told him that Josiah, the father, had died seven years before the date of the Memoir from which he was quoting.

Blanquart-Evrard's "Traité de Photographie sur Papier" (Paris, 1851) has an introductory sketch of the history of photography by George Ville. In this we read :

"La photographie est une découverte française." . . . "Elle est l'œuvre de deux hommes (Niépce et Daguerre)." . . . "L'idée de mettre à profit la propriété que possède la chlorure d'argent de noircir à la lumière, pour copier des dessins, et *fixer l'image de la chambre noire*, n'est pas venue pour la première fois à MM. Niépce et Daguerre. Déjà, Charles, physicien français, l'employait dans les cours qu'il faisait au Louvre, *il y a plus d'un demi-siècle* (this would mean before 1801), pour produire des silhouettes au moyen de la lumière. Wedgwood, le Palissy de l'Angleterre, l'avait employé de son côté pour copier des vitraux d'église, et Sir H. Davy, pour fixer l'image de la chambre noire." The time here indicated agrees with that mentioned by Arago in 1839, while the phraseology and the blunder as to the two Wedgwoods suggest that the writer is virtually copying from Arago's later account.

But the mention of chloride of silver does not accord with Arago's statement that Charles left no record of his method.

In a later book of M. Blanquart-Evrard, "La Photographie, ses origines, ses transformations" (Lille, 1870), we find yet a new account of Charles. Here, after mentioning Scheele's researches on the operations of light (1777), the writer says : "*Quelques années plus tard, vers* 1780, le Professeur Charles à exécuté, dans son cours public à Paris, le portrait en silhouette de ses élèves." . . . "Vers le même temps, mais un peu plus tard, un industriel Anglais, Wedgwood [again confusion of son and father], obtenait de son côté de pareils résultats ; " and he refers to Davy's Memoir of 1802. This is the earliest mention I have found of 1780 as the date of Charles's experiments. No authority is quoted for it.

In " La Photographie," by Mayer and Pierson (Paris, 1862), Charles is mentioned in connection with Wedgwood. "Charles, le professeur populaire, obtenait rapidement dans ses séances un grand nombre de silhouettes tracées en noir sur un papier enduit, *pour éprouver l'action lumineuse,* mais il mourut sans faire connaître le secret de sa préparation." It is added that "La couleur violacée pourrait faire croire à l'emploi de l'iode. L'ingénieux Wedgwood cherche aussi à utiliser cette singulière propriété que posséde la nitrate d'argent, etc." This account agrees with Arago's early version of the tradition, ignoring the later amplifications, but the addition of the surmise as to iodine is new. This substance was not discovered till well on in the nineteenth century.

The story of the silhouettes is set out at greater length in a book entitled " A History and Handbook of Photography," translated from the French of Gaston Tissandier, and edited by J. Thomson, F.R.G.S. (London: Sampson Low, 1876).* " About the year 1780, Professor Charles, the inventor of the hydrogen gas balloon, made the first use of the dark room for attempting to produce rudimentary photographs. By means of a strong solar ray, he projected a shadow of the head of one of his pupils on to a sheet of white paper which had previously been soaked in a solution of chloride of silver. Under the influence of the light it was not long in becoming black in the parts exposed, remaining white on that portion of the sheet which had been shaded, and then giving a faithful silhouette of the person's head in white on a black ground." A picture of the supposed scene in the lecture-room is given, which (says a footnote) "is based on the rather vague and incomplete accounts which were given of it at the time of its exhibition by Professor Charles." The picture represents a room, in one wall of which is a circular hole about a foot in diameter, through which streams horizontally a cylinder-shaped beam of light of

* I do not find the original book in the British Museum, and therefore quote from the translation.

the same diameter, so as to illuminate a screen. (This state of
things would imply either that the sun was on the horizon or
that a mirror was used.) Part of the light is intercepted by
the head of a sitting figure, thus throwing a shadow on the
illuminated disk. "The sheet of paper was passed from hand
to hand . . . but soon the light blackened it, and the profile
disappeared little by little as though blotted with ink. Professor Charles also reproduced, roughly, it is true, some engravings which he placed on a sensitised paper. The details of this
experiment are, however, for the most part, wanting in the
historical documents relating to his works. Wedgwood, a
clever English scientist, made a similar experiment to Professor Charles; he projected the image of the dark room on to
a sheet of paper similarly sensitised, and obtained a rough picture, which could only be preserved in the dark. In 1802
Wedgwood and Sir H. Davy published a remarkable treatise
on the reproduction of objects by light."*   There is a great air
of particularity about this account, but it gives no authority
for the additions made to the tradition reported by Arago,
namely, the mention of the chemical used and the alleged
reproduction of engravings. It is difficult, moreover, to understand M. Tissandier's account of what was done. He says
Charles made use of the dark room to produce his rudimentary
photographs. "Chambre obscure" (dark room) is the usual
French equivalent of "camera obscura." The experiment is
pictured as made in a darkened room, but the process is not
that of the camera. And one naturally asks, What or where
are the "historical documents relating to Charles's works," and
the "incomplete accounts given at the time?" These
phrases are virtually a confession that the story is a tradition
only ; for if M. Tissandier had known of such accounts, however incomplete, he surely would have quoted or referred to

---

* The words, "published a remarkable treatise, &c." are absurdly
inapplicable to Davy's dry little report in four or five pages, of
Wedgwood's experiment. We may be pretty sure M. Tissandier
never saw the "treatise."

them, instead of giving pages of hypothetical description. What he says as to Wedgwood is so hopelessly wrong that we cannot attach any weight to what he says about Charles. He represents Wedgwood as obtaining a rough picture by means of a camera, while we know Wedgwood failed to get any image from the camera. It is significant that in a later edition of the same book (1878) the translator and editor, in a chapter added by himself, says: "The story of the heliographic researches of Charles is altogether too vague and improbable to be taken into serious account."

Fabre's " Traité Encyclopédique de la Photographie " (Paris, 1889) says : " En 1780 le physicien Charles, dans ses cours du Louvre, dessinait les silhouettes sur papier recouvert de chlorure d'argent." This is a book which quotes authorities, and a footnote here mentions Blanquart-Evrard's book, " La Photographie, ses origines, etc. Lille, 1870," as to which see above.

Schiendl, in his "Geschichte der Photographie," 1891, gives 1780 as the date when Charles took his silhouettes " prepared with chloride of silver," but the authority he quotes is Fabre's book just mentioned, adding that Fabre's authority is Blanquart-Evrard's book, " La Photographie, etc., 1870," quoted above. This seems to show that neither Herr Schiendl, whose book indicates very wide research, nor Fabre, had found any earlier or better authority for the date 1780, or for the mention of chloride of silver, than the statement of Blanquart-Evrard.

Dr. Eder, in his important " History of Photochemistry and Photography " (Halle, 1891), quotes Arago's statement of 1839, but his verdict is, " The statement that Charles obtained silhouettes independently of, or before, Wedgwood is without foundation (entbehrt jeder Begrundung)." He points out the vagueness of Arago's phrase, " first years of the 19th century," and suggests that Charles, who was a member and librarian of the Academy of Sciences, and lived till 1823, may well have read the account of Wedgwood's experiments, published in 1802, and have taken from it the idea of the experiment shown to his class.

The English writers on Photography whom I have consulted treat the story of the silhouettes as of no account, as being purely traditional, but we cannot expect English books to tell us much in a case in which evidence could be looked for only from France. Robert Hunt, in his "Researches on Heat and Light," a work of authority in its time (1844), a time very near that of the discussions of 1839 on the beginnings of Photography, notices Charles thus : "This" (the account of Wedgwood's work published in 1802) "*was certainly the first published account of any attempt to produce images by the decomposing power of light.* It does, indeed, appear that, nearly about the same time, M. Charles in his lectures at Paris proposed to make use of a prepared paper to produce black profiles by the action of light, but he died without disclosing the preparation which he employed ; indeed, his countryman, the Abbé Moigno, admits that Charles 'left no authentic document to attest his discovery.'"

Mr. W. Jerome Harrison, in his "History of Photography," mentions the story of the silhouettes, but adds, "This statement is a mere tradition, and the best authorities have considered it 'too vague and improbable to be taken into serious account.'"

This review seems to show that no better authority for the story of the silhouettes has been brought forward than the statement of Arago in 1839, and that the only discoverable authority for the date 1780 is a statement given, without any supporting evidence, by M. Blanquart-Evrard. It must be remembered that Arago, whether he was accurate or not, had exceptional opportunities of knowing what was to be known on the matter. He was a foremost figure in the French scientific world. As Secretary of the Academy of Sciences he had at his command the Academy records, and we may presume that he had looked to see what they showed upon this subject. He not only says he knew of no record left by Charles, but asserts that Charles left none. He must have known Charles personally, and was writing only sixteen years after his death. It seems very improbable that any valid evidence should have been in existence for the date 1780, or for the accounts of the chemical used, and that this evidence should have been unknown to him. That Charles was lecturing "vers 1780" may be taken as probable, if not certain. His connection with the balloon ascents, and the adventure with Marat, point to a date before 1789. But if he lectured for thirty years (as Fourier asserts), the date of the lecturing would not show anything as to the date of the silhouette experiments; while it is easy to understand that an oral tradition might confuse one date with the other. If this point were worth further investigation, possibly a search among pre-revolution French newspapers might yield some evidence.

But, supposing the story of the silhouettes to be true, the question remains, has it any significance in regard to the history of photography? Was the experiment photographic, that is, photographic in intent? There is nothing to show that it was. It is much more simple to regard it as done only "pour éprouver," as MM. Mayer et Pierson say, "l'action lumineuse." It was a way of making pupils seize the already well-known fact that light has a darkening effect on certain substances. Charles, we know, took pains to get vivid illustrations, and this was just the kind of experiment to stick in the memory of an audience. It is, of course, possible that, after showing them the silhouettes, he went on to tell them that some means might conceivably be found of stopping the after-action of light on the space which remained white, and that if this could be done the silhouette would remain as a permanent profile portrait. If he said anything like this, and if he actually tried to get a "fixing" process, he was to that extent a photographer. If not, the idea of photography was not there; it was only an illustration of a known fact in photochemistry. But our most trustworthy report of the tradition gives no hint of his trying to fix the silhouette, or of his using the camera. This last point is important, for, if Charles had had in his mind the possibility of getting pictures of objects, he could hardly have failed to think of the camera, the familiar picture-making machine. If he told his class that what he showed them was a first step towards actually getting portraits by the mere operation of light it is difficult to imagine how an idea so new, so startling, so interesting to the common world, put forward by a man· who was, *quâ* lecturer, the Tyndall or Faraday of the Paris of his time, could have made so little stir as not to be noticed in any record of his life, or leave any trace beyond the vague tradition known to us. These considerations add force to Dr. Eder's supposition that the experiment was shown after 1802, and was suggested by a reading of the Davy Memoir. The volume containing that Memoir may well have been sent to the Paris Academy, of which Charles was (at some time) the Librarian. Arago evidently had it before him in 1839.

It is, of course, perfectly easy to account for the existence of the tradition without supposing that the experiment had any photographic meaning. For, on the announcement to the world in 1839 of Daguerre's method of applying the decomposing power of light to the making of pictures, nothing would be more likely than that people who had witnessed or heard of Charles's illustration of that fundamental fact should be reminded of his experiment, and should see in it, by the light of later knowledge, a significance which he himself had not given it.

My conclusions on the matter are these : from the nature of the case they can but be put in the language of probabilities :

1. The story of the silhouettes has probably a foundation in fact, though no record has been produced, contemporary or other, to show when the experiments were made, what was their object, or what method and materials were employed.

2. The assignment of the early date, 1780, would appear to rest on the unsupported statement of one author, writing nearly a century after that time.

3. There is no good reason for supposing that the experiments, if made, were photographic in character or intention, and it is not at all probable that they were so.

4. Assuming that they might have been photographic in character, no evidence has been adduced to refute the supposition

that they were prompted by the account published in 1802 of Thomas Wedgwood's work.

Thus there seems to be no solid ground for treating the story as relevant to the history of photography. It will probably remain an unverified tradition, as it is hardly likely that any one will think it worth while to search for documentary evidence of its truth.

A MYTHICAL ACCOUNT OF T. WEDG-WOOD'S PHOTOGRAPHIC WORK

THE story which, as mentioned in the preface, was put forward by Miss Meteyard in her book, called " A Group of English-men " (1872), and which has confused · the true story of Wedgwood's work by representing that he did what he certainly did not do, is in effect the same as had, some years earlier, made a stir among English photographers, and had been then proved to be a myth. It was known as the " story of the early photo-graphs," and was discussed at many meetings of photographers, of which reports may be found in the *Photographic News* and *Photographic Journal* of the years 1863 and 1864.

Miss Meteyard maintains that two photographs on paper, of which she gives engravings, one called a " Breakfast Table Scene," in her "Life of Josiah Wedgwood" (vol. ii. 585), and another called " A Savoyard Piper," which she makes the frontispiece of the " Group of Englishmen," were done by him in the years 1791–93. This is, of course, absolutely impossible in face of two facts clearly set forth by Davy in the paper of 1802 : First, that all Wedgwood's pictures faded away after a short exposure to light; secondly, that images formed by means of a camera obscura " were found too faint to produce in any moderate time an effect upon the nitrate of silver." The " Breakfast Table " picture must obviously have been made by means of a camera, and according to Miss Meteyard it was permanent enough to be copied by an engraver some seventy years after it was taken. There is nothing in the engraving of the "Savoyard Paper" to show that it was taken from a photograph, but if it was, the photograph could not have been Wedgwood's.

In the discussions of 1863 an attempt was made to show that the art had been invented, in the full sense of the term, about 1790–1800, or about forty or fifty years before the era of Niépce, Daguerre, and Talbot. It was said that, in clearing out some rooms at Messrs. Boulton and Watt's works at Soho, near Birmingham, there had been discovered two views on metal plates, showing a house at Soho, which views could be proved to have been taken before 1791 ; and that a camera had also been found whereby such pictures had been or might have been taken. There had been found also certain large coloured pictures of about the same date, which were copies of well-known paintings, evidently not done by hand, and these, too, were said to be photographic. All these various pictures were shown at meetings of the Photographic Society. The story was evidently put forward in good faith and at first was widely believed. The *Saturday Review* discussed it at length, and spoke of the "chain of evidence" as "nearly complete." But before long the so-called evidence proved to be worthless. The big coloured pictures, though the method of their production was a puzzle, were certainly not photographic. The two views of the house at Soho were admitted to be daguerreotypes, but the evidence for the early date went to pieces when carefully examined. As to the two alleged Wedgwoodian photos, no proof of date or authorship was offered beyond Miss Meteyard's statement that she had evidence to show they were Wedgwood's ; which evidence, it was said, *would appear in the forthcoming life of his father*. At the meeting of the Society on November 3, 1863, there was read a letter from her saying : "You may with safety put Wedgwood's experiments in 1790–1791," &c. At a later meeting, however (January 5, 1864), the secretary showed an old photograph belonging to himself, done by Mr. Fox Talbot about 1841, which corresponded exactly with that entitled by Miss Meteyard "The Breakfast Table at Etruria Hall, 1791." As this photograph showed a collection of twenty or thirty separate objects, cups and saucers, spoons, teapot, &c., disposed about a table, the existence of two views of the scene, exactly similar and yet of independent origin, would have been simply impossible. This evidence was confirmed by a letter from Mr. Fox Talbot, saying that he had taken the view at Lacock Abbey (where he lived), and that, no doubt, copies would be found there. These copies have since been found *—as also has the negative. No attempt was made to disprove the attribution of this picture to Mr. Talbot, nor was the origin of the "Savoyard Piper" explained.

The "story of the early photographs" was thus completely disposed of in 1864. But in 1866 it reappeared in Miss Meteyard's "Life of Josiah Wedgwood." She there described "The Breakfast Table" as an "Early Photograph by Thomas Wedgwood (Mayer Collection)," but of the promised evidence of authenticity there was not a word, not even a word to suggest that the origin of the picture had been questioned. Five years later, in 1871, she brought out her "Group of Englishmen." And again in that volume the exploded story was still more emphatically reasserted. An engraving of "The Savoyard Piper" there figures as the frontispiece, and is called a "facsimile of the earliest known heliotype, or sun-picture, taken by the Inventor of Photography, Thomas Wedgwood, 1791–93." But again no evidence is offered. We are only told that "Mr. Mayer derived it from an undoubted source," that "many of these 'heliotypes' were, it is said, scattered at one time about the Potteries"; that its "authenticity is undoubted," and that as the earliest known specimen of photography it is "considered to be of great value." It is curious that in both the volumes containing these statements there are

* I have seen one of them, kindly sent me by Mr. Fox Talbot's son.—R. B. L.

allusions which show that the authoress knew of the discussions of 1863–64. She alludes (Life, ii. 5) to the "Soho pictures," and in the "Group of Englishmen" the "Savoyard Piper" is mentioned as having been "shown at a meeting of the Photographic Society." It is not easy to imagine how she could have put the story into her books without taking the trouble to ascertain the issue of the discussions to which she herself had contributed materials. Such carelessness is nearly inconceivable; and yet one shrinks from supposing her to have been simply mendacious.

It may be worth while to mention here another theory which has found its way into books about Photography, and which was also started by Miss Meteyard. It purports to connect Daguerre's discovery with Tom Wedgwood's silver pictures, and turns on a guess that one Dominique Daguerre, a Paris shopkeeper or trader, who was (undoubtedly) old Josiah Wedgwood's agent, may have been the father of Louis Daguerre, the inventor of the Daguerreotype process. The guess is based entirely on the coincidence that the inventor and the agent had the same surname. Her "chain of evidence" is as follows: Daguerre, the agent, was once or oftener in London. "There is reason to think—indeed there is a tradition to the effect—that he visited Etruria, as was customary with most foreigners, and whilst there he probably witnessed some of T. Wedgwood's experiments on light and heat" (G. of E., p. 50). In a later page (157) this guess or probability appears as a fact: "Daguerre's son, who was with him in his visits to Etruria in 1791 and 1793, was about 20 or 21 years old in 1802. If he inherited his father's tastes, we may reasonably conclude that he was one and the same with the M. Daguerre who in 1824 improved the heliotype process . . . . and he may have been led to these researches either through memory of what he had seen or heard of T. Wedgwood's experiments."

This theory, which rests, as Miss M.'s words show, only on a series of guesses, is at once disposed of by the fact that Daguerre, the inventor, was born in 1787. If, therefore, he was the agent's son who "probably" heard of or saw Wedgwood's experiments in 1791 or 1793, he had developed a taste for physical science, and accompanied his father on business tours, when a babe of four or six years old! and if in 1802 the agent's son was "20 or 21 years of age," he must have been born in 1781 or 1782, or at least five years before the inventor. The biographical dictionaries do not give Louis Daguerre's parentage, but in a book written by M. Mentienne, Mayor of the place (Bry) where he died, what is said about his father could hardly apply to a Paris shopkeeper. The father was a rural functionary, "huissier of the bailliage of Cormeilles," and afterwards (1792) moved to Orleans, where he was employed on the crown domains.*

---

* "La Découverte de la Photographie en 1839." Paris, 1892.

D

ON SOME NOTICES OF TOM WEDGWOOD IN HISTORIES OF PHOTOGRAPHY

I GIVE here, by way of supplement to my account of Wedgwood's Photographic work, some notes on what is said about him by well-known writers on the subject. The earliest (known to me) of such notices, that by Arago (1839), has already been mentioned.

Dr. Eder, in his important History,* says : " The invention of photography on paper and leather by Wedgwood dates from the year 1802 [referring to Davy's Memoir of that year]. Many authors give this year as that of the invention of photography generally, which I, having regard to Schulze (1727), cannot admit." (As to Schulze, see Appendix A.) Dr. Eder points out that the work described in the Davy Memoir (which he summarises) should not be attributed, as it is by some writers, to Wedgwood and Davy, the latter having only described Wedgwood's experiments and furnished an Appendix. He considers Arago to have been wrong when, in his memoir laid before the French Academy in 1839, " he proclaimed these two men as the inventors of photography," though he (Dr. Eder) places them " in the rank of those enquirers in the province of

* "Geschichte der Photochemie und Photographie von Alterthume bis in die Gegenwart," von Dr. Josef Maria Eder, Direktor der K. K. Lehr und Versuchsanstalt für Photographie in Wien, &c. &c. Halle, a S. Wilhelm Krapp, 1891.

photo-chemistry who develop facts already known in a more or less new direction with more or less deep research (welche schon bekannte Thatsachen in einer mehr oder weniger tiefen Vorstudium weiter ausbildeten)." These last words seem to be a fair description of Wedgwood's work, but surely they are equivalent to saying that he was an inventor, though he left his invention incomplete ; for do not most inventions—nearly all, perhaps—consist in the application of known facts to new purposes ?

Dr. Eder mentions that Wedgwood's experiments became known in Germany in 1803, and from a reference made by Herr Schiendel I gather that Davy's account appeared in Gilbert's "Annalen" as early as 1811.

In Herr Schiendel's History* the notice of Wedgwood begins as follows : "In the year 1802 Wedgwood appears to have received a suggestion from a scientific society existing in Birmingham that called itself the ' Lunatic Society,' for making an attempt to copy pictures and drawings on glass, and to produce silhouettes in the same manner." (Im Jahre 1802, scheint Wedgwood von einer in Birmingham existirenden wissenschaftlichen Gesellschaft, die sich ' Lunatic Society ' nannte, die Anregung erhalten zu haben, Versuchte anzustellen, Gemalde und Zeichnungen mittelst Silbersalzen auf Glas zu copiren und auf ähnliche Weise Silhouetten zu erzeugen.) Herr Schiendel does not quote any authority for this story, and I know of no foundation for it. Dr. Eder also alludes to it, but doubtfully. He refers in a note (p. 60) to the tale of the "early photographs" current in 1863 and 1864, whence I conjecture that the supposed intervention of the society was part of that myth.

The word " Lunatic," which Herr Schiendel naturally thinks an odd epithet to be applied to men like Watt and Priestley, should be " Lunar." The reference is to a group of private friends, living about Birmingham and in the neighbouring

---

* " Geschichte der Photographie," von C. Schiendel. Wien, Hartlebeas, 1891.

counties, who were in the habit of spending a day together once a month at one or other of their houses in succession. Among them were James Watt, Boulton, Captain Keir the chemist, Dr. Erasmus Darwin, Priestley, Samuel Galton, Dr. Withering the botanist, and one or two more. Herschell the astronomer, Edgeworth, Sir Joseph Banks, and others are mentioned as having been occasional visitors. The meetings were held at or near the full moon, doubtless in view of the considerable distances which some of the party had to ride or drive, whence came the word " Lunar." * I do not know of anything to connect the Society with Tom Wedgwood (who was from thirty to forty years younger than most of the group), except the facts that most, if not all, were friends of his father, and that Tom corresponded with Priestley and Keir about his experiments on heat and light. Whatever be the origin of the story, it has a very apocryphal look. No one who knew the facts could have described the " Lunar " friends as a " Scientific Society existing in Birmingham," and the statement that the Society prompted Wedgwood to an attempt trying to " copy pictures *on glass*," an attempt which he did *not* make, must surely have arisen from a mis-reading of the ambiguous title of Davy's " account."

Herr Schiendel refers to the account as published after Wedgwood's death, a mistake which I suppose arises from his confusing the photographer with his father, the potter, who had died in 1795. Like Dr. Eder, he insists that Schulze was the real inventor of Photography, a view which I think is conclusively refuted by Schulze's own Memoir (Appendix A). He refers, as does Dr. Eder, to Beccarius and Scheele as " predecessors " of Wedgwood and Davy—a vague phrase, which might lead readers to suppose that these earlier physicists aimed at turning the facts they were investigating to some *graphic* use. This, as far as I can ascertain, was not the case. Priestley, in

---

* A lively account of the " Lunar Meetings " is given in the autobiography of Mrs. Schimmelpenninck, a daughter of Samuel Galton.

his "History and Present State of Discoveries relating to Vision, Light, and Colours" (1772), gives an account of the observations of Beccarius,* Scheele, Schulze, and others, but says nothing to show that any of their experiments were directed towards obtaining a representation of an object. Dr. Eder writes (p. 62) : "Schulze and Beccarius showed that, by patterns applied to opaque substances, writings and drawings can be copied on chloride of silver exposed to light" (dass man durch aufgelegte Schablonen aus undurchsichtigen Stoffen, Schriften und Zeichnungen auf Chlorsilber im Lichte copiren kann). But on referring to the Commentaries of the Bolognese Academy, which Dr. Eder quotes as his authority as far as relates to Beccarius (with date 1757), I find nothing there to fit such a description of his work: The experiments described relate to the effect of light on various substances, and the one in which its darkening effect on luna cornea is shown is very like Schulze's "Observation," including the artifice of sticking a piece of black paper on the side of the glass : but I find nowhere a word as to copying either patterns, or writings, or engravings, or anything else.†

I notice this apparent error of Dr. Eder's because, occurring in a work of high authority, it has probably misled other writers. In many of the histories of photography, especially the more popular books, one meets with loose statements as to the earlier physicists whose observations prepared the way for the art, without any attempt to distinguish between photo*chemical* and photo*graphic* experiments. I find, for instance, in one of these

---

* James Bartholomew Beccaria of Bologna, not, as Dr. Eder and Herr Schiendel call him, John Baptist Beccaria, Professor of Physics at Turin.

† Vol. iv. of the "Commentaries" (pp. 84–87) has an account of experiments by Beccarius and Bonzi on the effects of light on various substances. The heading is "De vi quam ipsa per se lux habet non colores modo, sed etiam texturam rerum salvis interdum coloribus, immutandi." These "Commentaries" include a number of tracts or papers by different writers or editors. The only one I find by Beccarius himself is one on phosphorescents : "De quam plurimis phosphoris nunc primum detectis." Tom 2, pars altera, p. 136.

popular histories (after an account of the invention of the camera obscura) a chapter beginning: "Nothing further appears to have been done in photography until T. Wedgwood, a son of the famous potter, *took up the subject.*" These last words are wholly misleading. Before Wedgwood "the subject" did not exist, no one, so far as we yet know, having thrown out the idea of making a picture by means of light.

E

AS TO WEDGWOOD'S DISCOVERY (p. 19) OF THE FACT THAT SOLID BODIES HAVE THE SAME TEMPERATURE AT THE POINT OF INCANDESCENCE

I HAVE not succeeded in finding any definite statement as to when, or through whom, this fact first became known. A paper by Professor Draper, of New York, printed in the *Philosophical Magazine* for 1847 (vol. 30, p. 345), contains expressions which seem to imply his belief that Thomas Wedgwood was in effect the discoverer of the law, whereof that paper was apparently intended to give a complete proof. Draper describes its objects thus :

1. To determine the point of incandescence of platinum and to prove that different bodies become red hot at the same temperature.

2. To determine the colour of the rays emitted by luminous bodies at different temperatures.

3. To determine the relation between the brilliance of the light and the temperature.

After describing some experiments which led him to put the temperature of incandescence at 977°, he says : " Against the No. 977° it may also be objected that antimony melts at a much lower temperature and yet emits light before it fuses. If this statement were true it would lead us to believe that all bodies have not the same point of incandescence. But I think the experiments of Mr. Wedgwood on gold and earthenware are decisive on that point ; and moreover, I have reason to believe that the melting-point of antimony is much higher than is commonly supposed."

In his preamble, Draper says : "Sir I. Newton fixed the temperature at which bodies become self-luminous at 635°, Sir H. Davy at 812°, Mr. Wedgwood at 947°, Mr. Daniel at 900°." Draper seems to be here confusing the two Wedgwoods, father and son. It was Josiah, the father, who, in a paper on his "Pyrometer," in the *Phil. Trans.* for 1784, gave a table of comparative temperatures, one entry wherein is "red heat fully visible in the dark 947°." If he had meant by this that all bodies become luminous at that temperature, his son certainly would not have used the language we find in his paper of eight years later. I have not discovered where it is that Newton makes the statement Draper ascribes to him. It is not in his "Scala graduum caloris" given in the *Phil. Trans.* for 1701.

A paper by Professor Kirchhoff in *Pogg. Ann.*, vol. 109, translated in *Phil. Mag.* for July 1860, on the relation between the radiating and absorbing powers of different bodies for light and heat, gives a more general treatment of the subject, extending, so far as I understand it, the law indicated by T. Wedgwood, and applying high mathematics to the problem. One of Kirchhoff's conclusions is thus expressed : "It follows that all bodies, when their temperature is gradually raised, begin to emit waves of the same length at the same temperature, and therefore become red hot at the same temperature, emit yellow rays at the same temperature, &c."

From all that I can learn on the matter, I infer that we may regard T. Wedgwood as the discoverer of this curious and important physical law.

F

PRIESTLEY IN AMERICA (P. 28)

PRIESTLEY's move to America was in 1794, just at the time when Coleridge, Lovell, and Southey were hatching the famous Pantisocracy scheme which was to "realize the age of reason" on the banks of the Susquehanna. They were hoping the philosopher would join them, but he set up his household gods at Northumberland, a little town or village in Pennsylvania.

> "Lo! Priestley there, patriot and saint and sage,
> Him, full of years from his loved native land,
> Statesmen bloodstained and priests idolatrous,
> By dark lies maddening the blind multitude,
> Drove with vain hate."
>
> (*Religious Musings.*)

This is Coleridge's fiery account of Priestley's exile, written in 1794, when he was in the white heat of his young revolutionary fervour. But it is curious, when we turn to Priestley's letters to his neighbours at Northumberland, to find him enlarging on the rancorous vehemence with which he was maligned and attacked in that land of freedom. Pennsylvania, equally with Warwickshire, had its "priests idolatrous," who "maddened the blind multitude" against the "saint and sage." "At a Baptist Chapel," we read, "the minister burst out and bade the people beware, for 'a Priestley had entered the land'; then, crouching in a worshipping attitude, exclaimed, 'Oh! Lamb of God, how they would pluck Thee from Thy Throne.'" (Life by Rutt, ii. 263.)

G

THE COLERIDGE ANNUITY—ITS AFTER-HISTORY

A CIRCUMSTANCE in the after-history of the annuity has been made the subject of speculation and criticism by various writers, for which reason I think it well to notice it here, though it occurred some years after T. Wedgwood's death. He bequeathed to Coleridge an annuity of £75 a year, being one half of the £150. No part of the annuity had previously been settled legally upon him. Mr. Dykes Campbell's statement that Tom's half had been so settled is an error. This is clearly shown by the language of the will. Moreover, there was no mode in which such a promise *could* have been made legally enforceable, in the absence of what lawyers call a " valuable consideration." This fact had been ascertained by T. W. in the case of the annuity which he gave to Leslie, and that promise was therefore embodied in a simple letter, which left it binding in honour though not in law. Josiah Wedgwood, indeed, in his letter of January 1798, alludes to " securing " the annuity to Coleridge, but by this he can only have meant arranging for its payment through a bank or otherwise. The brothers cannot have forgotten what passed in the Leslie case about a year previously.

Thus, after T. W.'s death, Coleridge received £75 a year from Tom's executors up to the time of his death in 1834. But at some time near the end of 1812 Josiah ceased paying the £75 a year which he had theretofore been paying on his own account. It is not known what reasons led him to do this, or what, if anything, passed between him and Coleridge on the subject. Nothing has transpired to suggest that Coleridge ever made any objection or remonstrance. A long and effusive letter of his to Poole (Feb. 13, 1813 : Letters, p. 611) is not only free from any trace of resentment or complaint, but overflows with expression of love and gratitude towards Josiah.

Josiah's act has been criticised as having the appearance of a breach of the promise made in the letter of January 1798 (p. 55). That view, however, rests on a strained interpretation of the language of the letter—an interpretation inconsistent with the essential facts of the case. "Without any condition annexed to it" was an unlucky phrase ; for it said, or seemed to say, what the writer could not mean, while it did not say what he did mean. The brothers could not have meant to promise that, under any conceivable circumstances, whatever Coleridge should do or not do, should be or not be, they would give him £150 a year for life. Such a promise would have been merely senseless. The annuity was given for a purpose, and the purpose necessarily made a condition, vague, but substantial. It was not annexed to the promise, but it was inseparably bound up with the transaction. Hazlitt, who was with Coleridge when he accepted the offer, describes it in the words " devote himself to the study of poetry and philosophy," and " to dissuade him from abandoning poetry and philosophy for the ministry." And nobody has ever read the story otherwise. Coleridge, in accepting the offer, was in fact undertaking to occupy himself in work of that kind, or at any rate in intellectual work of *some* kind. By taking the annuity he undertook to carry out its purpose, as really as the Wedgwoods undertook to give him the money. When Josiah wrote " no condition annexed " he simply meant to say, " We do not stipulate that you must write so many pages per annum of poetry, or such and such philosophical essays ; we shall not prescribe any specific task ; we wish you to be free to do the work you think best worth doing ; you will best judge how to work and what to work at." To read the words " with no condition annexed " as equivalent to " under all or any conceivable circumstances " is to make the promise absurd. Coleridge was about to become a Unitarian preacher. He might have taken orders and become Bishop of Durham, with twenty or thirty thousand a year. Or he might have turned out a wholly depraved character, might have forged the Wedgwoods names on bills of exchange, or become an irreclaimable profligate. Will any one say that in any of such cases the brothers would be bound in honour to go on paying him £150 a year for life because they did not "annex the condition " that he should not become a bishop, or a convict, or a debauchee ? But we do not know that the obligation he undertook was not something of a specific kind. For we have not before us all that passed between him and the brothers in January 1798. The most important sentence in Josiah's letter begins : "After what my brother Thomas has written : : . " That imports Tom's letter into the offer : but what his brother Thomas had written we do not know, nor do we know what Coleridge wrote in accepting the offer. It is possible that these lost letters might give some clearer indication of what the brothers hoped or expected him to do. At all events, without them we do not know all that passed in 1798, any more than we know what passed in 1812.

No one can now say exactly what prompted Josiah's action at the latter date. But we may, I think, assume that his view on the question of honour and obligation was that above expressed. If he had thought himself bound in honour to go on paying he would certainly have done so. He was not only a man of presumed probity and honour, but a man who, during the whole of a long life, was conspicuous for his large-minded generosity. Remembering what Charles Darwin wrote about him—(" the very type of an upright man—I do not believe that any power upon earth would have made him swerve an inch from what he considered the right course ")—we may dismiss the suspicion that his act was prompted by any mean or petty

motive. In view of Coleridge's utter failure, during'all the
fourteen years elapsed since 1798, to make his life in any degree
consonant with the obligation cast on him by the annuity, he
must have felt himself free to consider the question afresh. In
going on with the payment was he doing good or harm ? His
brother's moiety was irrevocably given as from 1805; but that
did not forbid his considering the matter afresh so far as it concerned his own action. Indeed he was bound so to do. That
he did consider it carefully is certain ; for we know, though
the fact comes to us only by oral tradition, that when one of his
sons, long afterwards, asked him why the payment ceased, he
replied : "I had ample reason for what I did," and would say
no more. He was the most reticent of men, and would
naturally hate to talk about that most miserable time in
Coleridge's life. What those words meant will be for ever a
secret. He probably knew much which we shall never know.
With such a man as Coleridge, and a man in such a state, no
imaginable possibility would be unbelievable. But I should not
myself read the words as implying any specific misdoing on his
part. A simpler explanation is more obvious. The most
essential fact in the case appears clearly in a letter of Southey to
Cottle, 17th April 1814. (This was a year or more after the
withdrawal, but Southey's statements evidently apply to the
immediately preceding years.) He is pointing out the futility
of a proposal made by Cottle to collect funds for giving
Coleridge £150 a year. "No part of Coleridge's embarrassment arises from his wife and children, except that he has
insured his life for £1000 and pays the premium. He never
writes to them, and never opens a letter from them. . . .
Perhaps you are not aware of the costliness of this drug. In
the quantity which C. takes, it would consume *more* than the
whole which you propose to raise. A frightful consumption of
spirits is added. Proposals after proposals have been made to
him by the booksellers, and he repeatedly closed with them.
He is at this moment as capable of exertion as I am, and would
be paid as well for whatever he might be pleased to do. There

R

are two Reviews—the 'Quarterly' and the 'Eclectic,' in both
of which he might have employment at ten guineas a sheet.
As to the former I could obtain it for him; in the latter they
are urgently desirous of his assistance. *He promises and does
nothing.* . . . Nothing is wanting to make him easy in
circumstances and happy in himself but to leave off opium, and
direct a certain portion of his time to the discharge of *his duties.*
Four hours a day would suffice."*

"My case," wrote Coleridge himself, "is a species of madness, only that it is a derangement, an utter impotence of the
volition, and not of the intellectual faculties." (To Cottle,
26th April, 1814.)

This had been his state for some years. In February 1810
we find Josiah writing to Poole: "It seems the 'Friend' is at
an end. I fear Col. is a lost man .. . . I see the wreck of
genius with tender concern, but without hope." Similarly
Wordsworth (March 1808): "He has no voluntary power of
mind whatsoever, nor is he capable of acting under any con-
straint of duty or moral obligation."

Evidently this terrible condition, a "madness" or paralysis
of the will and moral sense, was not to be mended by a money
subsidy. If the "pitiable slavery to opium" could be ended
there would be no lack of money. But the subsidy was only
aggravating the evil, by making it easier for him to indulge in
the pernicious drug, easier to acquiesce in the slavery. Josiah
Wedgwood must have known the facts, and who can say that
they did not justify his conclusion? We must not forget that,
at that time, the wreck of Coleridge's life must have seemed to
every one final and irrevocable; though only about three years
later there came the turning-point; when he summoned up
courage to seek for protection from himself, and at length, by
wonderful good fortune, found himself in that haven of rest,
under the care of the Gillmans, which made the last eighteen
years of his life comparatively happy.

* Cottle's "Reminiscences, 1848," p. 37. Another letter of
Southey's to the same effect is quoted by Dykes Campbell, p. 204.

Mr. Dykes Campbell's treatment of this incident (p. 192 of his book) seems to me—I write it with regret, remembering what we owe to him—rather lacking in the care and judgment which are generally so conspicuous in his work. I have noticed above the mistake of fact upon which it partly rests. He also remarks that "Mrs. Coleridge was the sufferer by the withdrawal, for the whole (of the annuity) had been for many years at her disposal." This may be true, but it hardly touches the main question Josiah had to decide. Any regular aid he gave the wife evidently went to remove, *pro tanto*, one of the husband's chief inducements to exertion. It may be said, indeed, that a man in his then condition would not be influenced by any such notice. But this is answered by the fact that he *did* afterwards make the effort which led to his recovery; and who can say that he was not helped thereto by what Josiah did?

H

T. WEDGWOOD'S WILL

THE following is a summary made from the copy Probate at Somerset House :

Will dated 13 June 1805. Proved 4 Jan. 1806.

Executors : Josiah Wedgwood, of Gunville, and Dr. Robert Waring Darwin, of Shrewsbury.

The main disposition is the gift of Residue to his two brothers, John and Josiah, and his three sisters, Susan Darwin, Catharine, and Sarah, in fifths.

There are a number of small legacies to servants and to village people at Gunville.

Bequest of furniture at Eastbury to his mother, and of plate to Catharine and Sarah : his watch and seals to his nephew, Josiah, son of his brother Josiah.

Bequest of annuity for life of £150 to John Leslie (to be £250 in case of his marriage), conditionally on his not having from other sources more than £200 a year ; or £300 if married.

Power to buy an annuity for him.

Bequest of annuity for life of £75 to "Samuel Taylor Coleridge, now or late of Stowey, near Bridgwater, gentleman," to be paid half-yearly, clear of all deductions except income tax, with power to the executors to purchase an annuity for him ; he not to have power to sell, assign, or mortgage it.

After this there is the following special bequest : "Whereas there are several persons to whom I have given assurance of pecuniary assistance towards their maintenance so long as the same shall be necessary and there may after my decease appear claims for pecuniary remunerations and advances which said several persons and the circumstances giving rise to such claims are well known to my said brother Josiah Wedgwood, I do therefore give and bequeath unto my said brother Josiah Wedgwood the sum of five thousand pounds Upon trust to assist such persons and satisfy such claims according to his own discretion."

I

A NOTE ON THE VALUE OF PHOTO-
GRAPHY TO THE WORLD

IF some competent person would take the pains to sum up the
multifarious uses now made of photography, the hundred ways
in which it aids study, research, and work of various kinds,
scientific, artistic, social, legal, and many more, such a list
would give us some measure of the importance of the art to the
world. But it would be a task demanding an almost encyclo-
pædic knowledge of modern activities. To take one illustration only, the use of the camera in observatories seems to be
daily disclosing fresh wonders in stellar astronomy, wonders
which no human eye, however laboriously applied to the eye-
piece of a telescope, could ever have discovered. A quite
different aspect of the question—may we not, perhaps, say
a higher? certainly one too often forgotten—is vividly set
forth in some words of John Richard Green, the historian,
which I will make the epilogue to this little book. They are
words which would have pleased the sympathetic soul of Tom
Wedgwood. Green was, it may be remembered, for many
years a hardworking clergyman in a very poor district of East
London. He is giving a sketch of the noble work of Edward
Denison in that region ("Stray Studies," p. 13) :

"What do you look on as the greatest boon that has been
conferred on the poorer classes in later years ?" said a friend to

me one day, after expatiating on the rival claims ôf schools, missions, shoeblack brigades, and a host of other philanthropic efforts for their assistance. I am afraid I sank in his estimation when I answered, "sixpenny photographs." But any one who knows what the worth of family affection is among the lower classes, and who has seen the array of little portraits stuck over a labourer's fireplace, still gathering together into one the "home" that life is always parting—the boy that has "gone to Canada," the girl "out at service," the little one with the golden hair that sleeps under the daisies, the old grandfather in the country—will perhaps feel with me that in counteracting the tendencies, social and industrial, which every day are sapping the healthier family affections, the sixpenny photograph is doing more for the poor than all the philanthropists in the world.

INDEX

Printed by BALLANTYNE, HANSON & CO.
London & Edinburgh

Ingram Content Group UK Ltd.
Milton Keynes UK
UKHW021846280423
420980UK00005B/94